CLARITY CONFIDENCE CODE

REWIRE YOUR MIND, MANIFEST YOUR VISION, LIVE UNSTOPPABLY

VANTAGE QUEST

CONTENTS

DISCLAIMER..1

CHAPTER 1: THE AWAKENING — WHY YOU'RE STUCK AND WHAT'S REALLY HOLDING YOU BACK....................3

CHAPTER 2: REWIRING SELF-IMAGE — THE TRUTH ABOUT WHO YOU REALLY ARE 33

CHAPTER 3: THE POWER OF INNER CLARITY — FROM MENTAL CLUTTER TO CRYSTAL VISION................................61

CHAPTER 4: THE CONFIDENCE BLUEPRINT — EMBODYING UNSHAKABLE SELF-WORTH....................................91

CHAPTER 5: BREAKING THE FEAR LOOP — HOW TO MOVE EVEN WHEN YOU'RE SCARED................................ 119

CHAPTER 6: DECISION MASTERY — HOW TO TRUST YOURSELF FULLY.. 147

CHAPTER 7: MAGNETIZING OPPORTUNITIES — ALIGNING WITH YOUR HIGHEST TIMELINE.................................. 175

CHAPTER 8: ENERGETIC BOUNDARIES — PROTECTING YOUR PEACE WITHOUT GUILT.. 203

CHAPTER 9: FROM DOUBT TO CERTAINTY — REPROGRAMMING YOUR MIND FOR SUCCESS................ 231

CHAPTER 10: ACTIVATED ACTION — TURNING CLARITY INTO ALIGNED RESULTS.. 261

CHAPTER 11: YOUR MAGNETIC MESSAGE — OWNING YOUR VOICE AND VISIBILITY 291

CHAPTER 12: LIVING THE CODE — INTEGRATION, EXPANSION & NEXT-LEVEL IDENTITY 321

BIBLIOGRAPHY 351

DISCLAIMER

The contents of this book, The Clarity Confidence Code - Rewire Your Mind, Manifest Your Vision, Live Unstoppably, The 8-Week Blueprint to Personal Power, Purpose, and Prosperity, are intended for informational and educational purposes only. The author and publisher are not medical, psychological, legal, or financial professionals, and the information contained herein should not be interpreted as professional advice, diagnosis, or treatment. No guarantees of specific outcomes or results are made.

While every effort has been made to ensure the accuracy and reliability of the information presented, the author and publisher make no representations or warranties regarding the completeness, accuracy, or applicability of any of the content. Readers are encouraged to consult with qualified professionals for advice specific to their individual circumstances.

Any exercises, meditations, visualizations, or identity-rewiring techniques described in this book are offered as tools for personal exploration and growth. They are not substitutes for professional therapy, counseling, medical treatment, or other health or wellness services.

By reading this book, you acknowledge and agree that you are solely responsible for your own decisions, actions, and results. The author and publisher disclaim any liability for any loss, damage, or disruption caused by the use or misuse of any information contained in this publication.

No part of this book is intended to create a coach-client, therapist-client, or any other fiduciary relationship. Results may vary, and your personal success will depend on individual effort, commitment, and other external and internal factors beyond the control of the author or publisher.

CHAPTER 1

THE AWAKENING — WHY YOU'RE STUCK AND WHAT'S REALLY HOLDING YOU BACK

Welcome & Book Overview

Clarity is power. But power without direction is chaos. That's why this book—The Clarity Confidence Code—is more than information; it's an identity upgrade. It's not about adding more to your plate; it's about *removing what never belonged*. You're not broken. You've just been operating under outdated programming. And the truth is, the system you've been running can be replaced—not by willpower alone, but by *rewiring your core* through neuroscience, conscious repetition, and embodied truth.

According to research from the University of Scranton, 92% of people fail to achieve their goals—not from lack of desire, but from using tools that weren't designed for their subconscious wiring. Most are applying surface-level tactics to a deep-rooted identity problem. The answer isn't to hustle harder—it's to *reprogram smarter*. Source

Neuroscientific studies from Stanford University reveal that your brain is capable of change at *any age*, provided the right emotional engagement and repetition are present. This is the science of neuroplasticity—the brain's ability to rewire itself. When you anchor new beliefs in the body and rehearse them through focused visualization, your internal operating system *updates*. You are not stuck—you're simply *unaware of your control panel*. Source

Clarity is the antidote to paralysis. When you lack it, you're buried in "what ifs," and crushed by perfectionism. But when you have clarity, you simplify decisions, eliminate noise, and act with conviction. Harvard Business School research confirms that clarity of purpose trumps external resources when it comes to sustained success. Confidence is not about pretending—it's about *knowing*. Source

This isn't about hype. It's about transformation. Every chapter in this book walks you through rewiring tools: emotional regulation, identity-based habits, and high-definition mental rehearsal. These aren't motivational gimmicks—they're grounded in proven cognitive strategies. You'll learn why affirmations don't work unless they are *felt*, and why willpower fails unless it's paired with *automatic identity alignment*.

Breakthrough doesn't begin when you "figure it all out." It begins when you *decide* that the old story ends here. The old self—rooted in doubt, survival patterns, and inherited beliefs—doesn't get to write your next chapter. As the ancient wisdom goes, "When the false self dies, the true self rises." This program is a resurrection—not of something new, but of who you *were before the world told you to forget*.

You'll discover how your subconscious has been scripting your life without permission. From the beliefs you absorbed in childhood to the identities you adopted for approval, your brain has been automating your results. But automation isn't the enemy—*misalignment is*. When you give your subconscious new blueprints—built on truth, not trauma—life begins to bend in your favor.

Each lesson will include stories of transformation, science-backed strategies, and soul-level truths that resonate deeper than logic. This isn't about collecting knowledge—it's about *embodying wisdom*. Because clarity without movement is fantasy. Confidence without integrity is performance. You are here to create *internal congruence*, where what you feel, say, and do are one.

You'll experience embodiment practices that speak to your nervous system, not just your intellect. When the body feels safe, the mind follows. You'll no longer be stuck in cycles of self-sabotage because your new identity will be reinforced with emotion, repetition, and aligned action. Change becomes natural when it is integrated—not forced.

Expect journal prompts that activate reflection, challenges that stretch you into visibility, and rituals that ground your truth into the present moment. You'll learn how to navigate fear, not by eliminating it, but by *redefining your relationship with it*. You'll walk away with the most valuable asset on Earth—*internal authority*.

By the end of this journey, you won't just have new habits. You'll have a *new relationship with yourself*. Your self-image will be elevated. Your clarity will be undeniable. Your confidence will be unshakable—not because you became someone else, but because you finally returned to who you were always meant to be.

This is your turning point. Not tomorrow. Not when circumstances feel perfect. *Now*. Because your life doesn't shift from more effort—it shifts from deeper alignment. And when you finally claim that alignment, you'll no longer chase power. You'll *embody* it. Welcome to the Clarity Confidence Code. Your breakthrough is not a fantasy. It's *inevitable*. Let's begin.

Why Clarity and Confidence Matter

There are two forces that shape your life more than any other: clarity and confidence. Clarity gives you direction. Confidence gives you propulsion. Without these two, you're like a Ferrari with no GPS and no gas. But with both, you become unstoppable. You don't just *hope* things change—you *create* the change. In a world that tries to sell confusion as complexity and doubt as realism, reclaiming your clarity and confidence is the most radical act of power you can make.

Clarity is not a luxury—it's a survival tool in a distracted world. According to a 2022 McKinsey study, leaders who embody clarity outperform their peers in decision-making, execution, and alignment. But this goes beyond boardrooms. When you're clear on who you are and what you value, your life begins to move in harmony. You stop chasing everything and start *becoming* someone worth following. McKinsey Source

When you lack clarity, every decision becomes a weight. You hesitate. You overthink. You ask ten people for advice when your soul already whispered the answer. But when you are clear—on your values, your desires, your vision—your life sharpens. Your voice deepens. Your movement becomes magnetic. That's not mysticism; that's the power of a focused nervous system trained to trust itself under pressure.

And clarity alone isn't enough. You must pair it with confidence—the grounded kind that doesn't need to shout. Confidence is what makes you speak up when fear says be quiet. It's what helps you walk into rooms where your past would've kept you silent. The University of Melbourne found that confidence—not talent—was the top predictor of success across careers. You don't need more credentials. You need more *conviction*. Melbourne Source

Confidence doesn't mean never feeling fear. It means acting anyway. It means trusting that even if it doesn't go perfectly, *you will be okay*. This is not about ego. This is about *agency*. You cannot lead a powerful life with a powerless mindset. Confidence gives you the courage to try, the resilience to rise, and the audacity to believe again—even after disappointment.

Here's the truth most never learn: both clarity and confidence can be *trained*. They're not traits you're born with. They're neurological *patterns*. Just like you learned self-doubt, you can learn self-certainty. Just like you downloaded confusion from childhood chaos, you can install a new mental operating system—one built on self-leadership and truth.

Your brain is plastic. It changes based on what you *rehearse*. According to the McGovern Institute at MIT, emotional repetition rewires the nervous system. That means the more you visualize your clarity and act with embodied confidence, the faster your identity begins to shift. This is not hype—it's *hardware rewiring*. MIT Source

You don't find confidence. You *build* it. You don't wait for clarity. You *create* it. Every question you ask, every truth you own, every step you take sends a signal to your brain: *this is who I am now*. Identity isn't passive. It's a project. And every project needs a blueprint. This book is your blueprint.

When clarity and confidence converge, life changes. You stop tolerating mediocrity. You stop entertaining drama. You stop betraying yourself to be liked. You speak with certainty. You choose with boldness. You rest with peace because your energy is no longer divided. You become *whole*. And wholeness is magnetic.

You will still have fear—but it will no longer run the show. You will still face uncertainty—but you'll move forward with grounded awareness. The difference? You'll know who you are, what matters most, and where you're going. That clarity becomes your compass. And your confidence becomes your vehicle.

Don't underestimate the power of internal alignment. A single aligned decision can undo years of self-doubt. A single moment of truth-telling can realign your trajectory. You don't need the world to validate you. You need your *own inner yes*. And once you give yourself that permission, the world begins to *respond accordingly*.

You're not starting from scratch. You're starting from *truth*. You're not building a new you. You're *remembering* the you that was buried under noise, fear, and expectations. And as you begin this journey, remember this: "The most powerful force in your life is a mind that knows where it's going and a heart that believes it belongs there." This is the moment your clarity activates, your confidence ignites, and your life begins to rise. Let's go.

The Cost of Staying Stuck

Let's start with brutal honesty. Being stuck isn't just inconvenient—it's *expensive*. It costs you more than just opportunities. It drains your energy, erodes your self-worth, and quietly suffocates your potential. Every moment spent in confusion, in fear, in indecision is a moment of your brilliance being held hostage by your own conditioning. And while you might think you're waiting for clarity, what you're really doing is *delaying your destiny*.

The World Health Organization has named burnout a global epidemic, stemming largely from people staying too long in environments, careers, and relationships that are misaligned with their truth. Chronic stress and emotional suppression aren't badges of honor—they're signs that something sacred within you has been ignored. You weren't built to survive. You were designed to *expand*. Staying stuck is not your default—it's your deviation. Source

The feeling of being stuck often disguises itself as procrastination, anxiety, or overthinking. But underneath it, you'll usually find one root cause: disconnection from your truth. You've been editing yourself for so long, you forgot who the original version was. And that creates emotional friction. It's like driving with the parking brake on—of book you're exhausted. Of book you're doubting everything. The vehicle was never meant to move that way.

You were not born hesitant. You were taught to hesitate. You learned to dim your light to make others comfortable. You were trained to question your knowing and abandon your instincts. But that training? It's reversible. The same neural pathways that were conditioned in fear can be rewired in clarity and conviction. That's not motivational fluff—it's biological fact. Your brain is plastic, and it *responds to repetition*. Source

The data backs this up. Research from Yale's Center for Emotional Intelligence confirms that suppressing your desires and ignoring your emotional truth makes you three times more likely to experience burnout and depression. You can look "successful" to the world and still feel like you're dying on the inside. That's not success. That's silent suffering. Source

Think of the opportunities you've already lost in the past year alone: the ones you didn't act on, the ideas you never voiced, the bold steps you delayed. A 2023 study in the *Journal of Behavioral Decision Making* shows that inaction regret causes more psychological damage than failure. It's not falling short that hurts—it's never trying. Because your soul doesn't crave safety. It craves *expansion*. Source

Being stuck is not your identity—it's a symptom. And symptoms don't need shame; they need *healing*. The longer you wait to address the internal misalignment, the more normal dysfunction begins to feel. You start calling self-betrayal "loyalty," calling fear "practicality," and calling delay "being responsible." But none of that is true. The truth is, you've just forgotten who you are. And this is the moment you *remember*.

Getting unstuck starts when you stop treating confusion like a life sentence and start treating it like a wake-up call. You don't need another book, podcast, or to-do list. You need a new identity—one rooted in clarity, built on confidence, and backed by *embodied truth*. You don't think your way into action. You *act your way* into a new way of thinking.

This book is a rescue mission—from the version of you that got too good at tolerating crumbs. It's a recalibration back to self-trust, to emotional sovereignty, to knowing. The kind of knowing that doesn't ask for permission and doesn't explain its choices. The kind that wakes you up in the morning with *vision* instead of dread.

And the good news? You can start today. You can rewrite your story—not someday, but now. You are not stuck because of your circumstances. You're stuck because of the *identity you've been rehearsing*. Shift the identity, and the results follow. You don't need more discipline. You need more *truth*.

From this moment on, you are reclaiming every lost opportunity, every wasted year, every silenced instinct. You're no longer the person who waits for clarity—you *embody it*. You don't chase confidence—you *generate it*. You don't escape fear—you *alchemize it*. This is your turning point. Not because everything is perfect—but because you've decided *you are*.

You were never meant to live a life of quiet compromise. You were built for impact. For expression. For greatness that doesn't just elevate your world—but *shakes the world around you*. The cost of staying stuck is everything. But the reward of breaking free? That's a life of peace, purpose, power, and *pure alignment*. Welcome back. Let's rise.

Common Myths That Keep You Paralyzed

Everything changes the moment you realize: you were never broken, just misled. Not by malicious people—but by well-meaning systems, cultural norms, and generational beliefs that were passed down as truth. These myths have shaped how you see yourself, what you believe is possible, and how much you allow yourself to pursue. But once exposed, these illusions can no longer hold power over you. You don't need to fix yourself—you need to *free* yourself from inherited lies.

The first myth that paralyzes potential is the belief that you must have everything figured out before you start. That idea is the enemy of movement. In reality, clarity is not a prerequisite—it's a byproduct. The most successful people begin with what researchers call "minimum viable clarity" and refine as they go. According to Harvard Business Review, taking small steps and adjusting along the way produces better outcomes than waiting for certainty. Action creates clarity—not the other way around. Source

Another myth says confidence is something you're born with. But science says otherwise. Confidence is not a trait—it's a skill. And all skills can be developed. The National Institutes of Health confirms that consistent action, emotional reinforcement, and positive self-talk literally rewire the brain's identity pathways. You're not lacking confidence—you're lacking repetition of empowered behavior. Every time you take action aligned with your truth, your self-concept strengthens. Source

Then there's the idea that you must feel "ready" before you leap. This one sounds responsible, but it's actually rooted in fear. You won't feel ready for most of your breakthrough moments. Courage often precedes readiness. Psychological Science published a study showing that people who act despite fear develop greater emotional resilience than those who wait to feel secure. Readiness isn't a feeling. It's a *decision*. Source

Perfectionism is another lie dressed as logic. You don't need to be flawless to be powerful. In fact, perfection is the fast track to paralysis. Research from the University of Kent revealed that perfectionists are more likely to experience burnout, anxiety, and procrastination—while those who embrace imperfection are more innovative and fulfilled. Your messiness doesn't disqualify you. It *humanizes* you. And in a world tired of polished facades, your realness is your resonance. Source

And let's dismantle the myth that you're too old, too late, or too far behind. Success is not a race—it's a rhythm. Some of the most impactful visionaries began their legacy after 40. Vera Wang designed her first dress at 40. Colonel Sanders started KFC at 62. The Stanford Center on Longevity has proven that many people do their most purpose-driven work after midlife, when wisdom and alignment meet. Source

These myths are seductive because they feel safe. But safety is not the goal—*liberation is*. You were not meant to shrink yourself to fit a narrative that wasn't built for you. You were born to expand into the fullness of your soul's design. The truth is, you don't need more time, more credentials, or more approval. You need to unlearn the beliefs that have been blocking your brilliance.

The mind doesn't operate in logic—it operates in *repetition*. And the most dangerous ideas are the ones you hear often enough to believe without question. That's how culture shapes self-worth. That's how school systems train obedience over originality. That's how families unconsciously pass down limitation under the guise of protection. But you don't have to perpetuate the programming. You can *interrupt the pattern.*

Your life changes not when you add more—but when you *release the lies.* The myth of perfection, the myth of delay, the myth of readiness—all of them are fragments of a story that no longer fits the identity you're here to embody. Let them go. Because behind every myth is the truth waiting to be reclaimed. The truth that says: your voice matters, your timing is divine, and your power is not in question.

You were hypnotized into believing you were powerless. But hypnosis can be reversed. When you expose the myth, you collapse its influence. And when you collapse the influence, your authentic self rises. Not the version that waits for permission, but the version that *moves in purpose.*

There is a voice inside you that has been whispering beneath the noise. It knows. It's been waiting for you to listen, to remember, to return. You don't have to shout. You don't have to prove. You simply have to *become.* Because once you see the lie, you're no longer bound by it. And once you reclaim your truth, your next chapter begins—not in fear, but in *fullness.*

You're not late. You're not behind. You're right on time to wake up, break the spell, and write a new narrative—one where clarity is your compass, confidence is your currency, and truth is your home. The myths have served their purpose. Now it's time for *you* to serve yours. Let the real journey begin.

The Identity Trap: Who You Think You Are

You don't live from your goals—you live from your identity. That one realization can unshackle decades of false starts and unfulfilled dreams. Most people are fighting to change their habits, routines, or mindset without ever addressing the root identity those patterns emerge from. It's like painting over rust—superficially better, but ultimately unstable. True transformation doesn't happen through willpower alone. It happens when you *align your behavior with your identity.* And if your identity hasn't shifted, your results never truly will.

Research from Stanford's Behavior Design Lab confirms that lasting change doesn't come from motivation or effort—it comes from alignment with identity. In other words, you act in accordance with who you believe you are. If deep down you believe you're the type of person who always fails, you'll sabotage your progress. If you see yourself as someone who's bad with money, you'll unconsciously resist wealth. This subconscious resistance isn't laziness—it's a self-protective pattern wired by your nervous system.

The truth is, we've all been hypnotized. From early childhood, we absorbed beliefs from our environment, our parents, teachers, media, and peers. If you were told you were too much, not enough, hard to love, or hard to succeed—you likely internalized it. And now, as an adult, you're running those beliefs on autopilot. Dr. Bruce Lipton, a pioneer in epigenetics, reports that up to 95% of our actions are driven by subconscious programming—not conscious intent. That means the story running your life wasn't even *written* by you.

But here's the miracle: anything installed can be *uninstalled*. Your wounded identity—the one that plays small, avoids risk, and hides behind perfectionism—is not your truth. It's a survival mechanism. A persona built to keep you safe in a world that once told you who you had to be in order to be accepted. But survival is not the same as success. And staying in the identity that once protected you will now *prevent* you from your full potential.

You weren't born hesitant, anxious, or disconnected. You were born bold, expressive, curious, and clear. What you're reclaiming isn't something new—it's something *ancient*. Something that's always lived inside you. And neuroscience backs this up. Studies published in *Nature Neuroscience* reveal that new identity pathways can be formed within 30 days of consistent focus, emotion, and aligned behavior. Your brain doesn't care who you used to be—it adapts to what you *rehearse*. You are not fixed. You are *fluid*.

The key isn't trying to become someone you're not. The key is *remembering* who you are underneath the noise. Beneath the programming. Beneath the roles you've had to play. There is a version of you that already knows how to lead, love, speak, and rise. That version doesn't need to be found. It needs to be *freed*. This book isn't here to teach you how to perform a new identity. It's here to help you *reclaim* the one you buried to survive.

Identity-based transformation is more than mindset work. It's about emotional healing, nervous system safety, and embodied practice. We don't change through logic alone—we change through *experience*. That's why this journey isn't just about information—it's about *integration*. It's about walking your truth, not just talking about it. Because when your identity shifts, action becomes natural. You stop forcing habits and start flowing with alignment.

This is not surface-level self-help. We're not layering affirmations on top of abandonment wounds. We're going to the root. We're identifying the hidden scripts that have shaped your life for decades. And we're choosing—intentionally, consciously, powerfully—to write new ones. Ones that serve your purpose. Ones that match your highest vision. Because no amount of action will compensate for an identity that resists it.

Your soul already knows the truth. That's why you've felt restless. You've outgrown the identity you've been operating from. You've sensed that your next level won't come from another strategy, but from a *shift*. A deeper alignment between who you are and how you live. That's the identity leap. And once you make it, everything changes.

This is how you escape the cycle of self-sabotage. It's not about being more disciplined. It's about becoming more *authentic*. When your identity matches your desires, resistance fades. Confidence becomes a side effect. Momentum becomes effortless. You stop trying to *fix* yourself and start trusting yourself. Because the goal was never to become someone else—it was always to *become whole*.

"You don't need to fix yourself. You need to remember yourself." That's the core of identity transformation. You don't need more pressure. You need more *permission*. Permission to release the outdated roles. Permission to be who you are without apology. And when you do that, not only will your results shift—your life will feel like *yours* again.

In the next session, we'll explore how to distinguish between fear and intuition—so you stop second-guessing and start *leading from your inner knowing*. Because clarity isn't found in the mind. It's anchored in your *identity*. And from this point forward, that identity is aligned with truth. Let's continue.

Fear vs. Intuition

Fear is persuasive. It dresses itself in logic, masquerades as caution, and often shows up first when you're about to stretch into something big. But fear is not your intuition. Confusing the two is one of the fastest ways to stall your growth. You'll find yourself calling fear "gut feeling" and resistance "discernment." You'll start justifying your shrinking as wisdom and mistake your trauma response as guidance. That's not discernment—it's disconnection.

Fear screams in urgency. It yells, "You're not ready," "What will they think?" or "What if you fail?" It plays reruns from the past and projects them onto the future. Its energy is chaotic, rushed, and defensive. Fear is a product of your survival brain, the amygdala, designed to detect threats. The problem is, it often can't distinguish between actual danger and emotional risk. And when that system dominates, your nervous system gets hijacked—and your clarity disappears.

Intuition, on the other hand, is calm. It doesn't argue. It *whispers*. It's the soft "yes" in your chest or the quiet "no" that brings peace. It's not rooted in logic—it's anchored in truth. According to research published in *Psychological Science*, people who trusted their gut often made faster and more accurate decisions than those who relied on logic alone. Intuition isn't magic. It's data—processed faster than your conscious mind can grasp. [Source](#)

The HeartMath Institute's research takes it deeper: your heart sends more signals to your brain than your brain sends to your heart. That means your *body* often knows before your mind does. When you ignore your intuition, you're not being practical—you're being *disconnected*. [Source](#)

We ignore intuition because we've been conditioned to. We were taught to prioritize authority, consensus, and approval over inner knowing. We've been trained to wait for logic to validate the whisper. But by the time logic speaks, intuition has already moved on. You're left chasing alignment that could've been claimed in a moment of trust.

The key to reclaiming your inner wisdom is learning to identify the signals. Fear is fast, shallow breathing. Tight chest. Racing mind. Pressure to decide *now*. Intuition feels grounded. Spacious. Sometimes uncomfortable, but never chaotic. When you feel a knowing in your gut or peace in your body despite no evidence—you're tapping into truth, not trauma.

According to a 2020 meta-analysis in *Frontiers in Psychology*, mindfulness and body awareness practices enhance your ability to detect these internal signals, also known as interoception. The more connected you are to your body, the more accurately you can access and trust your intuition. Source

Rebuilding your intuitive muscle doesn't happen overnight. It happens every time you choose alignment over approval. Every time you say yes to your knowing before you have evidence. Every time you act not from certainty—but from *connection*. You stop outsourcing your decisions. You stop debating your desires. You start moving in integrity with your highest self.

And this matters because every time you betray your intuition, your self-trust erodes. You start needing more validation to act. More evidence to decide. More noise to drown out the voice that was already clear. This is how clarity dies—not through confusion, but through *abandonment of the self*.

When you reclaim intuition, you reclaim power. You begin to walk differently. Speak differently. You no longer need consensus because you've built internal congruence. You don't need to be loud—you become magnetic in your quiet knowing. You stop needing permission because your path *feels like truth*.

Fear asks, "What's the worst that could happen?" Intuition asks, "What's the truth I'm not ready to admit?" And the moment you stop running from that truth, you begin to *remember* who you really are. This is the shift. From mental noise to embodied knowing. From survival to sovereignty.

In the next chapter, we'll break through the glass ceiling that keeps you in cycles of almost—almost confident, almost ready, almost successful—and help you expand into the version of you who lives from wholeness, not hesitation. Because now that you've learned to hear your truth, it's time to *honor it*.

The Internal Glass Ceiling

There's a ceiling you keep hitting, and it's not built by society, your job, or even your circumstances. It's internal. Invisible. Yet it shapes every decision, limits every win, and caps the level of joy and success you allow yourself to experience. This is what psychologists refer to as the internal glass ceiling—an unconscious belief system that says, "This is as good as it gets for someone like me."

This ceiling shows up not with alarms but with subtle sabotage. You might procrastinate just before a big opportunity, downplay your accomplishments to stay relatable, or feel mysteriously drained the moment things begin to go well. These aren't random behaviors. They're deeply embedded protective patterns created by your nervous system to keep you tethered to what feels familiar—even when what's familiar is suffering.

Stanford's Dr. Andrew Huberman explains that the brain is biologically wired to resist change—even positive change—when it threatens our emotional safety. The amygdala, responsible for detecting threats, doesn't differentiate between real danger and the perceived threat of outgrowing your past. So if you grew up believing success leads to isolation, your brain might literally trigger fear when you start rising. It's not a lack of capability—it's a misfired survival mechanism. Source

That's why you can set the goal, make the vision board, and still feel blocked. You want the dream relationship, the thriving business, the peaceful life—but something inside still believes "it's too much." These beliefs aren't based in truth. They're formed through trauma, conditioning, and inherited narratives from family and culture.

Dr. Gay Hendricks, in his book *The Big Leap*, calls this the Upper Limit Problem: the hidden thermostat that regulates how much success, love, and joy you're allowed to feel before you unconsciously pull back. You hit your upper limit, then life suddenly feels "off," so you create drama, distractions, or emotional chaos to bring yourself back down to your emotional set point. Source

Here's the truth: your external world can never rise above your internal self-permission. Until you expand the image of who you believe you're allowed to be, no amount of strategy will work. You'll always find a way to shrink. The real breakthrough isn't pushing harder—it's shifting your identity to believe that more joy, wealth, love, and peace is *safe* and *normal*.

This is where neuroscience meets embodiment. If your nervous system doesn't feel safe with abundance, it will reject it. That's why tools like breathwork, somatic experiencing, and safe exposure to success are critical. You have to *train your body* to hold more good without panicking. According to a 2022 study in *Clinical Psychological Science*, combining somatic regulation with self-worth interventions significantly increased goal completion and emotional resilience. Source

You must begin to name your limits. Where does it start to feel "too good"? Where do you tense up when things flow? Where do you subconsciously back away from visibility, abundance, or connection? That's your nervous system revealing the edges of your old identity—and inviting you to expand it.

Once you identify the cap, you can consciously rewrite it. Affirmations aren't enough—you must embody new truths. Step into rooms that feel expansive. Breathe into the fear. Practice receiving without guilt. Let your body learn that success can be *safe*, not stressful. That you can be loved without shrinking. That joy doesn't require a collapse to follow.

This isn't mindset work—it's identity evolution. And once you start expanding your emotional capacity to receive, the world mirrors that shift. You begin attracting opportunities that match your new ceiling. Not because the world changed, but because *you did*.

So many are waiting for their "big break" without realizing they first need an *internal breakthrough*. You don't need to force your next level—you need to *allow it*. Allow the joy. Allow the love. Allow the power. Not someday. Now. Because nothing outside of you is capping your potential. Only the story you've been loyal to.

In the next section, we'll dive deeper into dismantling self-sabotage—not by fighting it, but by understanding its root and replacing it with self-trust, emotional safety, and identity congruence. Because once your nervous system feels safe with greatness, it becomes inevitable. Let's break that ceiling—for good.

The Origins of Self-Sabotage

Let's tell the truth: you're not lazy, undisciplined, or unmotivated. What you've been calling "self-sabotage" is actually self-protection in disguise. That inner conflict—the one that shows up as procrastination, distraction, or avoidance—is not because you don't want success. It's because a part of you believes success might cost you safety, love, or acceptance. This isn't failure. This is your nervous system doing exactly what it was trained to do: survive.

Every time you delay your dreams or walk away from what you said you wanted, it's not because you're weak—it's because your subconscious is trying to protect you from perceived emotional risk. This is what psychologists call approach-avoidance conflict. You desire something deeply—visibility, abundance, love—but you simultaneously fear what that desire could bring. You want the spotlight but fear judgment. You want to rise but fear leaving people behind. That internal tug-of-war creates paralysis.

Your subconscious isn't resisting the goal—it's resisting the *story* it associates with that goal. If, as a child, being bold got you punished, your system learned that boldness equals danger. If being visible brought shame, then your nervous system believes that playing small is safer. These patterns don't mean you're broken—they mean you're *brilliant*. You adapted. You protected yourself. But what once kept you safe is now keeping you stuck.

This internal sabotage often looks like inconsistency, hesitation, or chaos just as things begin to go well. You start the project, then vanish. You build momentum, then backslide. This isn't random. According to clinical psychologist Dr. Nicole LePera, this behavior is rooted in trauma—not character. It's the child within, still trying to avoid pain. And until you make peace with that inner protector, you'll keep pulling the brakes every time you accelerate.

Here's the liberating truth: these patterns are not permanent. They're programs. And programs can be rewritten. A groundbreaking study published in *The Lancet Psychiatry* found that cognitive reappraisal—changing the emotional meaning behind a memory—can significantly reduce self-defeating behavior. Your nervous system isn't fixed. It's *trainable*. You don't need more hustle—you need *emotional safety*.

So the work is not in pushing harder. It's in asking deeper questions. What does achieving this goal subconsciously threaten? What part of you is afraid of being seen, loved, or fully expressed? What emotions have you been taught are dangerous to feel or express? This is where the true healing begins—not with discipline, but with *discovery*.

When you meet the inner protector with curiosity instead of criticism, you open the door to real change. That part of you isn't trying to ruin your life—it's trying to *save* you from repeating pain. But it's time to remind that part: this is a new chapter. You are no longer the child who had to hide. You are the adult who gets to choose.

Reprogramming begins when you create safety in your body—not just your mind. Somatic tools like breathwork, EFT tapping, and nervous system regulation teach your body that success, visibility, and abundance are not threats—they're *safe*. When your nervous system stops equating success with danger, sabotage dissolves. You stop shrinking to survive and start expanding to *thrive*.

You are not your past reactions. You are the awareness beneath them. And once you see that self-sabotage is just feedback, not failure, you become powerful enough to change the pattern. Not by force—but by love, by truth, and by choice. The pattern loses its grip the moment you name it and nurture the part of you that created it.

The world doesn't need a more perfect version of you. It needs the whole, present, *unapologetic* you. And that version only emerges when safety becomes your baseline—not stress. That's when consistency becomes natural. That's when confidence becomes embodied. That's when success becomes sustainable. Because now, your system isn't fighting you—it's *fueling* you.

What you once called sabotage was sacred. It was survival. But now you're not surviving—you're leading. And that leadership starts with leading yourself out of the loop of fear, into the life that reflects your truth. You are not behind. You are not broken. You are becoming. And from this moment on, the only thing you sabotage is the lie that ever said you weren't ready.

In the next chapter, we'll explore how awareness is the first and most essential tool in your transformation—and how to wield it not just for understanding, but for *liberation*. Because when you stop fighting yourself, you don't just move forward—you *fly*.

Awareness as the First Breakthrough

Awareness isn't just the starting point of transformation—it is the revolution itself. The moment you become conscious of a behavior, a thought, or a feeling, you step into the seat of the observer. And in that split second, you become more than the pattern. You become its witness. That shift alone dismantles the illusion that you are your struggle. You're not the fear. You're the one noticing it. And from that noticing, liberation begins.

Neuroscience validates this with precision. A landmark study from UCLA revealed that simply naming an emotion reduces amygdala activity—the brain's fear center—and activates the prefrontal cortex, the region responsible for reasoning and choice. In other words, when you say, "This is anxiety," you begin to separate from it. It loses its grip on your nervous system. You stop reacting and start responding. You're no longer the storm—you're the sky that holds it. (Source)

This is not philosophy—it's biology. And yet it feels spiritual, too. Because the practice of awareness echoes ancient truths. In Buddhist teachings, it's the foundation of mindfulness. In modern psychology, it's called metacognition. In your everyday life, it's that moment when you catch yourself before reacting and choose curiosity instead of criticism. That is presence. That is power.

Awareness turns the light on. And when you see what's been hiding in the dark—your fears, your guilt, your inherited beliefs—it can feel uncomfortable, even painful. But pain is not the enemy. Pain is information. Pain is your soul's siren, alerting you to the places that need your attention, not your avoidance. What you once numbed, you now *notice*. And what you notice, you can change.

It's easy to shame ourselves for our patterns. "Why can't I stop this? What's wrong with me?" But that inner war only deepens the wound. True power comes when you shift from self-punishment to self-permission. "Ahh… this isn't procrastination. It's fear of judgment." "This isn't laziness. It's grief." That level of honesty doesn't weaken you—it *reclaims* you. You stop being the problem and start being the *solution*.

Awareness replaces willpower. Willpower tries to override behavior with force. But awareness transforms it from the root. The reason why diets, routines, and habit hacks often fail is because they don't address the unconscious beliefs driving the behavior. If the mind is a computer, awareness is the debug tool. It locates the glitch in the code, the faulty line that says "I'm not good enough," "I always fail," or "Success isn't safe." And once that code is revealed, it can be rewritten.

Studies from Harvard confirm that awareness isn't just mental—it's *physical*. Eight weeks of mindfulness training has been shown to increase gray matter in brain regions responsible for self-regulation, compassion, and introspection. This means awareness doesn't just make you feel better—it reshapes your brain. You're not just changing your thoughts—you're upgrading your entire operating system. (Source)

But don't confuse awareness with detachment. This isn't about bypassing emotions or pretending everything is fine. True awareness invites you to feel more fully, not less. It lets you experience fear without becoming it, rage without being consumed by it, and grief without drowning in it. You're not avoiding emotion—you're *anchoring* in presence while it moves through you. This is emotional mastery. This is wholeness.

Awareness becomes your compass. It lets you navigate life not through unconscious reaction, but through aligned choice. You start asking better questions. You pause before speaking. You listen before leaping. And slowly, the chaos that once ran your life becomes a classroom. Every trigger becomes a teacher. Every pattern, a portal back to truth.

This is the most empowering truth: once you become aware, you are no longer a victim to circumstance. You are no longer hypnotized by conditioning. You have agency. You can choose a different thought, a different action, a different path. Not because you forced it—but because you *saw* it. You cannot heal what you're unwilling to see. But once you see it—you reclaim your power to change it.

Awareness is the shovel that unearths the real you. The version of you that was never broken, just buried under layers of programming, pain, and performance. With every moment of presence, you dig deeper toward that essence. You get closer to your core. And eventually, the noise fades, the masks fall away, and you remember: you were always whole. Just hidden.

In the next lesson, we'll uncover how the stories and beliefs you inherited—many of which were never yours to begin with—became the lens through which you see your life. And more importantly, how to break free from those lenses and reclaim the clarity and confidence that were yours all along. Awareness was the first step. Now we begin the reprogramming.

The Role of Conditioning and Programming

You weren't born afraid to speak your truth. You didn't show up on this earth with doubts about your worth or confusion about your power. Those weren't yours to begin with—they were installed. And like any code, they can be overwritten. From the moment you began absorbing the world around you, your subconscious became a sponge, soaking up messages from your environment, even when those messages were rooted in limitation, fear, or misalignment.

The most powerful conditioning happens early, long before logic kicks in. According to the Center on the Developing Child at Harvard, by age seven, the brain has already formed most of its neural architecture. It absorbs everything without discernment or filters. If you were praised for being quiet, you learned silence was safe. If love was conditional, you began to perform for acceptance. These weren't conscious decisions—they were adaptive strategies. Strategies that helped you survive emotionally, but now prevent you from expanding fully. Source

That conditioning forms the blueprint of your life. It determines what you think you're allowed to have, how you expect people to treat you, and how much abundance you're comfortable receiving. The National Institute of Mental Health confirms that early environmental influences shape adult behavior, stress responses, and self-worth. You are not failing—you are following programming you didn't choose. Source

Imagine trying to run next-generation software on outdated operating systems. That's what happens when you're living a bold vision through the lens of old survival patterns. You crash. You freeze. You self-sabotage—not because you're broken, but because the subconscious doesn't believe you're safe with success. Your inner child is still running the show, trying to protect you using strategies that once worked but no longer serve.

The good news is the mind is not static. It's neuroplastic. That means it can change—permanently—through conscious repetition and emotional engagement. A 2020 article in *Nature Reviews Neuroscience* emphasized that emotional intensity combined with repetition triggers synaptic plasticity, the process that rewires brain pathways. This is how we override old scripts—not through force, but through *felt transformation*. Source

This book exists to give you more than knowledge. It's designed for *remapping*. Through techniques drawn from neuro-linguistic programming, somatic release, and subconscious rewiring, you're not just going to think differently—you're going to *feel differently*. You'll begin to recognize when an outdated pattern is playing and interrupt it in real time. This is what it means to become sovereign over your own system.

You can't "think positive" your way out of deep programming. That's spiritual bypass. What works is embodiment—integrating new beliefs into your nervous system until they become your natural state. You feel them before you speak them. You act from them before you have evidence. That's when the outside world begins to rearrange in response.

Because here's the truth that changes everything: you weren't born with fear of rejection, fear of failure, or fear of being too much. You learned that. And if you learned it, you can unlearn it. The same way your brain was trained to play small, it can be retrained to rise. You are not stuck—you are *conditioned*. And conditioning can be reprogrammed.

You don't have to fight for your worthiness—it's already yours. What you do have to fight for is your focus. Your awareness. Your right to consciously choose who you become from this moment forward. The battle is not against your past, but against the unconscious loyalty to old scripts that no longer reflect your vision.

Repetition is how you got here. Repetition is how you get free. But this time, the repetition is not rooted in fear—it's rooted in *freedom*. Every time you affirm your worth, every time you choose your truth, you're installing a new identity. One that's based not in survival, but in soul.

This isn't about becoming someone else. It's about returning to who you were before the world told you to shrink. Before you were taught to earn your worth or perform for love. That version of you—the bold, intuitive, joyful one—is still there. Waiting. Not to be found. But to be remembered.

In the next section, we'll introduce the core framework of this journey: the Clarity Confidence Code. A transformative path designed to walk you out of confusion and back into power. Because now that you see the programming, you have the key to rewire it. Let's begin.

Introducing the Clarity Confidence Code

You've been taught to chase goals, set resolutions, and hustle harder. But if you've ever reached a milestone only to feel empty—or watched your efforts collapse under pressure—you've met the limits of behavior-first change. Most people try to change their lives by changing what they do. But transformation doesn't begin with behavior. It begins with *identity*. When who you are aligns with what you want, action becomes effortless. That's what the Clarity Confidence Code unlocks.

This isn't another mindset trick. It's not a five-step routine or a motivational high that fades after 24 hours. This is a complete identity recalibration system—built to rewire the deepest layers of your self-image and reboot your inner operating system. At its core are three truths: clarity is power, confidence is trained, and identity creates behavior. These aren't just slogans—they're scientifically backed principles of transformation.

Modern neuroscience shows that identity-based change is more sustainable than goal-based change. A 2016 study published in the *Journal of Cognitive Neuroscience* confirmed that behavior follows belief—especially the belief about who you are. When your identity is misaligned with your vision, sabotage is inevitable. But when your identity supports your vision, momentum becomes automatic. Source

That's why you can have the best intentions, the clearest plans, and still feel stuck. You're trying to build a future on a foundation of old programming. It's like painting a castle over a shack. It might look good temporarily, but it won't last under stress. The Clarity Confidence Code flips the entire approach—starting not with action, but with *alignment*.

In Phase One, you identify the real blocks—not just the habits that aren't working, but the beliefs underneath them. You learn how to locate the scripts that are running your subconscious and keeping you in cycles of hesitation, fear, or burnout. Once you see the false stories, you can separate from them—and choose new ones.

Phase Two is about nervous system stabilization. Because clarity means nothing if you're constantly hijacked by anxiety, overwhelm, or shutdown. Through somatic tools like breathwork, movement, and body-based anchoring, you teach your system that success is safe. That expansion doesn't equal danger. You build the emotional capacity to hold more—without breaking.

Then comes Phase Three: activating purpose and vision. But not just any vision. This isn't about status-driven goals that look good on paper. It's about soul-aligned desires that energize you at a cellular level. When your vision is emotionally charged and anchored in truth, your whole system gets on board. Your mind stops resisting. Your body says yes.

Phase Four turns everything into momentum. This is where flow replaces force. You don't have to wake up and hype yourself up with willpower anymore. Your actions now come from identity congruence. You begin to *do* what your future self would do—because you've already become that version inside. Your presence shifts. Your voice strengthens. Confidence becomes embodied, not performed.

And it works because it's based on wiring, not willpower. A 2018 meta-analysis in *Neuroscience & Biobehavioral Reviews* found that visualizing from identity—not just outcome—dramatically increases success rates. Why? Because the brain acts faster on beliefs than instructions. [Source](#)

This is what makes the Clarity Confidence Code different. It doesn't ask you to hustle harder. It shows you how to become the person for whom that vision is inevitable. You stop chasing goals. You start attracting alignment. Your choices, habits, and outcomes begin to match your identity automatically. Not because you're trying harder—but because you're living from your *truth*.

You stop second-guessing. You stop asking for permission. You stop wondering if you're ready. Because the identity you now operate from doesn't rely on validation. It generates clarity, magnetism, and certainty from the inside out. That's how deep, permanent confidence is built.

You're not becoming someone new. You're remembering someone ancient. You're stepping into the you who was always underneath the fear, the programming, the pretending. That version was never lost—just hidden. Now it's being reactivated. And with it comes a life that feels fully yours.

In the next section, you'll begin the process of anchoring this shift—through a transformational writing practice that guides you to declare your truth, embody your identity, and step fully into the next chapter of your evolution. Because now that the code is activated, everything changes. Starting now.

Journal Exercise: Your Stuck Story & Truth Reframe

You've tried willpower. You've tried discipline. You've even tried faking confidence until it felt real. But what if the real reason it didn't last wasn't because you lacked strength—but because you were applying pressure to the wrong place? Lasting transformation doesn't begin at the level of behavior—it begins at the level of *identity*. And until you change the code that runs your inner world, your outer world will always revert to the same loops, no matter how hard you push.

Most people try to build new habits on top of an outdated self-image. They download morning routines, follow motivational influencers, and hustle harder, hoping that a new behavior will create a new reality. But neuroscience has already proven that we don't act to achieve a goal—we act to remain consistent with who we believe we are. That belief lives in the subconscious. So if you believe you're not "the kind of person" who succeeds, stays confident, or follows through—you'll unconsciously create results that confirm it.

This is why traditional self-help often leaves people feeling worse. It promises change through action alone. But without internal rewiring, those actions never stick. The brain is a predictive machine, constantly filtering new information through old identity scripts. That's why success without identity congruence creates stress instead of fulfillment. You reach the goal, but your nervous system doesn't feel safe there. And what doesn't feel safe gets sabotaged.

The Clarity Confidence Code offers a different path. It's not about adding more pressure to perform. It's about removing the noise that distorts who you really are. It's about rewiring your nervous system to feel safe in expansion, training your subconscious to support your vision, and embodying the clarity that turns you from seeker into *creator*. You don't just *know* what to do—you *feel* ready to do it.

This transformation starts with awareness. You must identify the hidden programs keeping you stuck: the fears, the inherited stories, the outdated self-perceptions. Once seen, they lose their grip. Research from UCLA shows that naming an emotion reduces the brain's stress response. That's not just psychology—it's power. Because when you name the block, you reclaim the choice.

Next comes nervous system stabilization. Your capacity for clarity and confidence isn't just mental—it's physical. If your body is in a constant state of stress, your system won't allow growth. That's why somatic tools like breathwork, vagus nerve regulation, and embodiment practices are central to the Code. When your body feels safe, your soul can expand.

Then, you activate your true vision—not a goal based on ego, fear, or status, but a vision rooted in soul truth. A vision that excites your system so deeply, it becomes magnetic. Your decisions begin to align. Your habits shift naturally. You no longer need hype to move—you have *internal clarity* driving every step.

That's when momentum becomes inevitable. Because now your actions are congruent with your identity. You begin to move, speak, and choose from the future version of you—not the wounded self of the past. Confidence is no longer something you chase—it's something you *anchor* in your body and energy. You no longer have to earn permission to be powerful. You become power in motion.

And here's the key: it's not willpower—it's wiring. A study in *Neuroscience & Biobehavioral Reviews* found that people who visualized their identity while pursuing a goal had up to 60% higher success rates. Why? Because the subconscious responds to identity rehearsal. It believes what you embody, not just what you say. You don't affirm your way to change—you *become* the change.

This is the magic of the Clarity Confidence Code. It turns you from someone who's hoping for alignment into someone who lives from it daily. It transforms your presence, your voice, and your habits without forcing you to fake it. Because now, everything you do flows from who you *really are*—not who you were told to be.

This isn't self-improvement. This is self-reclamation. You're not becoming someone else—you're remembering someone ancient. Someone true. The version of you that existed before the world taught you to fear your power. Before doubt became your language. Before you settled for confusion instead of clarity.

That version is alive. And it's ready to lead. The Code simply hands you the map, calibrates your compass, and reminds you that you've had the key all along. In the next section, you'll use that key for the first time—in a writing activation designed to awaken your true self, ignite your internal power, and step into the identity that no longer waits... but leads. Let's begin.

If this book has stirred something deep within you—if you've felt even a flicker of recognition that you're meant for more—then don't just stop here. Reading creates awareness, but immersion creates transformation. That's why I created the full *Clarity Confidence Code Course*. This isn't just the next step—it's the shortcut to becoming the version of you who no longer hesitates, hides, or holds back. It's where the inner rewiring gets activated in real time—through high-definition coaching, embodiment exercises, and the identity recalibration rituals that shift your nervous system at the core. If you're ready to stop dabbling and finally lock in the breakthroughs you've tasted in these pages...

then step in. The door is open. The transformation is waiting. You just have to walk through it. Enroll now at https://clarityconfidencecode.com

Let's begin the next phase of your evolution—starting with the truth that's always lived inside you.

CHAPTER 2

REWIRING SELF-IMAGE — THE TRUTH ABOUT WHO YOU REALLY ARE

What Is Self-Image and Why It's Everything

You will never outperform your self-image. Not in your career. Not in your relationships. Not in your wealth, visibility, confidence, or peace. Your self-image is the internal thermostat that quietly governs what you believe is safe to have, do, and become. It is the boundary line of your life's possibilities—and most people never realize they're living inside a mental prison built before the age of ten.

The concept of self-image isn't new, but its importance is still wildly underestimated. Dr. Maxwell Maltz first introduced it in his book *Psycho-Cybernetics*, after observing how even drastic cosmetic surgery couldn't shift how his patients saw themselves. A beautiful face didn't equal a beautiful self-perception. That's because our lives follow the blueprint in our minds—not the mirror. Neuroscience has since validated Maltz's claim: change your self-image, and your behavior, personality, and outcomes transform accordingly.

Your self-image is hardwired into your brain's default mode network (DMN), the neural system responsible for internal storytelling and self-perception. Studies from the University of British Columbia reveal that the DMN activates most when we think about ourselves—even when we don't realize we're doing it. That means your brain is constantly reinforcing an inner narrative. And if that story says, "I'm not good enough," "I always fail," or "I'm not meant for more," those thoughts become your operating instructions.

Identity always dictates behavior. That's why it's possible to know exactly what to do and still not do it. Why people repeat the same toxic patterns even after therapy. Why affirmations often feel like lies when your inner identity screams the opposite. It's not a discipline problem—it's a self-image problem. You're trying to build a new life on an outdated self-concept. Until that shifts, everything else wobbles.

Most of our self-image was programmed before age ten. It came from adults who were themselves unhealed, school systems that rewarded obedience over authenticity, and social systems that defined value by performance. You didn't choose that story—you inherited it. And your subconscious made it law. But here's the truth: the past doesn't get to dictate your future unless you let it.

Self-image is not fixed. It's plastic. The brain can rewire through a process known as neuroplasticity. A 2020 meta-analysis in *Nature Reviews Neuroscience* showed that consistent visualization, emotional rehearsal, and belief updating can reshape the neural circuits tied to identity and self-concept. You can literally change how you see yourself—and by doing so, you change what's possible for you.

That's the foundation of the Clarity Confidence Code. It's not about tweaking your habits or setting better goals. It's about reconstructing the very image you hold of yourself—from one built on trauma, to one rooted in truth. From one shaped by survival, to one aligned with your soul. Because when your self-image shifts, your world does too.

When you begin to see yourself as powerful, worthy, and magnetic, you stop settling for environments that don't reflect that. Boundaries get stronger. Decisions get faster. Confidence becomes embodied. Results become inevitable. Why? Because now your actions match your identity. There's no longer friction between what you want and who you believe you are.

This is why lasting transformation can't come from hustle alone. If you're acting from a misaligned identity, you'll burn out or backslide. But when your identity and vision are congruent, your nervous system stops resisting and starts supporting your rise. It no longer feels like you're forcing change—it feels like you're coming home.

That's when life meets you at your new level. Because energy doesn't lie. When you upgrade your self-image, people respond to your new frequency. Opportunities open. Your voice strengthens. The old version of you no longer fits, and that's a beautiful thing. You didn't lose anything. You simply rose beyond it.

The work ahead is not about becoming someone else. It's about releasing the false self and reclaiming who you were before the world told you to shrink. That version is still inside you—intact, brilliant, powerful. It's time to let them lead. The next section will walk you through exactly how your identity was formed, how it's been hijacked, and how to rewrite the internal code with intention, clarity, and sovereignty. You're not here to perform. You're here to become. Let's begin.

How Identity Is Formed (and Hijacked)

You didn't choose the first version of who you became. It was formed quietly, behind the scenes, through repetition, emotion, and the need to survive. In your earliest years, your brain existed in a theta state—a deeply programmable frequency where information entered without filters, logic, or resistance. It was hypnosis in action. You absorbed the tone in someone's voice, the look in their eyes, the silence after you spoke. It wasn't just parenting. It was programming.

Every frown when you were bold, every reward when you stayed small, every withdrawal of love when you didn't perform—it wasn't just an experience. It was a script. And your brain, doing its best to keep you alive and accepted, turned those scripts into identity. You didn't realize it then, but your subconscious began constructing a narrative: "I am only lovable when I succeed," "My voice is dangerous," "Desires bring punishment." These weren't choices. They were adaptations.

And here's where it gets serious: those early adaptations formed the basis of up to 95% of your adult behavior. The subconscious doesn't negotiate—it executes. It's not judging whether your identity empowers you; it's repeating what it learned when you were too young to question. That's why you can want a bigger life and still sabotage it. Because deep down, you're trying to remain consistent with who you *believe* you are.

This is how identity becomes a prison. You adopt roles that once kept you safe: the pleaser, the achiever, the quiet one, the strong one. These roles earned love or approval—but now they cost you freedom. You stay in relationships that drain you because they fit the story. You shrink your dreams because expansion threatens the old pattern. You resist visibility, abundance, intimacy—not because you don't want them, but because they feel unsafe to the version of you that's still trying to survive.

It's not logic. It's identity conflict. Neuroscience proves that when behavior contradicts self-concept, the brain responds with discomfort, resistance, and self-sabotage. Even if the change is good. Even if the future is brighter. That's why you fall back into old patterns even after reading all the books, doing the affirmations, setting the goals. Your identity wins every time.

But here's the breakthrough: identity is not static. It's not cemented by your childhood. It's not defined by your past. It's flexible. It can evolve. And you can *choose* to become someone new—not by force, but by truth. The real you isn't buried. It's simply buried under conditioning. And when you dismantle the roles you never chose, you meet the you that was always meant to rise.

In this book, you're not here to perform for another version of success. You're here to strip away what isn't yours. You'll trace your behaviors back to the belief. You'll trace the belief back to the identity. And then you'll trace the identity back to the moment it was formed—so you can reclaim the truth. That you were never too much. Never not enough. Never a mistake.

From there, you'll construct a new identity. One based not on fear, but on freedom. Not on performance, but on purpose. Not on survival, but on soul. And that identity becomes the filter for every choice, every boundary, every habit, every result. You no longer have to hustle for outcomes. You become the person for whom those outcomes are natural.

Because your life doesn't rise to the level of your desires. It rises to the level of your identity. If you identify as powerful, confident, and magnetic—your life will begin to mirror that. Not because you're pretending, but because you're congruent. And congruence is magnetic. It attracts relationships, opportunities, and clarity that align with the truth you finally allow.

This is where the code activates. Not in a list of rules—but in a reprogrammed reality. You'll learn to shift in the moment. To speak from your empowered self instead of your wounded one. To take action not from fear, but from future. This isn't a tweak. It's a transformation.

You're not becoming someone else. You're returning to someone eternal. The version of you that was always worthy. Always wise. Always ready. In the next lesson, we'll contrast the Wounded Self with the Empowered Self—so you can recognize who's been running your life… and who's meant to lead it next. The past was programming. The future is *power*. Let's go.

The Wounded Self vs. The Empowered Self

There are two versions of you that show up in your life every day, whether you recognize them or not. One is rooted in protection, the other in power. One was created to survive, the other to thrive. These two selves—the Wounded Self and the Empowered Self—don't just influence your choices; they shape your reality. Your job isn't to destroy one and glorify the other. Your job is to recognize who's running the show, and to consciously choose who leads from this moment forward.

The Wounded Self was born from necessity. It was your internal bodyguard in moments of trauma, rejection, or shame. It said, "I'll protect you from ever feeling this again." And so it built walls. It made you people-please to stay liked. It made you dim your light to avoid judgment. It made you overachieve to feel worthy. It wasn't malicious—it was protective. But what protected you then may be imprisoning you now.

This part of you doesn't trust expansion. It avoids risk, stays small, and seeks safety in control. But you were not built for a life of avoidance. You were built for greatness. Your Empowered Self remembers that. It is your original self, your unshakable essence before the world told you to be something else. It doesn't hustle for validation. It doesn't shrink for comfort. It radiates certainty because it knows who it is.

Psychology now confirms that integrating these parts—not ignoring or suppressing them—is the key to healing. Internal Family Systems therapy has shown that when we acknowledge, speak to, and reparent our wounded inner parts, emotional regulation increases, confidence returns, and resilience skyrockets. This is not about becoming someone new. This is about reclaiming who you always were, beneath the layers of programming.

Even your brain agrees. A 2022 study by the National Institute of Mental Health found that embodying a confident identity—even before you fully believe it—activates the ventromedial prefrontal cortex, the area responsible for identity reinforcement and emotional regulation. In other words, your brain is wired to adapt to who you *practice* being, not who you used to be. You don't wait until you're confident to act—you act your way into the identity of confidence.

The signs are clear when your Wounded Self is in charge. You tolerate relationships that drain you. You say yes when your soul screams no. You procrastinate on your purpose because clarity feels too risky. You apologize for taking up space, charge too little for your worth, and seek approval like oxygen. But this is not your fault. It's your conditioning. And conditioning can be rewired.

When your Empowered Self takes the wheel, the game changes. You speak with authority. You set boundaries without guilt. You choose alignment over approval. You trust your vision even if no one claps for it yet. You act not to prove your worth, but to express it. People may not understand your power—but they will feel it. Because energy doesn't lie.

And here's what most people don't know: you don't become your Empowered Self by waiting. You become it by leading. By stepping in before you're ready. By saying, "I choose me," even when fear is loud. Every time you act from your truth, you reinforce that identity. Every time you soothe your Wounded Self instead of silencing it, you heal. Every time you trust your gut over the crowd, you grow stronger.

This book is a path to that identity shift. It's not about surface-level motivation—it's about structural rewiring. You'll learn how to notice the voice of fear, thank it, and still choose power. You'll be guided to act from soul, not shame. And you'll be challenged to embody confidence before life gives you permission—because that's when life responds in kind.

You don't need another strategy. You need a new self-perception. You need to stop outsourcing your authority and remember that you were born enough. That nothing needs to be earned for you to speak, lead, and rise. You are not waiting to be chosen. You are here to *choose yourself*.

The Wounded Self may have built your past, but it has no place designing your future. That role belongs to the version of you that remembers your truth.

The Empowered Self who leads with vision, moves with clarity, and magnetizes everything that matches their worth. That version is here now. Let's bring them to the surface. In the next section, we'll reveal the subtle signs that you've been living from a false identity—so you can reclaim the real one and rise without resistance.

Signs You're Living from a False Identity

There's nothing heavier than wearing a mask you forgot you were wearing. It's the quiet fatigue you carry, the subtle weight of constantly adjusting, editing, and performing. You smile when your soul wants to roar. You nod when your intuition screams no. You show up as the version of you that feels acceptable—but not alive. This is the cost of living through a false identity, and millions are paying it every single day without realizing it.

Your false identity wasn't chosen—it was assigned. It was shaped in the moments you didn't feel safe to be real. When expressing your emotions got you punished. When being too bold made you feel too much. When being your full self felt like a liability. In those moments, your subconscious stepped in and said, "Let me protect you." And so began the construction of a personality designed to survive—not thrive.

That identity was never supposed to be permanent. It was a mask, a defense mechanism, a social strategy. But over time, the mask became the mirror. You forgot who you were before the world taught you who to be. And if you've never consciously rewritten that script, chances are you're still operating under the old one. Research in *Developmental Psychology* confirms that early identity formation is shaped far more by social modeling and approval-seeking than authenticity.

The false self is a chameleon. It changes tones, tempers, and truths depending on the room. You become the "good child," the "reliable friend," the "overachiever," the "peacekeeper"—roles that earned love but cost you yourself. You feel like a performance even in your own life. It's exhausting not because you're doing too much, but because you're doing it from a version of you that's not rooted in truth.

And that's the red flag: when confidence feels conditional. When you only feel "enough" if you're producing, pleasing, or fixing something for someone else. Stillness makes you squirm. Silence feels dangerous. And success doesn't satisfy—it just moves the goalpost. That's not empowerment. That's the nervous system trying to earn safety through performance.

The price of a false identity isn't just burnout. It's disconnection. You lose the ability to hear your own voice. You second-guess what you know. You ask for opinions when your soul already has the answer. You shrink around people who feel familiar but unsafe. You fear that outgrowing your old self means losing your place in your tribe. But the truth is, your future can't be built by a version of you that was designed to survive your past.

You can't lead a soul-aligned life from a persona built in fear. The identity that keeps you relatable may also be the one that keeps you small. And you weren't born to blend in. You were born to embody your essence, to take up space with integrity, and to express the full power of who you really are. That power can't be accessed through the lens of a false self.

Here's the good news: identity is fluid. You are not stuck with the scripts you inherited. You can interrupt the loop. A 2019 study published in *Frontiers in Psychology* found that individuals who practiced authentic self-expression—by shedding false roles and integrating their true identity—experienced greater psychological well-being, confidence, and decision-making clarity.

You don't have to destroy the old identity. You just have to stop feeding it. That means you begin choosing truth over comfort, expression over performance, presence over perfection. It means speaking even when your voice shakes, choosing what aligns over what pleases, and allowing your body to feel safe as your real self. That's when the rewiring begins.

Your real identity doesn't demand perfection. It doesn't chase approval. It doesn't hustle for belonging. It simply is. It walks into rooms with quiet power. It makes decisions with calm authority. It leads not to impress, but to express. That version of you has been waiting patiently for permission. But now, it doesn't need permission—it needs *activation*.

The Clarity Confidence Code is that activation. It will guide you through seeing the false identity with compassion, understanding why it formed, releasing the need to maintain it, and reclaiming the identity that can hold your expansion. Because when you lead from truth, everything becomes lighter, clearer, and more magnetic.

In the next lesson, you'll discover the exact steps to dismantle the false identity loop—so you can stop living on autopilot and start living from power. You're not here to perform your life. You're here to embody it. And the shift begins now.

How to Interrupt the Old Identity Loop

You're not stuck because you're broken—you're stuck because a hidden loop is running the show. And that loop isn't random. It's precise. It begins with a belief, triggers an emotion, produces a behavior, delivers a result, and then—most critically—it *reinforces* the original belief. This is the architecture of the Identity Loop. It's not just how habits are formed; it's how identity is sculpted, repeated, and lived.

You don't even realize it's happening because it feels like truth. You believe "I'm not confident," so you feel anxious. You act small. You get mediocre results. And then you say, "See? I knew I wasn't confident." The loop confirms itself. Over and over. Until you forget it was ever a loop to begin with—and start thinking it's just who you are. But it's not who you are. It's who you've *practiced* being.

Modern neuroscience now confirms this. A 2020 study in *Nature Human Behaviour* showed that the brain is predictive, not reflective. It expects you to behave in line with your past and adjusts your choices accordingly. You're not just living your life—you're living your predictions of it. But when you interrupt that loop with even the smallest act of rebellion, you begin to rewrite your brain's default settings.

Disruption is more powerful than discussion. That means you don't need to talk your way out of the loop—you need to act your way out. Behavioral contradiction—deliberately doing something your current identity wouldn't—is one of the most effective neuroplasticity tools available. Studies show it rewires belief faster than affirmations because it creates evidence, not just theory.

So how do you break the loop? First, name it. Say it out loud. "I believe I am unworthy, so I shrink. I feel anxious. I stay quiet." Naming the loop breaks the trance. Awareness creates separation. You're no longer *in* it—you're observing it. That observation is the beginning of power.

Then, challenge its origin. Ask yourself: Who gave me this version of me? Who told me I had to stay small to be loved? Who rewarded me for silence, for obedience, for pleasing? More often than not, you'll realize that your loop was inherited—not chosen. And if you didn't choose it, you can choose to release it.

Next, do the opposite. Say no without a smile. Speak when you'd usually stay quiet. Publish what you've been hiding. Ask for more. These are not just courageous actions—they are neurological reboots. They interrupt the nervous system's pattern, and that disorientation is where the transformation begins.

But don't just act—*anchor* the action. Feel it. Feel the version of you who would act this way as their default. Breathe into it. Say to yourself, "This is who I am now." You're not faking. You're *claiming*. That shift in language embeds the action into identity. And now, you're no longer doing a thing—you're *being* someone new.

Reinforce the change by tracking the evidence. After each micro-win, pause. What did you do? How did it feel? What shifted? This documentation is what turns a moment of courage into a momentum of change. Harvard researchers have found that even small wins tracked consistently lead to higher confidence and increased risk tolerance.

Most people wait to feel "ready" before acting differently. But the truth is, readiness is a byproduct of action—not a prerequisite. You don't need to feel ready to become your future self. You just need to act like them—and let your nervous system catch up. That's how identity is built: action first, belief second, reinforcement third.

This is your invitation to stop waiting for permission and start disrupting the narrative. You've lived long enough in the loop of hesitation, doubt, and delay. Now it's time to build a new one—one that loops confidence, clarity, and courage. Not from hype. From embodiment.

Because identity isn't a fixed trait. It's a habit. A pattern. A choice, practiced into reality. You're not locked into the version of you that was built to survive. You're free to build the version of you who was born to lead, speak, create, and expand. In the next section, you'll meet that version through a powerful visualization—your authentic self, unfiltered and fully free. The loop ends here. And the real you begins.

Visualization: Meeting Your Authentic Self

You're not stuck because you're broken—you're stuck because a hidden loop is running the show. And that loop isn't random. It's precise. It begins with a belief, triggers an emotion, produces a behavior, delivers a result, and then—most critically—it *reinforces* the original belief. This is the architecture of the Identity Loop. It's not just how habits are formed; it's how identity is sculpted, repeated, and lived.

You don't even realize it's happening because it feels like truth. You believe "I'm not confident," so you feel anxious. You act small. You get mediocre results. And then you say, "See? I knew I wasn't confident." The loop confirms itself. Over and over. Until you forget it was ever a loop to begin with—and start thinking it's just who you are. But it's not who you are. It's who you've *practiced* being.

Modern neuroscience now confirms this. A 2020 study in *Nature Human Behaviour* showed that the brain is predictive, not reflective. It expects you to behave in line with your past and adjusts your choices accordingly. You're not just living your life—you're living your predictions of it. But when you interrupt that loop with even the smallest act of rebellion, you begin to rewrite your brain's default settings.

Disruption is more powerful than discussion. That means you don't need to talk your way out of the loop—you need to act your way out. Behavioral contradiction—deliberately doing something your current identity wouldn't—is one of the most effective neuroplasticity tools available. Studies show it rewires belief faster than affirmations because it creates evidence, not just theory.

So how do you break the loop? First, name it. Say it out loud. "I believe I am unworthy, so I shrink. I feel anxious. I stay quiet." Naming the loop breaks the trance. Awareness creates separation. You're no longer *in* it—you're observing it. That observation is the beginning of power.

Then, challenge its origin. Ask yourself: Who gave me this version of me? Who told me I had to stay small to be loved? Who rewarded me for silence, for obedience, for pleasing? More often than not, you'll realize that your loop was inherited—not chosen. And if you didn't choose it, you can choose to release it.

Next, do the opposite. Say no without a smile. Speak when you'd usually stay quiet. Publish what you've been hiding. Ask for more. These are not just courageous actions—they are neurological reboots. They interrupt the nervous system's pattern, and that disorientation is where the transformation begins.

But don't just act—*anchor* the action. Feel it. Feel the version of you who would act this way as their default. Breathe into it. Say to yourself, "This is who I am now." You're not faking. You're *claiming*. That shift in language embeds the action into identity. And now, you're no longer doing a thing—you're *being* someone new.

Reinforce the change by tracking the evidence. After each micro-win, pause. What did you do? How did it feel? What shifted? This documentation is what turns a moment of courage into a momentum of change. Harvard researchers have found that even small wins tracked consistently lead to higher confidence and increased risk tolerance.

Most people wait to feel "ready" before acting differently. But the truth is, readiness is a byproduct of action—not a prerequisite. You don't need to feel ready to become your future self. You just need to act like them—and let your nervous system catch up. That's how identity is built: action first, belief second, reinforcement third.

This is your invitation to stop waiting for permission and start disrupting the narrative. You've lived long enough in the loop of hesitation, doubt, and delay. Now it's time to build a new one—one that loops confidence, clarity, and courage. Not from hype. From embodiment.

Because identity isn't a fixed trait. It's a habit. A pattern. A choice, practiced into reality. You're not locked into the version of you that was built to survive. You're free to build the version of you who was born to lead, speak, create, and expand. In the next section, you'll meet that version through a powerful visualization—your authentic self, unfiltered and fully free. The loop ends here. And the real you begins.

Building a New Inner Narrative

Every word you speak is a spell—whether it builds your future or binds you to your past depends entirely on your intention. Most people don't realize that language is not simply communication; it is creation. When you say, "I am," you're not describing your reality. You're instructing your subconscious mind on how to behave, what to expect, and what kind of life to prepare for you. This is the science behind verbal imprinting. Your words are not just sounds—they are commands.

Your nervous system is always listening. It doesn't debate your self-talk. It doesn't filter truth from fear. It simply obeys. Neuroscience confirms this: a 2019 study in *Neuropsychologia* showed that self-referential language—the phrases you say about yourself—activates the medial prefrontal cortex, the same area that governs identity, motivation, and behavior. This means the moment you say, "I am stuck," your brain adjusts your emotional and behavioral responses to match stuckness.

This is why change doesn't start with doing. It starts with declaring. Your tongue becomes your wand. And the words you repeat—especially with emotional charge—become the new neural pathways that define your self-concept. Speak limitations, and you live them. Speak power, and you rise into it. This isn't motivational fluff. It's biology.

Consider the language you use when you mess up. Do you say, "I'm such an idiot," or "I never get it right"? That's not humility—that's hypnosis. It's reinforcing a loop where your identity becomes entangled with error. Instead, when you say, "I am learning," or "I am growing stronger from this," you shift the narrative and signal your brain to anchor resilience over shame.

Auditing your language is the first step to liberation. Over the next 24 hours, notice your reflexive phrases. When challenged, what do you say? When someone compliments you, how do you receive it? These patterns are windows into your subconscious script. You can't rewire what you don't recognize. Awareness precedes transformation.

Then rewrite your script deliberately. Choose five core areas of your life—confidence, wealth, relationships, purpose, and health. For each one, write a new identity statement. Not a hope, but a declaration. "I am a calm and confident speaker." "I am a magnetic force for aligned abundance." "I am loved deeply and reciprocally." These statements aren't meant to feel true right away. They're meant to feel possible. Possibility is where the brain begins to shift.

Speak them daily—out loud. A 2022 study in *Brain and Language* revealed that vocal affirmations, especially when combined with physical expression (like posture and tone), create stronger neural responses than internal affirmations alone. This is because embodied speech activates mirror neurons and strengthens emotional learning. Don't whisper these. Declare them.

Stack your verbal imprinting with visualization. After speaking your affirmations, close your eyes and see yourself living from them. Don't just imagine the scene—feel it. Let your body experience the emotion of success, confidence, abundance. Your brain doesn't distinguish between imagined and real when the emotion is vivid. This is how you create memory before it happens.

Throughout the day, anchor your identity. Set reminders on your phone with phrases like "I am unstoppable," or "I lead with clarity." Leave sticky notes on your mirror or computer. Before meetings, say one of your identity statements aloud. These micro-repetitions carve new grooves into your subconscious. The more your brain hears it, the more it believes it—and the faster it aligns.

Remember: your old identity was built the same way. It was programmed with repetition. "I'm not good enough." "I always fail." "I'm too sensitive." You didn't consciously choose those beliefs. But now you can consciously *change* them. And that change begins at the level of language.

Declare it until it becomes second nature. Repeat it until it's hardwired. Speak it until you no longer have to think about it—because you've become it. This is not fake it 'til you make it. This is *declare it until you embody it*. Speak from your future self. Act like the person you're becoming. Let your words pull you into your destiny.

In the next session, we'll go even deeper. You'll craft a personalized identity script tailored to your vision. You'll learn how to adjust it in real-time, use it in moments of fear, and build it into your morning and evening routines. Because the life you want doesn't begin with a goal. It begins with a declaration. And your new declaration begins now.

Anchoring Positive Identity Shifts

Your subconscious isn't moved by your hopes. It's moved by your instructions. If your subconscious is the software running your life, then your words are the keyboard. Every phrase you speak programs the identity you live from—either reinforcing the version of you built on fear, or activating the version aligned with power, purpose, and presence. This is the foundation of identity scripting. It's not about positive thinking. It's about identity-based alignment, where language, emotion, and embodiment converge to shape who you are becoming.

What you say about yourself becomes what your brain expects. A 2021 study in *Cognitive Therapy and Research* revealed that people who rewrote their identity-based language for just 21 days experienced measurable increases in confidence, clarity, and goal fulfillment—especially when they paired those statements with vocal repetition and visualization. That's because the brain doesn't just remember words. It reconfigures behavior to match them.

Your mind doesn't respond to vague declarations like "I'll try." It responds to certainty. It responds to language that signals identity, not just desire. When you say "I am," you are not reporting your circumstances. You are commanding your subconscious to reinforce a belief as if it were fact. Stanford neuroscientists confirm that "I am" language activates the brain's valuation and motivation centers, directly influencing resilience, confidence, and focus.

That's why generic affirmations don't work. "I'm trying to feel good enough" only reinforces the idea that you're still trying. Instead, emotional power words like "I am magnetic," "I am a force," or "I am built for expansion" shift your neurology. Your body listens. Your nervous system adapts. And your behaviors begin to reflect your new identity.

But the first step is honesty. You must define the old script. What beliefs have you been repeating that keep you small? "I always mess it up." "I'm not good with money." "I can't speak confidently." Write these down without judgment. These are the codes you've been running in the background—often inherited, not chosen.

Then write the opposite. If you weren't operating from fear, who would you be? "I am a calm and confident communicator." "I command presence and radiate clarity." "I am safe to be seen and to speak." These aren't just words. They're truth activated. They are how your Empowered Self speaks.

Now embody it. Don't just say these in your head. Speak them out loud. Look yourself in the mirror. Adjust your posture. Say it with energy. When you combine repetition with somatic anchoring, you accelerate identity installation. *Psychological Bulletin* published findings showing that verbal repetition plus emotional intensity reshapes cognitive and behavioral patterns in 30 days or less when practiced consistently.

Every morning and evening, script five core "I am" statements across five pillars: confidence, voice, worth, power, and purpose. Let them guide your day, anchor your focus, and reset your self-perception. Examples: "I am a powerful and grounded presence." "I am safe to express my truth." "I am worthy of overflow." Let them become your new normal.

You can also script identity statements for key moments in life. Before speaking: "I am a heart-centered communicator." Before sales: "I am safe to offer and receive value." In conflict: "I am emotionally anchored and sovereign." Before expansion: "I am the version of me who holds more joy, love, and success." These micro-scripts shift your default response in real time.

What you repeat, you reinforce. The more you speak these new identity codes, the more your subconscious will accept them as truth. The more your body feels them, the more your nervous system will normalize them. And the more you act from them, the more your results will rise to meet them.

This isn't about becoming someone else. It's about removing who you were never meant to be and returning to the truth you forgot. The future version of you already exists. Your words are the bridge that take you there. Declare them boldly. Script them precisely. Anchor them daily.

In the next lesson, we'll take these scripts and bring them into your environment. Through ritual and repetition, you'll embed your new identity into your daily rhythm—until it becomes automatic, natural, and unshakable. Because your identity isn't just who you are. It's the story you've decided to tell—one phrase, one breath, one empowered declaration at a time.

Mirror Work and Affirmation Tools

Your identity does not stick because you think it once. It sticks because you repeat it in motion, in practice, and in presence. The brain rewires through repetition, but the soul anchors truth through ritual. Real transformation is not about hype; it's about consistency. When your environment, habits, and body all echo your new self, the shift from possibility to inevitability is no longer theory—it's reality.

You don't need more motivation. You need a system. The most successful people in the world don't rely on emotional highs to move forward. They use rituals. As one renowned behavioral scientist once said, "You do not rise to the level of your goals. You fall to the level of your systems." Systems make expansion automatic. And the most powerful system for identity change is ritual anchoring.

Ritual anchoring is the daily practice of locking your identity into your physical, emotional, and behavioral routines. It's not about willpower—it's about wiring. A Duke University study showed that 45% of our behavior is not conscious—it's habitual. If your habits don't carry your future self, your past self will keep winning. This isn't just about discipline. It's neuroscience.

To start, choose a time each day—5 to 10 minutes—to tap into your Empowered Self. This could be the moment after waking up or just before sleep. Speak your identity statements aloud. Visualize yourself already living them. Journal a few sentences as if you were already that version of you. Breathe deeply while affirming, "This is who I am now." The magic isn't in doing it perfectly. It's in doing it daily.

Next, change one object in your physical space. Swap your phone background to something that reflects your highest self. Tape your favorite "I AM" phrase to your mirror. Use a notebook titled "Becoming" to track wins. Why? Because the brain responds to visual cues. If you see it, you believe it. If you believe it, you behave from it.

Habit stack your identity cues. Say your affirmations while brushing your teeth. Visualize success while sipping coffee. Listen to your recorded voice notes while walking. These small changes compound. According to Stanford's Behavior Design Lab, habits stick best when they're emotional, frequent, and anchored in a real environment. This isn't extra work. It's intentional automation.

Movement accelerates change. Don't just speak your affirmations—stand tall, breathe deep, stretch wide, and move your body as you say them. Studies in *Frontiers in Psychology* reveal that combining motion with affirmation activates motor memory and cements identity shifts faster. When the body feels it, the brain memorizes it.

Set up emotional checkpoints throughout your day. Ask yourself: "Am I acting from my past self or my Empowered Self?" or "What would my future self do right now?" These small questions act like pattern interrupts. They re-center you into intentional living, pulling you out of autopilot and back into your aligned self.

This isn't about more hustle. It's about more harmony. Rituals don't demand you to push harder—they invite you to be deeper. To show up as the version of you who's already worthy, already ready, already equipped. You're not creating a new you. You're creating space for the *real* you to show up consistently.

Rituals rewire self-trust. Every time you show up for your ritual, you teach your brain, "I'm dependable. I follow through. I act like my future self today." That's not mindset. That's embodiment. You become someone who doesn't just talk about confidence—you live it, moment by moment, breath by breath.

If you've struggled to stay consistent in the past, it's not because you lack discipline. It's because your rituals weren't aligned with identity. When the ritual matches the self you want to become, it stops feeling like effort and starts feeling like integrity. And that shift makes consistency sustainable.

Ritual anchoring isn't another to-do list item. It's the container that holds your transformation. You're no longer just hoping to change. You're rehearsing your future into the present. One breath, one affirmation, one morning at a time. In the next lesson, you'll learn how to close the gap between your inner transformation and your outer expression—so the world sees what you now know to be true. You are becoming. And this is how you make it stick.

Daily Identity Rewiring Habits

You don't wake up confident. You *become* confident through deliberate design. Every day, with every thought and action, you're sending a broadcast to your nervous system about who you are and what's possible. That signal becomes your identity. And your identity creates your reality. Confidence is not an emotion you wait to feel—it's a character you *choose* to play until it becomes who you are.

Repetition is the language of identity. It's not what you do once that rewires your life—it's what you rehearse. Identity is not formed in chaos or crisis. It's formed through steady, intentional action. According to research from University College London, it takes an average of 66 days to form a new habit, with emotional investment being a critical factor in its success. That means your future self isn't some distant dream. It's a repeated decision away.

When you move, speak, and act from the version of you who already owns their confidence, your nervous system recalibrates. You teach your body that it's safe to take up space, to speak boldly, to choose differently. Identity is not fixed. It is programmable. It is a pattern. And patterns are rewritten through consistency, not intensity.

The most powerful time to shape that pattern is in the morning. Your brain is most suggestible in the first 60 minutes of your day. A 2020 study in *Cognitive Behavioral Therapy Today* found that individuals who engaged in morning routines combining movement, positive self-talk, and visualization experienced increased focus, mood regulation, and goal achievement. Mornings aren't just rituals—they're recalibrations.

That's why a morning formula matters. First, read your Identity Script aloud—declare with power who you are becoming. Next, engage in somatic activation. Stand tall. Breathe deep. Move like someone who believes in themselves. Then, close your eyes and visualize your future self in motion—see them making decisions, handling challenges, speaking clearly. Finally, journal a quick reflection on how you led from that self yesterday. Reinforce what you want repeated.

Why this process works is simple: it hits all four identity anchors—language, emotion, body, and memory. Most people focus only on mindset. But identity lives in the body. In how you sit, walk, breathe, and respond. When you speak it, feel it, move it, and record it—you become it faster. That's not hype. That's neurobiology.

Visualization isn't imagination. It's instruction. When you vividly picture yourself doing something, your brain lights up the same regions as if you're physically doing it. Research published in *Neuropsychologia* shows that mental rehearsal activates the motor cortex, which means your mind begins to build muscle memory from thought alone. That's the power of intentional vision.

And don't underestimate the power of journaling. Writing as your future self has been shown to significantly boost emotional regulation, motivation, and task execution. A study in *Frontiers in Psychology* found that just 10 minutes a day of future-self journaling enhanced goal follow-through and personal alignment. You're not just writing words—you're encoding identity.

But confidence doesn't stick if you don't protect it. Every scroll of comparison, every disempowering conversation, every mindless moment of self-doubt erodes the self you're building. That's why your night ritual matters too. End the day with reflection. Acknowledge the wins. Speak truth before sleep. What you imprint into your subconscious before rest determines what is strengthened during REM.

Sleep, in fact, is not passive—it's a prime time for consolidation. A 2021 neuroscience study revealed that identity-linked beliefs are stored during REM cycles. This means your bedtime language, thoughts, and intentions become part of your long-term self-concept. Speak your truth before sleep. Let your future self echo in your dreams.

Daily rewiring isn't about perfection. It's about persistence. You've practiced your old self for years. The awkwardness you feel when stepping into your future self isn't a sign it's wrong—it's a sign it's *new*. That tension is growth. And every time you choose the new self—especially when it's hard—you make that identity more real.

So each morning, ask: "Who do I choose to be today?" Answer not with wishes, but with your voice, your breath, your steps, your posture. Confidence isn't built on motivation. It's built on installation. One repetition at a time. Because the new you is not born. They are *installed*. One breath. One action. One choice at a time.

Your New Self-Declaration

You don't wake up confident. You *become* confident through deliberate design. Every day, with every thought and action, you're sending a broadcast to your nervous system about who you are and what's possible. That signal becomes your identity. And your identity creates your reality. Confidence is not an emotion you wait to feel—it's a character you *choose* to play until it becomes who you are.

Repetition is the language of identity. It's not what you do once that rewires your life—it's what you rehearse. Identity is not formed in chaos or crisis. It's formed through steady, intentional action. According to research from University College London, it takes an average of 66 days to form a new habit, with emotional investment being a critical factor in its success. That means your future self isn't some distant dream. It's a repeated decision away.

When you move, speak, and act from the version of you who already owns their confidence, your nervous system recalibrates. You teach your body that it's safe to take up space, to speak boldly, to choose differently. Identity is not fixed. It is programmable. It is a pattern. And patterns are rewritten through consistency, not intensity.

The most powerful time to shape that pattern is in the morning. Your brain is most suggestible in the first 60 minutes of your day. A 2020 study in *Cognitive Behavioral Therapy Today* found that individuals who engaged in morning routines combining movement, positive self-talk, and visualization experienced increased focus, mood regulation, and goal achievement. Mornings aren't just rituals—they're recalibrations.

That's why a morning formula matters. First, read your Identity Script aloud—declare with power who you are becoming. Next, engage in somatic activation. Stand tall. Breathe deep. Move like someone who believes in themselves. Then, close your eyes and visualize your future self in motion—see them making decisions, handling challenges, speaking clearly. Finally, journal a quick reflection on how you led from that self yesterday. Reinforce what you want repeated.

Why this process works is simple: it hits all four identity anchors—language, emotion, body, and memory. Most people focus only on mindset. But identity lives in the body. In how you sit, walk, breathe, and respond. When you speak it, feel it, move it, and record it—you become it faster. That's not hype. That's neurobiology.

Visualization isn't imagination. It's instruction. When you vividly picture yourself doing something, your brain lights up the same regions as if you're physically doing it. Research published in *Neuropsychologia* shows that mental rehearsal activates the motor cortex, which means your mind begins to build muscle memory from thought alone. That's the power of intentional vision.

And don't underestimate the power of journaling. Writing as your future self has been shown to significantly boost emotional regulation, motivation, and task execution. A study in *Frontiers in Psychology* found that just 10 minutes a day of future-self journaling enhanced goal follow-through and personal alignment. You're not just writing words—you're encoding identity.

But confidence doesn't stick if you don't protect it. Every scroll of comparison, every disempowering conversation, every mindless moment of self-doubt erodes the self you're building. That's why your night ritual matters too. End the day with reflection. Acknowledge the wins. Speak truth before sleep. What you imprint into your subconscious before rest determines what is strengthened during REM.

Sleep, in fact, is not passive—it's a prime time for consolidation. A 2021 neuroscience study revealed that identity-linked beliefs are stored during REM cycles. This means your bedtime language, thoughts, and intentions become part of your long-term self-concept. Speak your truth before sleep. Let your future self echo in your dreams.

Daily rewiring isn't about perfection. It's about persistence. You've practiced your old self for years. The awkwardness you feel when stepping into your future self isn't a sign it's wrong—it's a sign it's *new*. That tension is growth. And every time you choose the new self—especially when it's hard—you make that identity more real.

So each morning, ask: "Who do I choose to be today?" Answer not with wishes, but with your voice, your breath, your steps, your posture. Confidence isn't built on motivation. It's built on installation. One repetition at a time. Because the new you is not born. They are *installed*. One breath. One action. One choice at a time.

Exercise: Rewrite Your Self-Image Script

Your self-image is not a reflection—it's a rehearsal. Every time you think a thought about who you are, you're casting yourself in a role. And the more you rehearse that role, the more it feels real. But just because you've rehearsed playing small doesn't mean you're meant to live that script. It only means that a version of you has been allowed to take the stage who wasn't qualified to direct the show. That ends now.

The science is clear: identity is malleable. Neuroplasticity—the brain's ability to rewire itself—means that your personality isn't fixed, it's practiced. According to *Nature Reviews Neuroscience*, the pathways in your brain that carry self-beliefs grow stronger the more you repeat them. If you've practiced powerlessness, the brain becomes fluent in that language. But practice empowerment, and your neurology reshapes to match.

What you think, you feel. What you feel, you believe. And what you believe, you become. This is not opinion. It's psychology. Your subconscious doesn't argue with you—it obeys. When you say "I'm not confident," your nervous system says, "Got it. Let's act shy, dim the voice, avoid risk." But when you say, "I lead with presence," your body adjusts its breath, your eyes lift, and you speak with authority. The command rewrites the chemistry.

This is the moment you take the pen back. No more letting past stories or childhood wounds write your identity. This is the authoring of your future self, in real time, with your own voice. The first step? Radical honesty. Write down what you've believed about yourself that no longer serves you. Let it be raw. "I've been acting like someone who stays silent to avoid rejection." That awareness unlocks the ability to rewrite it.

From there, flip the script. Create a declaration that embodies who you are becoming. Write it in the present tense. Not "I want to be confident," but "I am a calm, grounded, and magnetic communicator." Your nervous system doesn't respond to what you hope for—it responds to what you command. This is the language of identity leadership.

Read your script out loud. Yes, out loud. A 2022 study in *Brain and Language* found that verbal affirmations, when paired with emotion or movement, activate deeper neural pathways than silent thoughts. So say it with conviction. Stand up. Breathe deeply. Speak your truth into the room like it's already law. Because it is.

Once you've written your empowered script, anchor it into your life. Post it on your mirror. Record it on your phone and listen daily. Make it your morning soundtrack. Let it be the first and last voice your nervous system hears each day. This is not a motivational routine—it's identity training. Repetition becomes recognition. Recognition becomes reality.

It's important to understand this isn't about "fake it till you make it." It's about *faith it till you become it*. You're not pretending to be someone new—you're remembering the version of you that was always there beneath the noise. This script is not a fantasy. It's your true voice, finally freed from conditioning.

The old self was never the problem. It was a protective performance based on outdated beliefs. But survival mode is not your default anymore. Now you lead with presence. You speak with clarity. You decide from worth. And the more you practice this script, the more that version becomes automatic. That's the real definition of confidence: congruence with your chosen identity.

So say it now. Say it daily. Say it even when it feels awkward. Especially then. Because identity change feels unfamiliar—not because it's fake, but because it's new. And everything new feels like resistance at first. Push through. Your nervous system is not your enemy. It's your ally. But it must be led.

You're not broken. You've just been running a script that's expired. But this is your rewrite. And in this new draft, you don't wait for permission, worthiness, or approval. You speak. You lead. You act. And most of all—you *become*. Because from this moment forward, you're not reacting to life. You're rehearsing your highest self, until it becomes the only version of you left standing.

Let the old version rest. Let the new one rise. And each time you read your script aloud, remember: you're not just saying words. You're rebuilding a reality. One that finally fits the power you've had all along.

What you've just experienced in these pages is only the beginning. You've tapped into clarity. You've glimpsed confidence. But real transformation—deep, lasting, undeniable confidence—is forged through repetition, immersion, and identity reprogramming at the subconscious level. That's exactly what the *Clarity Confidence Code Course* delivers. This isn't just another course—it's a complete mind shift, a proven system to rewire how you think, feel, and act from the inside out. If you're ready to master the inner game and lock in the new you—not just for a day, but for life—then it's time to go all in. Don't leave your breakthrough half-finished. Step fully into your power at 👉 https://clarityconfidencecode.com

Because the next chapter of your life deserves nothing less than the most powerful version of you.

CHAPTER 3

THE POWER OF INNER CLARITY — FROM MENTAL CLUTTER TO CRYSTAL VISION

Understanding the Cost of Confusion

Confusion is not harmless—it's a silent killer of dreams. Every moment you hesitate in indecision, you bleed energy, income, and belief in your own power. And yet, so many accept confusion as a casual byproduct of life, not realizing it's a thief. Neuroscience proves that uncertainty triggers your brain's fear center—the amygdala—as if you're under threat. That means every time you say "I don't know," your body goes into survival mode. (UC Berkeley) This isn't just a mental fog—it's biological warfare on your confidence.

You weren't born to live in hesitation. You were born to move mountains, shift rooms, and walk boldly in purpose. But clarity doesn't appear like magic—it's summoned. Waiting for clarity is like waiting for permission to live. The truth is, your next level isn't hidden. It's just buried under layers of fear that masquerade as logic. Every second you delay a decision, you reinforce the belief that you can't trust yourself. And that identity? That's what keeps people stuck for decades.

Studies confirm it—indecision robs your self-trust. Even when people later make the correct choice, they feel less confident if they hesitated too long. (Psychological Science) Imagine that. Your confidence has less to do with being "right," and everything to do with how quickly you act. That means the goal isn't to be perfect—it's to move. Because momentum builds mastery.

Confusion often becomes a shield we hide behind. Saying "I don't know what to do" can sound humble or responsible, but it's often just fear dressed up as thoughtfulness. We use confusion as a cover—so we don't have to risk failure, rejection, or radical success. It's not that you're unclear. It's that the truth feels scary. But you weren't designed to play small. The fear you feel is the signal that you're close to something powerful.

Most people wait for confidence to act, not realizing that confidence is built through action. It's like trying to get warm without starting the fire. Research in decision-making psychology shows that certainty increases not with accuracy—but with repeated action. (Organizational Behavior and Human Decision Processes) The more you decide, the more you trust your ability to decide. Action isn't the enemy—it's the cure.

This means clarity is not something you stumble into. It's something you generate. Each decision you make, no matter how small, becomes a stepping stone out of the fog. You learn by doing. You grow by deciding. Insight doesn't come from overthinking—it comes from engaging with life. You get data. You adjust. You align. And that's when momentum kicks in. That's when purpose becomes a force.

Without clarity, you end up saying yes to things that drain you. You chase careers, relationships, or goals that were never meant for you. You burn energy climbing ladders that lead to nowhere. But when you live from clarity, you become magnetic. Your presence shifts rooms. People listen differently. Doors open without you knocking. That's not luck—that's alignment.

The world doesn't respond to hesitation—it responds to conviction. When you walk in clarity, your energy changes. You don't need to sell yourself—you simply show up, and the right opportunities recognize you. You become the invitation. You become the example. That's how leaders are made—not from perfection, but from powerful clarity.

There's a question most never dare to ask: What am I pretending not to know? What truth have I buried under the noise of doubt? Your life changes the moment you stop waiting for guarantees and start trusting your inner compass. The answers are already within. You don't need another book or certification. You need courage.

Courage to choose. Courage to act. Courage to trust. Because the pain of staying stuck is always greater than the risk of moving forward. The discomfort of change is temporary, but the regret of inaction lasts a lifetime. There's no clarity coming later—it's waiting on your decision right now. The fog lifts when you move.

And here's the truth most people never hear: power doesn't come from having all the answers—it comes from choosing in spite of not having them. From moving when it still feels messy. From stepping out while the fear still whispers. That's real power. That's unshakable confidence.

Clarity isn't something you find. It's something you claim. And the moment you claim it, your life shifts. Not because the world changed, but because you did. You stopped waiting. You started leading. And that's when everything begins to move.

Why Clarity Precedes Confidence

Confidence doesn't appear out of thin air. It's earned through clarity—the kind of clarity that lights your soul on fire and puts your feet on solid ground. The world will tell you to "just believe in yourself," but neuroscience tells a deeper truth. Your brain is hardwired to freeze when the path ahead is foggy. According to a 2021 study in Nature Reviews Neuroscience, ambiguity triggers the anterior cingulate cortex, the region that governs emotional conflict and hesitation (Nature). That means hesitation isn't weakness—it's biology reacting to lack of direction.

When you're confused, your system interprets it as danger. Your nervous system slams on the brakes, not because you're incapable, but because it hasn't received the green light called clarity. Once that light turns on, everything changes. Your vision sharpens. Your actions align. You move with conviction. You lead not because you feel fearless, but because you finally know where you're going—and why it matters.

You can't chant your way into confidence. You must define what you stand for. Clarity is the foundation that lets confidence grow tall. When you're clear on who you are, what you want, and what you refuse to tolerate, self-doubt loses its grip. That's not opinion—that's proven. Studies show that a strong sense of self and life purpose significantly boosts confidence, especially under pressure (Psychological Bulletin).

You've seen people who appear confident, but crumble under challenge. That's what happens when confidence is built on performance, not purpose. Real confidence is rooted in identity. When your voice echoes your values and your actions mirror your truth, you no longer seek validation. You radiate alignment. And that alignment—more than applause or results—is what creates unshakable self-belief.

The tragedy is this: too many people are exhausting themselves in motion with no direction. They take book after book. Chase every new opportunity. But without clarity, their energy is scattered. They confuse busyness with progress. But clarity brings precision. And precision is power. As author James Clear puts it: "Motion feels like progress. But action with clarity creates results."

What matters most is not how much you do, but whether it's aligned with who you are. A powerful meta-analysis in Motivation and Emotion confirms this: people who are clear on their values and goals sustain higher levels of motivation and self-confidence over time—even more than those with raw talent (Springer). That means the edge isn't ability—it's alignment.

And when your mind is aligned, your inner voice changes. You stop second-guessing. You stop looking outside for answers. You stop living in delay. Clarity quiets the noise of fear. It silences the inner critic. It gives you permission to trust the person you're becoming. You begin to speak not just with certainty, but with authority. And that authority becomes your energy signature.

What's wild is how many people chase confidence when what they need is clarity. They set goals without knowing who they are. They pursue success that doesn't align with their soul. But you can't outrun confusion—you must confront it. You must get still enough to ask: "What do I truly want? Who do I need to become to receive it? What beliefs no longer belong on my journey?"

This isn't about perfection. It's about direction. Clarity gives your pain a purpose. It gives your past a frame. It gives your future a pull. And when you walk in that clarity, you walk differently. You speak differently. People treat you differently. Because the world responds to someone who knows who they are and where they're going.

Everything you want is downstream of clarity. The love you crave. The wealth you deserve. The impact you were born to make. It all hinges on your willingness to get crystal clear. And here's the secret: the clearer you are, the faster life organizes around your vision. That's not spiritual fluff—that's psychology, physics, and biology in harmony.

So instead of asking how to be more confident, ask where you need to get clearer. What decision are you delaying? What dream are you negotiating with fear? What version of you is ready to lead? Because clarity isn't a privilege—it's a choice. And once you choose it, the universe takes notice.

Confidence isn't a gift you wait for. It's a fire you ignite by stepping into the truth of who you are. And the moment you claim that truth with clarity, the world will move to meet you. Not because you're loud—but because you're aligned. Not because you have all the answers—but because you've stopped running from the ones already within you.

Inner vs. Outer Clarity

Outer clarity might impress the crowd, but it's inner clarity that transforms your life. The world celebrates productivity, aesthetics, and external success—but what's the point of looking like a leader if you feel lost on the inside? People chase titles and trophies hoping they'll fill a void, only to find themselves more anxious, disconnected, and unfulfilled. Research from Harvard psychologist Daniel Gilbert reveals that when our decisions aren't aligned with our core selves, we become poor predictors of our own happiness (Harvard Scholar). That's not just disappointing—it's disempowering.

When you know who you are at the core, the world stops being so loud. You no longer rely on applause to validate your path. You no longer edit yourself to be accepted. That shift is called identity congruence—the psychological alignment between your values and your behaviors. A study from the Journal of Personality and Social Psychology proves that people with high internal self-concept clarity experience greater emotional resilience and decisiveness, especially during chaos (APA). That means the clearer you are on the inside, the calmer you move through the storms.

This isn't theory—it's strategy. Inner clarity becomes your GPS. It tells you which direction aligns with your purpose, not just your pressure. It whispers when something isn't right, even when it looks good on paper. Because outer clarity without that inner compass is a trap. It becomes performance. You check every box, hit every goal, and still feel empty. You're not confused—you're disconnected. And no amount of hustle can make up for that.

If you're feeling burnt out, overwhelmed, or misaligned, check this first: are your goals truly yours? Or are you living someone else's blueprint, trying to earn worth through achievement? A 2021 study in Occupational Health Psychology confirms that misalignment between inner values and outer goals leads to job-related anxiety and emotional fatigue (APA). That means burnout isn't just about workload—it's about living without soul alignment.

Once you get clear on the inside, your outer world starts to make sense. You stop second-guessing. You stop asking for permission. You stop needing a committee to validate your intuition. Decisions become quicker. Priorities become sharper. You move from noise to knowing. And knowing is where real power lives. The kind of power that doesn't need to yell to be heard. The kind of power that changes lives in silence.

So how do you find that kind of clarity? You interrogate your identity. You ask the questions most people avoid. What do I truly value? What am I done tolerating? What do I stand for, even when it's inconvenient? These aren't affirmations. They're activations. Acceptance and Commitment Therapy (ACT) has proven that when people align their behavior with personal values, clarity and motivation increase dramatically (NIH). That's not mindset talk— that's measurable neuroscience.

The mistake most people make is thinking clarity is a bonus. Something you get after you've succeeded. But clarity is not a luxury—it's a launchpad. The clearer your internal blueprint, the more unstoppable your external reality becomes. You don't chase success. You become someone who success chases. You don't push harder—you align deeper. That's the difference between effort and embodiment.

This is why clarity feels magnetic. When you walk into a room clear on who you are and what you're here to do, the room adjusts. People respond differently. Life organizes around conviction. That's not charisma—it's coherence. Your internal world becomes so aligned, it shapes the external without force. You become the cause, not the effect. You become the signal, not the noise.

You won't get there by being busy. You get there by being bold enough to ask what really matters. You have to be willing to burn the false versions of yourself to uncover the real one. That's the only clarity that lasts. The kind that holds firm when everything else is shaking. The kind that can't be bought, borrowed, or broken. That's what makes it powerful. That's what makes it rare.

The truth is, most people are afraid of clarity. Because clarity demands change. Once you see the truth, you can't unsee it. Once you know what you're here for, settling becomes suffering. But the pain of clarity is the beginning of power. It calls you higher. It breaks the cycle. And it dares you to become the person you were born to be, not the one the world trained you to be.

You've been taught to value noise. But power is found in stillness. In asking better questions. In building from the inside out. So stop outsourcing your destiny. Stop editing your voice. Start with truth. Start with values. Start with clarity. Because once you get the inside right, the outside can't help but rise to match it.

Outer clarity follows inner conviction. When you build from the inside, the world bends to match your truth. That's not motivation. That's physics, biology, psychology—and destiny—working together. So step into it. Boldly. Unapologetically. Unstoppably.

Common Clarity Blocks

You didn't come into this world confused. You came in clear—fully connected to who you are and what you're here to express. There was no self-doubt, no hesitation, just pure alignment. But somewhere along the way, the signal got scrambled. Layers of conditioning, fear, and expectation blurred your vision. And now, when you try to take bold steps, something unseen holds you back. Not your potential. Not your intelligence. But the inner blocks to clarity that quietly run the show.

Clarity isn't missing—it's buried. And the deeper tragedy is this: most people never stop long enough to recognize that they're not actually confused—they're blocked. These clarity blocks wear many disguises. They sound like logic, responsibility, or humility. But make no mistake—confusion is not your personality. It's a symptom. And until you name it, it will rule you.

One of the most common blocks is the fear of being wrong. You delay decisions because you're terrified of making a mistake. But neuroscience confirms that clarity improves through motion, not mental rehearsal. A 2020 study in the journal Cognition shows that taking decisive action—whether right or wrong—strengthens your decision-making ability over time (source). The brain builds clarity through experience, not avoidance.

Then there's perfectionism, the master manipulator of momentum. You tell yourself you're just being careful, but perfectionism is just procrastination with a better pitch. Research from the University of Kent reveals that perfectionists are more likely to be mentally exhausted and stuck in confusion due to overanalysis (source). It doesn't make you better. It just makes you paralyzed.

Another major block is emotional attachment to your past. You can't fully envision a new future while clinging to an outdated identity. This is called identity inertia. Until you let go of who you were—especially the version of you that was shaped by guilt, failure, or trauma—your subconscious will resist clarity. A 2019 meta-analysis in Clinical Psychology Review confirmed that unresolved shame reduces goal clarity and self-efficacy (source). To move forward, you must release the weight of old roles.

Sometimes the block isn't internal—it's external noise. Advice. Opinions. Expectations. When you ask others for guidance before asking yourself, you're not seeking clarity—you're outsourcing your power. There's a time for wise counsel, but if you can't hear your own voice above the crowd, then clarity can't breathe. The loudest voice in your life must be your own.

Another clarity thief is identity conflict. You say you want change, but part of you is afraid of what that change might cost—relationships, approval, or stability. This internal conflict creates a fog. You're torn between expansion and comfort. A 2017 study in Frontiers in Psychology found that identity conflict leads to indecision, anxiety, and avoidance behaviors (source). You don't lack vision—you lack alignment.

And then there's emotional overwhelm. When your nervous system is dysregulated, your clarity collapses. Chronic stress shuts down the brain's ability to plan, organize, and take inspired action. This isn't a mindset flaw—it's biology. Studies show that long-term stress impairs cognitive clarity and goal setting (source). Before you can think clearly, you must feel safe.

Information overload is another silent block. You consume endlessly—books, podcasts, books—but never integrate. You mistake research for readiness. But clarity doesn't come from volume. It comes from depth. As Cal Newport says, "Clarity comes from doing deep work, not drowning in noise" (source). The more information you absorb without action, the more disconnected from your intuition you become.

Then there's the block of disembodiment. You try to think your way into clarity, but clarity is not just cognitive—it's somatic. If you're not connected to your emotions, your body, or your intuition, you'll ignore the subtle signals guiding you toward alignment. Clarity is felt before it's defined. You don't just know it—you sense it.

But the most dangerous block of all is waiting for permission. You stall not because you lack direction—but because you're waiting for someone else to validate it. You want confirmation before you move. But clarity is self-issued. No one is coming to approve your vision. That's your job. And the moment you stop waiting, the fog begins to lift.

Clarity doesn't arrive when you force it. It arrives when you remove the blocks that are suffocating your truth. It's not about trying harder—it's about trusting deeper. The minute you stop believing the lie that you need someone else's approval to move forward, you realign with your power. And when you return to that place, everything changes. You remember what you've always known. You were never confused. You were just disconnected.

The Power of Asking Better Questions

You don't need more time, more talent, or even more tools. What you need is a better question. Because clarity doesn't come from overthinking—it comes from asking the kind of question that activates your deepest intelligence. Science confirms this. Harvard researchers found that when you ask a question, your brain automatically starts looking for answers—even if the question is disempowering. This is the "question-behavior effect" (Harvard Business Review). Which means every time you ask, "Why can't I do this?" your brain goes to work proving your limitations. But when you ask, "What would this look like if it were simple?" your brain starts building pathways to possibility.

You've been trained to think the answer is out there. That the solution lies in the next book, the next expert, the next breakthrough. But the truth is, answers are shaped by the questions you dare to ask. Ask low-quality questions, and you'll get low-quality clarity. Ask questions rooted in fear, and your clarity will be filtered through anxiety. But ask questions rooted in identity and vision—and your whole perspective shifts. You move from guessing to knowing. From reacting to leading.

The most confident people don't have fewer problems. They just ask better questions. Questions like: "What is this moment trying to teach me?" "How would my future self navigate this?" "What am I pretending not to know?" These aren't affirmations. They're activations. They bypass the noise and speak directly to the wisdom within you. A study in the Journal of Cognitive Enhancement found that people who asked themselves future-anchored questions daily experienced greater clarity, motivation, and emotional strength (Springer).

You don't rise by knowing all the answers—you rise by holding better inquiries. Because a single question can change your focus, your mood, and your life's trajectory. When you ask, "What would this look like if it were aligned?" you give yourself permission to stop chasing someone else's dream. When you ask, "What version of me is ready to emerge right now?" you ignite transformation.

Elite athletes, visionary leaders, and world-class therapists all use the same core tool: precision questions. They don't waste energy on "What if I fail?" Instead, they ask, "What would I do if I couldn't fail?" That kind of question disrupts fear, rewires belief systems, and reconnects you to your power. It's not self-help fluff—it's neurological fact. Questions reprogram perception, and perception shapes results.

Even therapeutic frameworks like Motivational Interviewing are built on the power of questions. Instead of telling clients what to do, therapists ask targeted, open-ended questions that activate inner clarity faster than external advice ever could (PubMed). Because when the answer comes from within, it sticks. It lands. It activates action.

The mind is a question-answering machine. And what you feed it determines what it creates. Feed it questions like "Why am I always behind?" and it will construct a story of defeat. But feed it "What would success feel like today?" and it will start rewriting your story in real time. You don't need a new life. You need a new lens—and questions are how you clean the glass.

There is a version of you that already has full clarity. They're not confused. They're not stuck. They're not waiting. They're just buried under years of disempowering inquiries. The key to unlocking that version of you isn't in working harder—it's in asking bolder. Bolder questions lead to bolder identities. And bold identities shape extraordinary lives.

Try this: start each day by writing one powerful question in a journal. Not a to-do list. Not a plan. Just one bold, clear, identity-expanding question. Ask it with intention. Let your mind and heart respond without filters. In 21 days, you won't just think differently—you'll lead differently. Because clarity isn't a skill. It's a frequency. And questions are the tuning fork.

Stop asking for guarantees. Start asking for wisdom. Instead of "What should I do?" ask "What aligns with who I'm becoming?" That question alone can end years of confusion. Because the future isn't waiting to happen—it's waiting for you to ask better questions about it. And the moment you do, clarity rushes in like a flood.

Asking better questions isn't about hype—it's about rewiring your destiny. It's how you trade confusion for confidence. How you upgrade your mindset without waiting for motivation. It's how you move from trying to trusting. The power is already inside you. It just needs the right prompt.

You don't get better answers by working harder. You get better answers by asking better questions. So ask yourself this right now: "What am I not seeing that would change everything?" And let that question become the beginning of your breakthrough.

Clarity Framework: Truth, Desire, Direction

You can't build a powerful life on a foggy foundation. Clarity isn't a luxury—it's oxygen. It's what separates the aligned from the exhausted, the fulfilled from the frustrated. Without it, you'll mistake motion for progress. You'll say yes to obligations that drain you, follow goals that don't belong to you, and end up wondering why you're so busy, yet so empty. But with clarity? You become magnetic. Grounded. Unshakable. And it all starts with one framework: truth, desire, and direction.

Truth isn't what the world told you. It's not what you were conditioned to believe. It's what exists beneath the noise, beneath the roles you play, beneath the masks you wear. When you confront the truth—not the convenient story, but the honest one—you reclaim your power. Research shows that self-confrontation increases goal attainment and authenticity, enhancing long-term well-being (Frontiers in Psychology). The moment you stop lying to yourself, clarity doesn't trickle in—it floods in.

Most people aren't confused—they're avoiding the truth. Because truth demands change. It exposes where you've been settling. It highlights the gap between who you are and who you've been pretending to be. But truth is never your enemy—self-deception is. And the sooner you name it, the sooner you free yourself from the emotional weight of pretending.

After truth comes desire—not the shallow wants sold by consumerism, but the soul-deep desires that whisper who you were before the world taught you to be realistic. Desire is not a distraction—it's a compass. According to Harvard psychologist Daniel Gilbert, when you live in alignment with your desires, even uncertain outcomes lead to more meaning and motivation (Daniel Gilbert, Harvard Scholar). Desire is the language of your destiny trying to speak through you.

Desire is sacred. It's the fire that reminds you you're alive. It's the voice that says, "You're meant for more." When you suppress your desires to be safe, you shrink. When you express them, the world begins to bend in your favor. It's not magic—it's physics. Energy flows where clarity grows. Desire opens portals. It calls your future into your present.

But desire alone isn't enough. Without direction, desire turns to frustration. You feel the energy but don't know where to place it. That's why direction matters. Direction isn't about having the whole path—it's about knowing your next bold move. A study published in the Journal of Applied Psychology found that people who define their next step with specificity are 91% more likely to follow through (APA). Specificity sharpens intention. Intention accelerates execution.

Direction is emotional targeting. It's the point where passion meets precision. It takes your fire and gives it form. It turns vague dreams into practical momentum. When you know your next step—exactly what, when, and why—you stop asking for permission. You stop second-guessing. You move with conviction. And conviction is contagious.

This is why all three—truth, desire, and direction—must be aligned. Truth without desire creates obligation. You'll do what's right but feel lifeless. Desire without direction creates chaos. You'll feel inspired but lack focus. Direction without truth creates burnout. You'll chase goals that don't feed your soul. But when all three are aligned? You enter a state of flow. A zone where life feels guided, not forced.

This framework isn't theory—it's science-backed strategy. It activates your brain's executive network, the same region responsible for decision-making, identity, and long-term vision (NIH). In this state, clarity becomes your default. You stop chasing clarity and start living from it.

To tap into this power, begin each day by asking: "What truth am I avoiding?" "What desire am I suppressing?" "What direction am I afraid to move toward?" These questions aren't just reflective—they're revolutionary. They pull you back into alignment. They break through the mental fog and reignite your inner compass.

You don't need a five-year plan. You need five seconds of courage to admit what's true, honor what you want, and take one aligned action. That's how clarity is built—brick by brick, choice by choice. You won't get there by overthinking. You'll get there by aligning.

Clarity lives at the intersection of truth, desire, and direction. Stand in that intersection long enough, and you don't just change your life—you become the type of person who creates lives worth following. Because once you know who you are, what you want, and where you're going, the world doesn't just respond. It rearranges.

The Art of Soul-Based Visioning

There is a powerful difference between chasing goals and living from vision. Goals are often constructed from logic, pressure, and societal programming. Vision—true, soul-level vision—comes from a deeper place. It's not what looks good on paper. It's what feels right in your spirit. The mistake most people make is confusing ambition for alignment. That's why they burn out. That's why they build lives that fit someone else's mold and wonder why success feels hollow. Fulfillment doesn't come from hitting milestones. It comes from honoring your inner blueprint.

When your life is guided by meaning rather than metrics, something shifts. According to Dr. Michael Steger of Colorado State University, people who live purpose-driven lives experience greater emotional resilience, higher satisfaction, and mental clarity (source). Purpose is not a luxury—it's fuel. Without it, you're running on fumes, chasing deadlines that have no soul behind them. But when your vision is rooted in meaning, motivation becomes effortless.

You don't need to hustle when you're aligned. Neuroscience proves that your brain's dopamine pathways fire more powerfully when goals are connected to personal values and emotional resonance—not just rewards or praise (source). That means the energy you're looking for doesn't come from trying harder. It comes from tuning deeper into what truly matters to you. When vision is soul-aligned, you move from pressure to pull. The future calls you forward.

But most people craft vision from fear. They ask, "What can I afford? What's realistic?"—when the real question should be, "What would set my soul on fire?" True visioning bypasses logic and activates truth. It's not about surviving—it's about expanding. It asks, "If I wasn't scared, what would I build?" "If I trusted myself fully, who would I become?" These questions don't just spark ideas—they summon your essence.

Research confirms this. A meta-analysis in Neuroscience & Biobehavioral Reviews showed that vision-based mental rehearsal—when done with elevated emotion and future-self identity—reshapes the brain, increases motivation, and improves goal execution (source). This isn't daydreaming. It's neurological reprogramming. It's your biology catching up to your destiny.

When you emotionally connect to your future, your nervous system begins to believe it's already real. Your subconscious doesn't know the difference between imagined and experienced. That's the power of vision. When you write it, speak it, and feel it as if it's already true, your body, brain, and behavior start aligning automatically. This is called identity installation, and it's not motivational hype—it's backed by research (source).

To tap into this force, you must slow down. Create stillness. Get out of the head and into the heart. Ask truth-centered questions. Write your vision as if it's already happening. Feel it. Speak it. Don't just describe what it looks like—describe what it feels like to live it. Do this daily. Not as a ritual, but as a recalibration. Let it become your internal GPS.

That GPS is real. Your brain's reticular activating system (RAS) filters your perception based on what you've declared is important. When you feed it soul-aligned vision, it starts filtering the world differently. You begin to see resources, opportunities, and people that match your energy. You're no longer just chasing outcomes—you're drawing them to you by who you've become internally (source).

This is why alignment beats effort every time. Vision makes you magnetic. When your frequency matches your future, you don't need to convince the world—you simply show up, and the world adjusts. This isn't fantasy. It's the law of resonance at work. You attract what you are in harmony with. You don't get what you want. You get what you are.

So when someone asks about your five-year plan, don't just list outcomes. Speak vision. Speak energy. Speak alignment. Describe the kind of life your soul wants to live—not the life your fear told you was safe. Because real success isn't about climbing ladders—it's about building one that's leaning on the right wall.

You don't need more steps—you need more soul. You don't need another system—you need deeper surrender. The future you desire isn't something you create from scratch. It's something you remember. Your spirit already knows. Your job is to listen, align, and act as if it's already true.

Your soul already wrote the vision. Your mind's job is to stop interfering. And when you align your choices with that inner truth, life begins to reflect what your higher self already decided. That's when you stop chasing success—and start embodying destiny.

Creating Your Life Vision Map

A dream without direction is just noise in a world already drowning in distractions. It's not enough to wish, want, or hope—you must map. Not the rigid kind filled with to-do lists and obligations, but a living, breathing blueprint aligned with who you are at the deepest level. You were not born to drift with the tides of life. You were born to design a destiny that mirrors your soul, not society's expectations. And those who live with purpose—spiritually, emotionally, and financially—aren't just lucky. They're clear. They have a map.

Writing down your vision isn't fluff—it's science. A study from Dominican University found that individuals who write their goals and revisit them are 42% more likely to achieve them than those who merely think about their dreams (Dominican University Study). When you write your life into existence, you activate parts of your brain that begin to filter reality differently. You stop hoping and start honing. That's the difference between the average and the aligned.

But here's the secret: you must build your Life Vision Map from the inside out. Most people chase what they think they should want—titles, money, approval—never realizing they're building castles on someone else's land. Real design starts with your core: truth, identity, values. It asks, "What matters to me—not what impresses others?" It's not about looking successful. It's about feeling in alignment.

Break your vision into key life categories: self, health, relationships, purpose, wealth, and environment. Then ask the real questions. "What does radical alignment look like here?" "What would I build if fear wasn't running the show?" "What would life look like if I believed I couldn't fail?" These are not motivational mantras. They are truth triggers—designed to bypass ego and activate soul-level clarity.

Science backs this approach. A 2019 study in *Psychological Science* found that visioning tied to personal values and intrinsic motivation activates the brain's identity and reward center, the ventromedial prefrontal cortex—leading to better emotional regulation and follow-through (Source). In plain terms, when your goals align with your core, you stay committed longer—and feel more fulfilled along the way.

But don't just write your map—visualize it. Your brain processes images 60,000 times faster than text (Source). That means your map should include symbols, visuals, affirmations, and colors that spark emotional resonance. This isn't arts and crafts—it's neuroprogramming. It trains your subconscious to act as if the vision is already happening.

Every area of your map must contain two power pieces: emotion anchors and embodiment actions. Ask yourself, "How do I want to feel in this part of my life?" Then ask, "What daily action would my future self already be doing?" This is how you shift from fantasy into frequency. You don't just dream it—you start living it. One micro-action at a time.

This isn't a vision board you forget in the back of a drawer. It's a blueprint for your becoming. Research in *Applied Psychology: An International Review* shows that people who regularly engage with their identity-based vision increase life satisfaction and goal consistency by up to 78% (Source). That's not wishful thinking. That's commitment made visible.

But clarity without consistency fades. You must revisit your map daily. Speak it. Feel it. Walk through it in your mind. Because when you activate that vision repeatedly, your brain's reticular activating system (RAS) starts filtering reality to match your intention (Source). Suddenly, the world begins to reveal opportunities, people, and decisions that were always there—but now you can see them.

Don't wait for the world to validate your vision. Give yourself permission now. Update your map as you grow. As your soul evolves, so will your blueprint. That's the beauty of a living vision—it breathes with you. It expands with your courage. And it evolves with your clarity.

A life by design doesn't happen by accident. It is born when you stop reacting to life and start architecting it. Your soul is not asking for perfection—it's asking for participation. And when you get organized at the level of your truth, the universe responds at the level of manifestation. What once felt impossible becomes inevitable.

So stop waiting for clarity to strike like lightning. Build it like a muscle. Map your life like it matters—because it does. You're not just here to survive. You're here to design, to lead, to create a legacy that echoes beyond your years. And it all starts with one question: "What would my life look like if my soul was in charge?" Let the answer become your map.

Eliminating "Maybe" Energy

"Maybe" might sound harmless, but it's the silent assassin of dreams. It slips into your language unnoticed, disguised as patience or politeness, but underneath it's pure paralysis. When you say "maybe," you split your power. You fracture your intention. You stall the energy that wants to move through you. Neuroscience proves that indecision spikes cortisol and disrupts focus by activating stress pathways in the brain (Cognitive Brain Research). That's not clarity. That's self-sabotage masquerading as thoughtfulness.

You were not built to live in limbo. Your spirit wasn't designed to waver endlessly in doubt. Every time you delay a decision, your subconscious interprets the inaction as danger. This leads to what psychology calls "learned helplessness"—a state where your brain stops believing that resolution is possible (PMC). "Maybe" becomes a feedback loop that feeds confusion and fear. The longer you stay there, the more powerless you feel.

But here's the truth: "maybe" is comfort in disguise. It allows you to dodge risk, avoid rejection, and shield yourself from responsibility. But the cost is staggering. Because while you're hiding from discomfort, you're also hiding from power. And power only flows to those who choose. Decision is the key that unlocks momentum. Until you make one, you stay stuck in neutral—engine revving, but going nowhere.

There is a biochemical price to indecision. Dr. Tara Swart, a neuroscientist and leadership coach, explains that uncertainty forces your brain to burn more glucose as it tries to calculate all possibilities, which drains energy and reduces willpower (HBR). This is why you feel tired even when you haven't done anything. It's not your schedule—it's your unresolved choices.

"Maybe" doesn't just delay action—it delays identity. Because identity is built through decision. When you choose, even imperfectly, you reinforce to your nervous system: "I trust myself." A study in *Personality and Social Psychology Bulletin* found that people who made quick, value-aligned decisions experienced higher confidence and reduced anxiety long-term (SAGE Journals). It's not about being right—it's about being committed.

Most people think clarity leads to action. But it's the reverse—action generates clarity. The more you move, the clearer your path becomes. You don't get confident by waiting for the perfect answer. You get confident by moving with the truth you have, and adjusting along the way. Confidence isn't found in perfection. It's found in the power of a clean decision.

You must learn to say "Yes" and mean it. Say "No" and stand in it. Every clean choice frees your bandwidth, sharpens your identity, and strengthens your leadership. The difference between stagnation and expansion often lies in one word: "Maybe." Eliminate it, and you'll start to feel your life move again.

This isn't about rushing—it's about trusting. Your future self already knows what to do. Ask: "What would the version of me who already achieved this choose right now?" That question bypasses the confusion of your current emotions and plugs into the wisdom of who you're becoming. That version doesn't entertain endless debate. They decide, and then they align.

The universe doesn't reward hesitation. It responds to clarity. Your indecision sends mixed signals to life itself. But when you commit—fully, boldly, unapologetically—doors open. Not because life suddenly changed, but because your energy became undeniable. You stopped tiptoeing and started transmitting certainty.

If you want to reclaim your momentum, start by removing "maybe" from your vocabulary. Replace it with decisive energy. Not every decision needs to be perfect. It just needs to be made. Power lives in motion. Motion creates momentum. And momentum builds belief faster than logic ever will.

Clarity isn't a matter of having all the answers—it's about being willing to move with the ones you have. Most people wait for permission. Winners give themselves direction. The moment you stop outsourcing your clarity, you start embodying your power. That's when people feel your shift. That's when opportunities find you.

Confidence isn't something you wait for. It's something you claim through commitment. Kill the "maybe," and you cut the cord to indecision. Your future doesn't need you to be perfect. It needs you to decide. Decide who you are. Decide what you want. Decide to move—and let life respond.

Aligning with Your Soul's Desires

You were never meant to play it safe. The dreams that live in your heart weren't installed—they were remembered. They came with you. They didn't arrive through education, career, or culture—they've always been there, coded into your spirit. But somewhere between rejection and responsibility, you were taught to mute them. To water them down. To call them silly, selfish, or "too much." But make no mistake—your soul's desires are not weaknesses. They're sacred instructions.

Desire is not greed. It's guidance. It's the internal GPS of the human spirit. As legendary psychologist Carl Rogers discovered, the people who feel most alive are the ones who live in congruence—when their actions reflect their inner desires (Positive Psychology). When you live out of sync with what matters most to you, your body tells you. You feel tired. You feel scattered. You feel like a stranger in your own life. But when you live aligned with what your soul longs for, you feel energized even before the results arrive.

There is a major difference between ego desires and soul desires. Ego desires chase applause. They hunger for validation. But soul desires create quiet power. You're not chasing attention—you're becoming more of yourself. These desires don't beg the world to notice you. They call you to remember who you already are. They aren't about achieving—they're about aligning. The pursuit itself feels like coming home.

Science backs this up. The Journal of Personality and Social Psychology confirmed that people who pursue "self-concordant goals"—goals aligned with their core values—report higher levels of fulfillment and are more resilient under pressure (APA Source). That means this isn't philosophy—it's neuroscience. Your brain and body thrive when you pursue what is true for you, not what looks good to others.

If you feel stuck, if you feel overwhelmed or disconnected, it's likely because you've been trying to force a life that doesn't fit. Maybe you're following someone else's version of success. Maybe you've been loyal to survival, not vision. You must pause and ask, "What is mine to create?" "What lights me up when no one's clapping?" These questions don't just reveal goals—they uncover your essence.

The real proof? The way your body responds. You'll know a soul-aligned desire because it will feel like breath returning to the lungs. It won't stress you—it'll stretch you. It won't feel like pressure—it'll feel like freedom. That's how truth sounds: expansive, not heavy. And you don't need outside permission to pursue it. You only need to listen inside.

Modern neuroscience confirms what your spirit already knows. Dr. Andrew Huberman of Stanford explains that dopamine—the brain's reward and motivation molecule—isn't just released when you achieve a goal. It's released every time you take a step aligned with your internal values (Huberman Lab). That means desire isn't a risk—it's a neurochemical advantage. Your biology is wired to support you when you walk your truth.

Every time you suppress a soul desire, you signal to your nervous system that it's unsafe to expand. But every time you honor it, even in a small way, you activate the systems responsible for courage, clarity, and decision-making. It's not just about fulfillment—it's about function. You become more mentally sharp, emotionally grounded, and physically alive.

So how do you start? You stop carrying what was never yours. Let go of the "shoulds." Let go of the identities that were shaped by fear. Ask yourself, "What would I create if I wasn't afraid?" Because fear is often the last layer protecting your deepest calling. If it scares you and excites you at the same time, that's the one to follow.

Now name it. Speak it. Declare it. Naming a soul desire turns confusion into clarity. Research shows that when we name our inner states—our longings, our emotions—we reduce stress and increase emotional intelligence by activating the brain's clarity centers (<u>Behavioral Brain Research</u>). Unspoken desires stay powerless. Spoken ones become pathways.

And then take one action. Not tomorrow. Not when it's perfect. Now. Why? Because action affirms identity. When you act on what your soul wants, your body learns that it's safe to dream. Your subconscious stops bracing for rejection and starts building for expansion. That's when miracles happen—not because you forced them, but because you finally aligned with the version of you that was waiting all along.

Desire is not something you earn through worthiness. It's something you remember through truth. And the moment you trust it, life starts to organize around your expansion. You no longer survive your story—you start writing a new one. One that feels like freedom. One that feels like you.

Clarity Meditation Practice

Clarity isn't something you find out there. It's something you uncover within. You're not broken, lost, or behind—you're buried. Beneath layers of stress, fear, and societal conditioning. What you're really looking for is already in you, waiting to be heard. But it doesn't scream—it whispers. And the only way to hear it is to get still. That's why meditation isn't a luxury or a New Age trend—it's a necessity. A neurological and spiritual technology for returning to truth.

Meditation isn't about escaping reality. It's about meeting it without distortion. According to a study by Johns Hopkins University, regular meditation reduces anxiety, enhances emotional regulation, and dramatically improves clarity in decision-making (<u>JAMA</u>). When you're spinning in confusion, the answer isn't another strategy. It's space. It's silence. It's learning to listen to what's underneath the noise.

Your brain is not wired to think clearly under stress. When you're in fight-or-flight mode, your prefrontal cortex—the part responsible for vision, logic, and planning—goes offline. Meditation reactivates it by calming the amygdala, your brain's fear center. Harvard research confirms that mindfulness meditation increases gray matter in the hippocampus (linked to memory and focus) and shrinks the amygdala, improving emotional stability and perception (Harvard Gazette).

So when your mind feels foggy, don't reach for caffeine, chaos, or content. Sit. Breathe. Listen. That stillness isn't weakness—it's wisdom in disguise. Meditation becomes the place where your scattered thoughts come home. It's not passive. It's powerful. You're not doing nothing—you're realigning with everything that already knows.

Start your "Clarity Meditation" with one clear intention. Ask yourself powerful questions before you close your eyes: "What's my next aligned move?" "What truth am I pretending not to know?" "Where am I leaking energy?" These are not just self-help prompts. They are neurological cues that activate your inner vision. Then breathe. Let the inhale clear static. Let the exhale bring you deeper into presence.

Within minutes, your brain shifts into alpha and theta waves—states tied to creativity, memory, and subconscious insight (NCBI). This is where your highest guidance lives. In this space, your subconscious isn't reacting to fear—it's responding to your truth. This is the point where insight breaks through. Not loud. Not dramatic. Just unmistakably clear.

Want to amplify the practice? Add visualization. See yourself already embodying the clarity you're craving. Watch your highest self walk through today with ease, making decisions with calm confidence. Say, out loud or in your mind, "I already know what to do," "I move with calm certainty," "I trust my inner knowing." These are not affirmations. They are neurological reprogramming. Imagery meditation activates the same brain circuits as real-world action, preparing your body and mind to follow through in reality (PMC).

And when the meditation ends, it's not over. Write it down. Capture what surfaced. The ideas. The nudges. The clarity that arrived without effort. This is not journaling for the sake of expression—it's transcription. It's taking dictation from the highest version of yourself. When you write it down, you ground it. You give it form. You make it harder to forget.

But don't stop there. Choose one insight you received—and act on it. Right now. Because clarity without movement fades into memory. But clarity with action becomes transformation. When you take that aligned step, no matter how small, your nervous system learns that expansion is safe. That's when you shift from knowing into becoming.

Stillness is not inactivity. It's the most profound form of activation. In silence, you finally make space for wisdom. You're not stuck—you're saturated. Saturated with noise, options, pressure, and performance. Meditation clears the clutter so truth can rise. So purpose can breathe. So direction can emerge not from your mind, but from your essence.

The world may scream, but your clarity always whispers. It doesn't need to convince you—it just needs you to pause long enough to hear it. When you tune in regularly, you stop looking outside for answers. You realize the compass was always inside, quietly pointing home. Meditation doesn't give you clarity. It reveals that you never lost it in the first place.

You were not designed to live reactive. You were designed to live responsive—to live tuned, aligned, and empowered. So take your seat. Return to your breath. Let the silence speak. Because in that stillness lives the answer you've been waiting for all along. And when you listen, really listen, clarity isn't something you find. It's something you finally remember.

Exercise: 5-Year Vision from the Soul

Most people approach their five-year plan like a negotiation with their fears. They ask what's possible based on their limitations, not what's aligned with their potential. They write cautious goals, shaped by the past, designed to keep them safe—not free. But the truth is, your soul doesn't speak in small talk. It doesn't whisper in fear. It calls you into expansion. And this five-year visioning process isn't about survival—it's about remembering who you really are beneath the noise.

There's a reason five years is powerful. Psychologically, it's distant enough to override the grip of your current circumstances, but close enough to activate the brain's planning centers. According to research from Stanford's Dr. Kelly McGonigal, visualizing a compelling future self activates the dorsolateral prefrontal cortex—the same part of the brain responsible for long-term focus, discipline, and goal-directed action (Stanford). When you connect emotionally to your future identity, your brain begins to build it into reality.

But clarity can't come from chaos. If you try to design your future while you're in survival mode, you'll only recreate the present with prettier packaging. That's why this process begins in stillness. Before anything else, get quiet. Get grounded. Let your nervous system settle. Because a dysregulated state cannot dream—it can only defend.

Now imagine this: it's five years from now. And everything is aligned—not perfect, but true. You didn't betray your intuition. You didn't shrink for safety. You built a life that reflects your values, your purpose, and your deepest truth. Close your eyes and ask: Where am I waking up? What does my body feel like? Who's with me? What am I creating and contributing to the world?

This isn't daydreaming—it's neural programming. A 2018 meta-analysis in Neuroscience & Biobehavioral Reviews found that when you mentally rehearse your future with vivid detail and emotional connection, you increase cognitive motivation, emotional regulation, and strategic clarity (ScienceDirect). Your brain can't tell the difference between imagination and memory—so give it something worth remembering.

Now write your five-year vision as if it's already real. Use present tense. Describe your mornings, your work, your relationships, your financial flow, your travel, your peace. Don't just think it—feel it. This activates your reticular activating system (RAS), which filters your perception of the world to match your dominant identity and intentions (NIH). Your future becomes magnetic when your brain starts looking for it everywhere.

This is not about hustle. This is not about impressing anyone. This is about becoming more honest with yourself than you've ever dared to be. A study in *Psychological Science* confirmed that people who have emotionally driven future visions show greater resilience, lower stress, and higher consistency in goal pursuit (SAGE Journals). The soul doesn't need to push—it pulls. And that pull is your compass.

Speak your vision out loud. Record it. Make it your morning soundtrack. Every time you hear your future self speak, you strengthen neural pathways of belief. You shift from "someday" to "inevitable." Repetition doesn't just reinforce—it rewires. You begin to act like the person you wrote about. And that's when everything starts to change.

But don't stop at inspiration. Ground it in action. Take one bold step today that's in alignment with the person you're becoming. It doesn't need to be big. It just needs to be honest. Because movement creates proof. Proof creates confidence. And confidence builds momentum faster than any motivational speech ever could.

This isn't about controlling every outcome. It's about creating coherence between your soul and your schedule. When your actions match your vision, the universe begins to rearrange itself around your alignment. You stop chasing opportunities—they start chasing you. Not because of luck, but because clarity is magnetic.

You don't need to become someone new. You need to remember the version of you that was never conditioned out of greatness. That self is already living five years ahead. She's already free, focused, and full of purpose. Your job is not to invent her. Your job is to listen to her, align with her, and walk toward the life she already lives.

You are not five years away from the life you want—you're one aligned decision away from setting it in motion. Write it. Speak it. Move toward it. And let the future version of you be the loudest voice in your mind. She's already waiting. All you have to do is show up.

You've just unlocked one of the most powerful mindset shifts most people will never even hear about—let alone implement. But reading about it isn't enough. Transformation only happens when information becomes *activation*. That's why I created the full **Clarity Confidence Code Course**—to guide you, step by step, through rewiring your beliefs, dissolving inner resistance, and programming your mind to operate on the frequency of certainty, success, and unstoppable confidence. If you're serious about mastering your emotions, reconditioning your subconscious, and finally breaking free from the invisible limits that have held you back, this course is your gateway. Don't just read the code—**live it**. The full experience awaits you at https://clarityconfidencecode.com

Now let's dive into the next layer of your evolution...

CHAPTER 4

THE CONFIDENCE BLUEPRINT — EMBODYING UNSHAKABLE SELF-WORTH

What Real Confidence Looks Like

Confidence isn't about volume—it's about vibration. It doesn't need to raise its voice because it already knows its worth. Real confidence walks into a room and changes the atmosphere before a word is spoken. It doesn't perform. It doesn't posture. It simply radiates a frequency of certainty that comes from deep alignment. The kind of certainty that says, "I trust myself. Fully. Quietly. Boldly."

What most people call confidence is really performance. It's the loud laugh, the curated image, the perfect delivery. But that's not confidence. That's compensation. When you know who you are, you don't need to over-explain or over-impress. Real confidence is quiet power. It's the kind of presence that doesn't hustle for attention because it isn't dependent on it.

Scientific research confirms what the soul already knows. A 2021 study in *Frontiers in Psychology* revealed that the strongest predictor of authentic confidence is self-concept clarity—not extroversion, not charisma, not charm (Frontiers in Psychology). That means when you're clear about who you are and what you stand for, confidence is the natural result—not a mask you wear, but a truth you live.

Confidence isn't perfection—it's resilience. It doesn't mean you never fall. It means you trust your ability to rise. According to the American Psychological Association, resilience is one of the most consistent predictors of long-term confidence (APA). That's because real confidence isn't built in your highlight reel—it's built in the dark, in the detours, in the days you choose to keep going when no one is clapping.

Real confidence doesn't chase approval. It doesn't need a trophy or a "like." It's rooted in internal validation. When your worth comes from within, you stop negotiating it. You stop outsourcing your identity to opinions. Confidence built on applause is fragile. The moment people stop clapping, it collapses. But confidence built on truth? That's unshakable.

It also looks like radical ownership. The ability to say, "This is mine. I own my choices. I own my growth." A study from the University of Georgia showed that leaders who took personal accountability were more respected and trusted by their teams and peers (University of Georgia). Because people can feel when your confidence is real—and nothing builds trust like responsibility.

Confidence isn't competitive. It's collaborative. It doesn't shrink in the presence of greatness—it celebrates it. When you're truly confident, you know that someone else's light doesn't dim your own. You don't fear being overshadowed because you know no one else can occupy your exact assignment. That's what makes you irreplaceable.

Here's the paradox that most miss: confidence is vulnerable. It has nothing to prove. It's secure enough to say, "I don't know yet." Or, "I'm working on that." That kind of humility isn't weakness—it's wisdom. According to self-compassion expert Dr. Kristin Neff, people who show themselves kindness in failure consistently demonstrate higher confidence and better decision-making (Self-Compassion Research). Because when you trust yourself, you don't shame yourself into growth—you love yourself there.

And confidence isn't just mental—it's physical. It lives in your breath, your eyes, your posture. Harvard researchers discovered that adopting a "power pose" for just two minutes—standing tall, arms open—can boost testosterone and lower cortisol, significantly increasing confidence (Harvard Business Review). That's the mind-body connection in action. When your physiology changes, your psychology follows.

True confidence doesn't perform for an audience. It's the same in the dark as it is in the spotlight. It doesn't need to be seen to be strong. It doesn't need applause to feel anchored. Because it knows that who you are when no one's watching is what determines how you rise when everyone's looking.

So what does real confidence look like? It looks like integrity. It looks like courage without arrogance. It looks like consistency between your values and your voice. It's walking into every room as if you belong there—because you do. It's knowing that you don't need to be chosen—you were born chosen.

Confidence isn't the loudest voice in the room. It's the clearest. The one that knows: I am enough. I have what it takes. And I don't need to prove it—I am living proof. When you walk in that truth, you don't just attract opportunities. You command them. Not through force, but through frequency. That's the power of real, radiant, soul-rooted confidence.

Confidence vs. Performance Persona

There's a version of you the world applauds—and then there's the real you. One is rehearsed, curated, filtered for performance. The other is grounded, calm, and anchored in truth. The sooner you learn to separate the performance from the presence, the sooner you stop mistaking applause for alignment. Because confidence is not found in how you're perceived—it's found in how you stand when perception no longer matters.

Most people aren't truly confident. They're skilled performers. They've learned how to smile through uncertainty, talk through anxiety, and look polished while their internal world is unraveling. But performance doesn't equal peace. It might win you admiration, but it will never give you rest. A 2021 study in the *Journal of Personality* confirmed this: people who project a performance persona experience higher anxiety and lower life satisfaction than those grounded in self-acceptance (Journal of Personality).

Performance-based confidence is conditional. It needs likes, approval, and recognition to feel worthy. It thrives on the next win, the next deal, the next compliment. But the moment that stream dries up, so does the illusion. That's why so many successful people feel like frauds. Because they're living on the edge of their last result, trapped in a loop of proving and performing.

Here's the trap—they get rewarded for the act. The world claps for the mask. It reinforces the image. But that kind of success is rented, not owned. And the rent is high. A meta-analysis published in *Emotion Review* found that emotional labor—constantly managing your outward identity—leads to cognitive fatigue, higher stress, and eventual emotional burnout (Emotion Review).

That's why burnout isn't always about workload. It's about misalignment. It's about the gap between who you are and who you think you have to be. And the bigger that gap, the heavier the mask. The longer you wear it, the harder it is to breathe. No wonder so many high achievers collapse emotionally while climbing professionally. They've built success that's disconnected from self.

Real confidence doesn't seek applause—it seeks truth. It asks, "Who am I when no one's watching? Who am I without the title, the praise, the performance?" And that answer—that clarity—is what gives you peace. Because you're no longer chasing validation. You're moving from alignment. You don't need to convince the world when you're no longer negotiating with yourself.

True confidence is stable. It doesn't shift based on circumstances. It doesn't crumble under silence. It's rooted in self-concept clarity—the psychological foundation of knowing who you are and what you stand for. That's why Olympic coaches and high-performance psychologists now prioritize internal confidence over external results. Because sustainable excellence only comes when your identity fuels your output—not the other way around (Frontiers in Psychology).

So ask yourself, honestly: Am I living with confidence—or performing it? Do I speak from truth—or from what's popular? Do I feel free in my success—or confined by my image? These questions aren't criticisms. They're invitations. Invitations to drop the performance and reclaim the presence that was always powerful underneath.

There's no shame in the mask. You built it to survive. To belong. To win. But what once protected you might now be imprisoning you. And the cost of carrying it too long is steep—your authenticity, your connection, and your peace. The world might praise the mask, but your soul will always crave the truth.

To step into real confidence, you must take the risk of being seen—not as a persona, but as a person. Not as a brand, but as a being. You must trust that your rawness has power. That your voice, your truth, your essence—unfiltered—is more than enough. That's not weakness. That's the ultimate flex.

Let your real self lead. The one who isn't afraid to be vulnerable. The one who knows that honesty heals. The one who doesn't need a script to stand tall. When that version of you steps forward, you don't just walk in confidence—you walk in liberation.

Confidence isn't about pretending to be more. It's about remembering you never needed to be anything else. The power isn't in your performance. It's in your permission. And the moment you stop performing and start showing up as you—fully, honestly, unapologetically—that's the moment the world meets your true power.

Why Confidence Is Built, Not Born

There's the version of you the world applauds, and then there's the version that wakes up with you each morning—the unfiltered, unedited, unscripted version. The first one is polished for performance, crafted to fit in, to succeed, to be safe. The second is pure power. Not loud, not boastful, but grounded and real. And when you begin to let that version lead, everything changes—not because you become more, but because you finally stop pretending to be less.

Most people aren't living confidently—they're performing confidence. They've mastered the art of looking strong while feeling uncertain. They've learned how to project success while silently battling self-doubt. But performance is not peace. It can win applause, but it can't build inner stillness. The danger isn't in pretending for a moment—it's in forgetting who you were before the act began.

Research backs this up. A 2021 study in the *Journal of Personality* showed that authentic self-confidence—rooted in self-acceptance—produces higher well-being and mental clarity than illusory self-assurance built on external image management (source). Translation? The deeper you know yourself, the less you need to prove yourself. Confidence isn't the result of validation—it's the reward of alignment.

Performance-driven confidence feeds on approval. It needs to be seen, liked, shared, and praised. But authentic confidence needs none of that. It's not dependent on applause because it isn't performing. It's simply being. The more your identity is tied to what you do or how you're perceived, the more fragile it becomes. One missed opportunity, one bad day, one criticism—and it shatters.

The trap is, the world rewards the mask. The performance gets likes. It gets promoted. It gets invited. And so, the mask gets reinforced. But underneath, emotional exhaustion builds. A meta-analysis published in *Emotion Review* found that this kind of emotional labor increases cortisol, drains mental energy, and leads to burnout (source). You can only carry a persona for so long before it starts to carry you—into anxiety, into fatigue, into disconnection.

That's why so many high achievers feel like imposters. They're killing it on the outside but crumbling on the inside. Success built on performance creates prisons made of expectations. And the moment you stop performing, the applause fades—and with it, your sense of self. Unless your confidence is built on something deeper than the echo of other people's approval, it won't survive the silence.

True confidence is quiet but certain. It doesn't demand attention, because it doesn't need it. It doesn't collapse when unrecognized, because it never depended on recognition. It stands because it knows. It breathes because it trusts. And it leads because it listens—to soul, not ego. That kind of power doesn't need to prove itself. It lives in peace, not performance.

Elite performers and Olympic coaches now train their clients in internal confidence as a predictor of sustainable excellence—not just technical skills, but emotional alignment. They've found that people perform best when they're grounded in who they are—not who they're pretending to be (source). Excellence is not born from ego—it's born from essence.

This is the turning point. The moment you stop asking, "How do I look?" and start asking, "Am I aligned?" The moment you stop chasing applause and start following your own voice. Because real freedom is found in the space where performance ends and authenticity begins. The space where you trust yourself enough to stop editing your truth to fit a mold you've outgrown.

There's no shame in the mask. It served you. It helped you rise. But what protects you at one level can imprison you at the next. And there comes a time when removing the mask is the bravest move you can make. Not to expose your weakness—but to reclaim your strength. The strength to say, "This is who I am, with or without the spotlight."

When you let your real self lead, you move differently. You speak without rehearsing. You walk without bracing. You create from alignment, not obligation. And suddenly, the results don't define you—the integrity does. You don't just look confident. You feel free. Because you're no longer selling a performance. You're standing in your presence.

Confidence isn't who you pretend to be. It's who you allow yourself to become when the script is burned, the mask is off, and the applause no longer matters. That version of you—the raw, real, radiant one—isn't waiting to be built. They're waiting to be remembered. And when you live from that place, you don't need to impress anyone. You become undeniable.

The Shame-Confidence Inverse

There is a version of you that the world celebrates—the polished one, the one who performs, who fits the mold, who says the right things at the right time. But there's another version, deeper and more powerful. The real you. Unfiltered, grounded, present. And when you learn to let that version lead, you stop chasing validation and start commanding respect. You stop performing for approval and start showing up in truth.

Confidence is not performance. It is not the smile you put on when you're scared. It's not the posture you strike to look the part. Most people are acting out confidence, not living it. They've learned how to function in fear while presenting strength. But pretending isn't peace. It might win the crowd, but it won't quiet the mind. True confidence doesn't need a stage—it needs a mirror and the courage to look into it without flinching.

Science confirms what the soul already knows. A 2021 study in the Journal of Personality found that people with authentic confidence—rooted in self-acceptance—experience greater clarity, emotional stability, and life satisfaction than those wearing a performance mask. On the surface, the persona may look successful, but behind the scenes, it produces anxiety, confusion, and emotional exhaustion (source).

Performance confidence is outcome-obsessed. It needs followers, titles, and applause to feel secure. But the moment external validation fades, so does the illusion. Real confidence is identity-based. It's not dependent on how well you perform—it's anchored in who you are when the lights are off and the audience is gone. That's the kind of confidence that doesn't just look strong—it stays strong.

The tragedy is that the performance persona is praised. It gets likes. It gets hired. It gets reposted. And so, the mask becomes the norm. But this kind of emotional labor—constantly managing your image—takes a toll. Research published in Emotion Review shows that maintaining a false persona depletes your mental bandwidth, spikes cortisol, and leads to burnout (source). The mask may fool others, but it slowly starves the soul.

That's why so many high-achievers quietly suffer. They're admired publicly and anxious privately. They're celebrated externally and suffocating internally. Because when your worth is based on performance, rest feels dangerous. Stillness feels like failure. And silence feels like invisibility. But your peace was never meant to be earned—it was meant to be claimed.

True confidence is not built on how you perform—it's built on how you align. It doesn't rise and fall with praise. It doesn't shatter with rejection. It stands in clarity. It says, "I am who I am, and I don't need to edit that for the room I walk into." That's not arrogance—it's freedom. And freedom is the soil in which real power grows.

Even in elite spaces, the top performers are shifting. Olympic athletes, CEOs, and creators at the highest levels are now investing in what researchers call "internal self-assurance"—the ability to perform from presence, not pressure (source). Because they know sustainable excellence doesn't come from being someone else—it comes from being fully yourself.

So take a moment and ask yourself: Am I confident—or am I acting confident? Do I speak what's real—or what's safe? Do I feel empowered in my life—or trapped in the image I've built? There's no shame in the mask. You created it to survive. But the same armor that once protected you can now keep you from your next level.

To break free, you must lead with the part of you that doesn't need to perform. The part that knows, "I don't need to impress—I just need to express." Real confidence is not about being the best—it's about being the truest. And when you're willing to be seen without the performance, something beautiful happens: people don't just admire you—they trust you.

And trust, real trust, is more powerful than any standing ovation. Because when people trust your authenticity, you don't have to prove anything. You simply have to be. And from that place, you don't compete for influence—you attract it. Not because you're polished, but because you're real. Not because you're loud, but because you're clear.

Confidence isn't who you pretend to be. It's who you allow yourself to be when you no longer need to pretend. And the moment you stop performing and start aligning, you discover a strength that's unshakable, a presence that's unforgettable, and a peace that finally feels like home.

How to Cultivate Internal Validation

The greatest freedom you'll ever experience doesn't come from financial abundance or even from external success—it comes from no longer needing anyone's permission to trust yourself. That is the core of internal validation. It is the shift from living for applause to living in alignment. It's waking up each day and knowing, with or without the spotlight, you are enough. You are clear. You are qualified. And you don't need the world to confirm it before you claim it.

Most people are wired to chase approval. It's not a personal flaw—it's societal conditioning. From the moment you could walk, you were trained to earn praise. Grades, trophies, likes, promotions. Your self-worth got braided into performance. But the problem with that wiring is simple: if your identity is rooted in applause, it collapses in silence. If you only feel worthy when others approve, then your power is always leased—never owned.

Internal validation means you stop renting your self-worth from the opinions of others. It means you become the source. You define your identity. You choose your standards. You validate your path. A study in the *Journal of Personality* revealed that individuals with strong internal validation—often referred to as self-determination—experience significantly more emotional stability, authenticity, and overall life satisfaction (source). When you trust yourself deeply, external opinions stop steering your life.

The shift happens when you separate who you are from what you produce. Your value is not your résumé. Your worth is not your results. You can fall short and still be whole. You can be doubted and still be destined. That's not delusion. That's alignment. True confidence comes not from getting it right all the time, but from knowing your essence doesn't change with your outcomes.

One of the most effective ways to cultivate internal validation is self-reflection. Daily journaling helps you acknowledge your wins without waiting for someone else to notice. A 2018 study from *Psychology of Consciousness* found that individuals who practiced daily self-acknowledgment developed higher internal confidence and significantly reduced their need for external reassurance (source). You don't need a cheerleader when your own voice becomes enough.

Ask yourself powerful questions. What did I do today that aligned with my values? Where did I choose integrity over popularity? What truth did I honor even when it went unnoticed? These aren't just journaling prompts—they're rewiring tools. Because every time you reflect from self-ownership, you build the mental blueprint of someone who no longer needs validation to breathe freely.

But internal validation doesn't thrive in self-criticism. You can't trust a voice that constantly tears you down. That's why self-compassion is essential. According to Dr. Kristin Neff's research, people who practice self-compassion show stronger motivation, better emotional resilience, and more authentic confidence than those who rely on inner judgment as a form of discipline (source). When you stop beating yourself into growth and start supporting yourself through it, everything shifts.

There's also a physical component to this shift. Embodied anchoring—like standing tall, breathing deeply, making eye contact with your reflection—sends signals to your nervous system that say, "We are safe. We are steady." Harvard's research on power poses revealed that posture can significantly boost your internal sense of confidence even before you speak or act (source). Confidence isn't just a mindset—it's also a somatic language.

Internal validation doesn't mean you don't care what others think—it means their opinions no longer dictate your direction. You can listen without obedience. You can receive feedback without losing yourself. You're open, but you're not empty. You're flexible, but you're not formless. Because now, your roots run deeper than your reactions.

This work isn't built overnight. It's a muscle. Every time you say yes to your truth without polling the room, that muscle gets stronger. Every time you trust your gut instead of outsourcing your decisions, your power grows. This doesn't make you hardheaded. It makes you grounded. Because the most magnetic people in the world aren't those shouting to be seen—they're those so anchored in their authenticity, the room calibrates to their presence.

There will still be noise. There will still be people who misunderstand, judge, or underestimate you. That's not your cue to shrink. That's your confirmation that your voice is finally distinct. You're no longer echoing what's expected—you're embodying what's real. And nothing is more powerful than a person who has chosen themselves fully.

You don't need the world to validate what your soul already knows. The moment you approve of yourself—fully, without compromise—your energy changes. You walk differently. You speak differently. And life, people, and opportunities begin responding not to who you were trying to be, but to who you've finally decided to become.

Anchoring Confidence in the Body

Confidence doesn't begin in your mind—it begins in your body. Long before you say a word, your posture, breath, and energy already said everything. That's because confidence is more than a thought—it's a physiological signal. It's not just what you believe. It's what your nervous system believes. When your body reflects certainty, the world responds differently. And more importantly, so do you.

Your body is a broadcast tower. It transmits signals louder than any sentence you speak. According to research published in *Trends in Cognitive Sciences*, embodied cognition reveals that your physical state influences your thoughts, decisions, and self-perception (source). That means your body doesn't just reflect how you feel—it creates it. Movement, breath, and posture become tools to program your mind.

This is where the game changes: confidence can be trained from the outside in. It's not just about rewiring beliefs through journaling or affirmations—it's about anchoring those beliefs in motion. Because when you stand differently, you think differently. When you breathe with intention, you act with conviction. Confidence isn't just something you think your way into—it's something you move your way into.

Let's start with posture. In a well-known Harvard study, participants who held "power poses" for just two minutes experienced a 20% increase in testosterone—the hormone linked to dominance—and a 25% decrease in cortisol—the stress hormone (source). Their confidence didn't increase because they changed their mindset. It increased because they changed their stance. The body told the brain, "We are ready."

This is not fake it till you make it. This is encode it until you embody it. When you stand tall, shoulders back, chin lifted, your body sends a powerful signal to your brain: "I am safe. I am capable. I am ready." That single physical shift doesn't just change how others see you. It changes how you see yourself. It rewires your decisions, your courage, and your capacity to lead.

Breath is your secret weapon. When your breathing is shallow and rapid, your nervous system goes into survival mode. But when you breathe deeply—slow, intentional diaphragmatic breaths—you shift into your parasympathetic system. A 2017 study published in *Frontiers in Human Neuroscience* confirmed that slower breathing increases emotional clarity, self-control, and higher-order thinking ([source](#)). Breath isn't just calming—it's catalytic.

If you want to access unshakable confidence, start moving like the version of you who already has it. Walk with power. Breathe like a grounded leader. Speak from your chest, not from hesitation. The body carries memory. When you make this physical pattern your new default, your identity evolves to match it. Confidence isn't something you find. It's something you embody.

Repetition turns movement into memory. That's why muscle memory is not just for athletes—it's for anyone who wants to live from their higher self. When you anchor affirmations with breath and posture, you create a neural bridge between identity and physiology. This is how elite performers access flow states. They don't wait for confidence. They trigger it. They condition it.

Every day, give yourself that moment. Stand in front of the mirror. Feet grounded. Spine lifted. Eyes locked with your reflection. Say out loud, "I trust myself. I lead with clarity. I am already enough." This isn't motivational fluff. It's neurological reinforcement. A 2022 study in *Body Image* found that affirmations combined with confident posture significantly improved emotional resilience and self-esteem—more than words alone ([source](#)).

This is how you create confidence that doesn't fade with failure. That doesn't wait for the room to approve. This kind of confidence is built into your bones, your breath, and your stride. You no longer have to "get into the zone." You live there. Because your body has become the evidence. Your state is no longer a visitor—it's your home.

The most magnetic people in the world didn't start with louder voices. They started with louder presence. Their confidence was not created in their mind alone—it was carved into their movements. They trained their body to believe the future they were building before it ever arrived. And the world followed their energy.

The body remembers. And when you train it to remember strength, stillness, and certainty, everything else follows. The mind quiets. The doubts dissolve. The room shifts. You stop chasing power—and you start becoming the proof. Confidence isn't an idea you reach for. It's a frequency you step into. And your body is the key.

Nervous System Rewiring for Confidence

Confidence is not just a mindset—it's a physiological state, rooted deep in the patterns of your nervous system. You can declare affirmations all day, but if your body is locked in a stress response, those words won't land. You'll say "I am powerful" while your breath shortens, your chest tightens, and your voice shakes. That's not a lack of willpower—that's a sign your body doesn't feel safe enough to believe what your mind is saying.

Real confidence begins with nervous system regulation, not hype or hustle. When your body feels safe, your brain unlocks higher functions: clarity, creativity, courage. But when it's stuck in fight, flight, or freeze, all your energy is redirected toward survival. That's why the most effective strategy for building true, unshakable confidence doesn't start in the mirror—it starts in the body. This isn't soft work—it's strategic rewiring.

The science backs it up. According to Dr. Stephen Porges' Polyvagal Theory, the vagus nerve is the central switchboard between your nervous system and your emotional experience. High vagal tone—meaning better vagus nerve function—is directly linked to better emotional regulation, resilience, and social engagement (source). In short, the calmer and more connected your nervous system, the more confidently you show up.

The first rewiring tool is breath. Deep, slow, diaphragmatic breathing activates the parasympathetic nervous system—your internal calm switch. A study in *Frontiers in Psychology* found that just five minutes of intentional breathing improved emotional stability and increased performance under stress (source). This isn't just relaxation—it's regulation. And regulation is the gateway to self-trust.

Another proven method is cold exposure. Whether it's a cold shower, ice bath, or even splashing cold water on your face, short-term cold exposure activates the vagus nerve and boosts dopamine by up to 250%. It teaches your body to stay steady in discomfort. That's how you train for real confidence—by building stress resilience in controlled environments (source).

Movement is not optional—it's essential. Confidence lives in rhythm. Walking, dancing, or even gentle swaying engages the cerebellum—the part of the brain that governs balance and action-oriented decision-making. A 2019 study revealed that movement therapy was more effective at reducing anxiety and boosting confidence than talk therapy alone (source). Why? Because confidence isn't just cognitive—it's kinetic.

Touch is another form of healing. Simple gestures like placing a hand over your heart or on your belly release oxytocin, calm the nervous system, and increase emotional safety. According to research in the *Journal of Psychosomatic Research*, self-holding exercises reduce internalized stress and improve somatic confidence (source). You don't just think your way to safety—you touch your way into it.

This work also involves reprogramming how you handle emotional triggers. When your nervous system is regulated, you pause before reacting. You create space between stimulus and response. That space is where power lives. Instead of repeating the old loops of fear and shutdown, you start rehearsing strength. You start choosing groundedness over panic.

True confidence isn't the absence of fear—it's the mastery of presence. It's having a body so familiar with safety that it doesn't flinch when challenge arises. That's the kind of confidence that doesn't just show up in a meeting—it shows up in the silence, in the setbacks, in the moments you choose not to abandon yourself.

This is the confidence your ego avoids. Because it's not performative—it's embodied. It requires you to feel instead of fake. To slow down instead of speed up. To breathe through the discomfort instead of run from it. That's the real work. That's the deep work. That's where unshakable self-trust is built.

So the next time you want to feel more confident, don't look for the perfect quote or the loudest hype track. Sit in stillness. Breathe slower than your fear. Move like you belong. Speak from your gut, not your panic. And let your body show your mind what it means to truly believe in yourself.

Because when your nervous system feels safe, your confidence becomes inevitable. Not because you've conquered fear, but because you've stopped collapsing under it. The body believes it first. And when the body believes, the voice strengthens, the decisions sharpen, and the world begins to mirror back what you finally know to be true.

Speaking Up Without Shrinking

Your voice is more than sound—it's a signature. It carries your truth, your energy, your power. Every time you speak, you're not just communicating words—you're announcing who you are. But the tragedy is, most people don't speak from power. They speak from permission. They shrink, silence themselves, or soften their truth, not because they lack wisdom, but because they've been trained to doubt their right to be heard.

This shrinking doesn't happen by accident. It's nervous system conditioning. When self-expression is linked to pain—like judgment, rejection, or ridicule—the body treats visibility as danger. According to the Polyvagal Theory by Dr. Stephen Porges, your nervous system will always prioritize safety over self-expression. So staying silent isn't weakness—it's self-protection masquerading as politeness. The solution isn't to yell louder. It's to heal the fear that speaking will cost you connection or safety.

Reclaiming your voice isn't about volume—it's about safety. When your nervous system feels secure, your voice unlocks naturally. It flows with conviction instead of force. That's embodied expression. It's when your tone and truth align. You don't perform—you present. You don't debate your worth—you declare it. And in that moment, your presence becomes undeniable.

Studies confirm this truth. A 2020 study in *The Journal of Communication* found that people who consistently expressed their needs and boundaries out loud had higher self-esteem, lower anxiety, and stronger relationship dynamics. Self-expression doesn't break connection—it strengthens it when it's anchored in truth. But you'll never feel this power if you continue to betray your voice just to be accepted.

The lie we were told is that speaking up ruins relationships. But the real betrayal is abandoning yourself to maintain a connection built on silence. Because what good is being accepted if the version of you they love isn't real? True connection doesn't require self-abandonment. It requires mutual respect. And respect begins when you decide you're no longer shrinking for people who only accept your silence.

To speak from power, you must switch from approval-seeking to truth-telling. Ask yourself, "Am I speaking to be liked, or to be authentic?" "Am I filtering my truth to avoid discomfort, or am I standing for what I believe?" Neuroscience shows that speaking your truth activates the medial prefrontal cortex—the same part of your brain responsible for identity, confidence, and motivation. Truth isn't just freeing—it's literally rewiring your brain to recognize your own worth.

One of the most transformative practices is vocal rehearsal in safety. This is where you practice speaking your truth out loud—alone, to the mirror, or with someone who sees you without judgment. According to research published in *Frontiers in Psychology*, vocal rehearsal improves speech clarity, emotional resilience, and perceived self-worth. It's not about being perfect—it's about being present. Being real. Being unshrunk.

You must also confront the shame that taught you to whisper. Shame is the voice that says, "Don't be too much." But the truth is, you were never too much—you were just in environments that couldn't hold your magnitude. That couldn't digest your clarity. That confused your confidence with arrogance. And now, your healing is reclaiming what the world couldn't handle: your full, uncensored voice.

Speaking with power doesn't mean you're fearless. It means you speak anyway—even if your voice shakes. Even if your palms sweat. Because confidence isn't built in silence—it's built in expression. And every time you speak your truth, you send a message to your body: "It's safe to be me." That's how self-trust grows. That's how voice becomes power.

You were never born to shrink. You were born to resonate. To shift energy in rooms. To plant clarity in confusion. To be the voice someone else didn't even know they needed to hear. Your words don't just express your identity—they activate your destiny. But only when you stop negotiating your voice in exchange for belonging.

This is your moment. Not to speak louder for attention—but to speak clearer from truth. Your voice was always meant to move mountains. To set boundaries. To call things forward. It doesn't have to be perfect. It just has to be yours. Speak it. Stand in it. Don't whisper your way through life when you were built to resound.

Your voice was never meant to be silenced. It was born to echo truth into silence. Born to carry conviction, not conditioning. Born to shift atmospheres, not shrink to fit them. So speak—not to impress, not to please—but to liberate. Because the world doesn't need your compliance. It needs your clarity. At full volume. Unapologetic. Unshaken. Unshrunk.

Reframing Mistakes and Criticism

Most people live in fear of failure as if it's a verdict, not a vehicle. They avoid mistakes like landmines, terrified of the judgment that might follow. But here's the truth: if you don't learn to reframe failure, you'll never unlock your full power. Every icon, every trailblazer, every person who changed the game didn't avoid failure—they leveraged it. They didn't get lucky. They got curious. They made mistakes, and then they made momentum.

You weren't born afraid to fail. That fear was taught. It was encoded into you by systems that punished imperfection and rewarded only performance. But neuroscience is rewriting that script. A study in *Scientific Reports* found that when people make mistakes and reflect on them, their brain's learning centers, especially the anterior cingulate cortex, light up—literally enhancing growth and adaptability. Mistakes don't mean you're off track. They mean your brain is on fire with potential.

Every time you fail, you're expanding. You're testing the edge. You're leaving the comfort zone and entering the arena. That is where transformation happens—not in the planning room, but in the pressure. Real mastery doesn't come from avoiding error. It comes from confronting it, analyzing it, and extracting wisdom from it. Your mistakes are not your enemies. They are your milestones.

Criticism, too, has been misunderstood. Most people receive feedback as an attack, not a gift. They shrink. They defend. They spiral. Why? Because they've attached their identity to their performance. But your worth is not your last win. Your power is not your last praise. You are not what went wrong. You are what you do next. Separate who you are from what you did, and you'll stop reacting—you'll start refining.

Harvard Business Review research confirms it: those who develop feedback resilience—who learn to listen without defense and reflect without ego—experience higher leadership growth, better decision-making, and deeper self-awareness. The most powerful people are not immune to criticism. They are immune to being defined by it. They listen for the truth, even when it's buried under someone else's tone.

Reframing criticism doesn't mean swallowing everything whole. It means asking three questions: What's true here? What can I learn? And how can I grow—even if the delivery was flawed? This is the mindset of transformation. You're not just collecting opinions. You're mining for refinement. You're choosing evolution over validation.

This is where neuroplasticity becomes your ally. A 2014 study in *Educational Psychology* found that people who reflected on their mistakes and asked growth-oriented questions improved their performance by up to 25% in future tasks. That's the science of reflection. It's not about guilt. It's about recalibration. Every time you pause and process instead of panic, your brain rewires for greatness.

But when you beat yourself up, you block that growth. Shame shuts down learning. Reflection accelerates it. Guilt tells you, "You're not enough." Growth says, "You're getting there." That's the power of reframing. It takes the sting out of the stumble and turns it into strategy. That's not motivational fluff—it's mental discipline.

So when failure shows up, don't flinch. Don't retreat. Say, "Thank you for the redirection." When criticism lands, don't collapse. Say, "I'll take what's useful and leave the rest." Your ego might resist. But your evolution requires it. You don't rise by being flawless. You rise by being flexible enough to fail forward.

This is how champions are built. Not by getting everything right, but by refusing to let anything keep them wrong. They study their losses. They extract patterns. They find the data in the disappointment. They don't let failure define them—they let it inform them. And that's why they keep climbing, long after others have quit.

You weren't designed to be perfect. You were designed to be powerful. That power isn't born in your highlight reel—it's forged in the rewiring of your low points. The moment you stop resisting failure is the moment it becomes your fuel. And when you learn to turn criticism into your curriculum, nothing can stop your rise.

You weren't built for applause—you were built for mastery. And mastery multiplies every time you reframe failure as feedback, every time you welcome criticism as clarity. Your next level isn't on the other side of perfection—it's on the other side of perspective. So rise—not because you never fell, but because you finally realized what the fall was for.

The Power of Presence and Embodiment

Power doesn't exist in some distant moment or forgotten chapter—it lives in the now. The most magnetic individuals on this planet don't need to speak first or loudest to command attention. They do it through presence. Not the kind you fake or fabricate, but the kind you feel. When someone walks in rooted in their truth, everyone knows it. That's presence. And presence is power in motion.

True presence isn't about dominating a room. It's about anchoring to the moment. Your body, your mind, and your energy must all arrive together. That is when influence becomes effortless. Harvard research led by Dr. Ellen Langer shows that mindfulness—the ability to remain anchored in the present—directly correlates with increased confidence, creativity, and leadership effectiveness. Being here fully isn't just good for your peace. It's a performance edge.

Presence is not just about mental clarity. It's about embodied clarity. It's when your posture, your breathing, your tone, and your gaze all echo the same message: I am here. I am enough. I am grounded. A 2018 study in *Social Cognitive and Affective Neuroscience* confirmed that body language and posture influence your brain's emotional state before a single word is spoken. That means how you carry yourself changes how others feel you—and how you feel yourself.

Your nervous system speaks louder than your words. Before your lips move, your body is already transmitting signals of safety, strength, or stress. People pick up on these cues in milliseconds. If you are distracted, scattered, or tense, your influence diminishes. But when your nervous system is regulated and you are fully present, your energy becomes undeniable.

When you're embodied, you activate your somatosensory cortex—the part of the brain responsible for integrating physical awareness with emotional regulation. Movement with intention, breathing with rhythm, speaking from the belly instead of the throat—these aren't just habits. They're tools that shape your state. You're not performing power. You're embodying it. And neuroscience supports it.

Presence requires participation. It demands that you stop living through a screen or future scenario and fully engage with the here and now. It's not passive—it's power with precision. And when you live that way, people trust you more. Because truth only lives in the present. That's why authenticity can't be faked. The nervous system knows the difference between performance and congruence.

To cultivate this magnetic presence, you need rituals that train your body to stay present under pressure. Breathwork that roots you. Mirror work that reaffirms you. Grounded movement that centers you. Vocal affirmations that reprogram your identity. You are not just rewiring your mind—you're training your body to carry your leadership like a frequency, not a function.

Even your tone begins to shift. When you speak from presence, your words carry weight. A study in the *Journal of Nonverbal Behavior* found that speakers who embodied calm presence—not forceful charisma—held greater audience trust, message retention, and influence. This isn't about having the best words. It's about having aligned energy behind the words.

You don't have to memorize every line of your message. You just have to become the message. That's the secret. When your body, your beliefs, and your breath all align, people feel something deeper than sound. They feel congruence. And congruence builds trust. That's when influence flows without effort. Because people aren't following what you say. They're following what you're anchored in.

Check in with yourself often. Ask, "Am I fully in my body or lost in my head?" "Am I rushing through this conversation or being in it?" "Is my leadership posture rooted in presence or performance?" These aren't just reflective questions—they are recalibration tools. Tools that bring you back to the moment where your power actually lives.

There's a reason presence is so magnetic. It's rare. It's real. It can't be scrolled past or faked. It is the energetic proof of someone who knows who they are and isn't trying to be anywhere else. In a world that runs from stillness, your ability to be fully here becomes revolutionary. You stop pushing. You start attracting.

Because presence is the gateway to power. Embodiment is the evidence of truth. And when you live fully in the now—not in the noise, not in the performance—you don't chase influence. You become it. And that is when the world no longer needs to be convinced. It simply begins to respond.

Confidence Habits for Daily Practice

Confidence is not an emotion you stumble into—it's a habit you build. You don't wait for it to show up. You train it. Every day. Just like strength is earned in the gym, confidence is earned through daily reps of belief, presence, and action. It's not about being in the right mood. It's about becoming the kind of person who acts from power before you even feel it. That's how confidence stops being a concept and starts becoming your identity.

Your day doesn't start when you open your eyes. It starts with what you feed your subconscious in those first thirty minutes. Neuroscience shows that upon waking, your brain operates in a theta-alpha state—making it highly receptive to suggestion. A 2019 study in *NeuroImage* revealed that this window can rewire your emotional baseline and shape your motivation throughout the day. What you tell yourself in this state doesn't just inspire—it imprints.

That's why identity priming is non-negotiable. Look in the mirror and speak the version of you that already exists on the other side of self-doubt. Say, "I move with clarity. I am already enough. I am grounded." These aren't just words. They're neural instructions. A 2022 study found that combining mirror work with auditory affirmations significantly strengthens brain pathways tied to self-trust and emotional regulation. This isn't woo. This is rewiring.

After your words come your breath. Confidence can't live in a nervous system stuck in panic. Deep, controlled breathing activates the vagus nerve, which signals to the body, "We're safe. We're steady." Research in *Frontiers in Psychology* confirmed that three to five minutes of diaphragmatic breathing can lower cortisol by up to 40% and improve executive function. This isn't relaxation—it's regulation. And regulation is the foundation of courage.

Next comes posture. Before you speak a word, your body has already made the introduction. Are you walking like you've already won? Are your shoulders saying, "I belong here"? Harvard studies on power posing reveal that just two minutes of upright posture can increase testosterone levels and reduce stress hormones significantly. The body is a teacher. And when it stands like a leader, the mind begins to follow.

But confidence isn't built in theory—it's forged in discomfort. Daily exposure to what makes you hesitate is how fear loses its grip. This is not reckless bravery—it's psychological exposure therapy. Neuroscience proves that when you repeatedly face fear and survive it, the amygdala rewires, reducing future threat response. Each small step into the unknown becomes a vote for your expansion.

Your speech is another daily practice. Speak slower. Breathe through your sentences. Take up space with your voice, not your volume. A study published in the *Journal of Nonverbal Behavior* found that people who spoke with deliberate pacing were consistently rated as more credible and confident—regardless of their message. You don't need to rush your words. You need to own them.

Journaling isn't just for reflection—it's a tracking system for your evolution. Gratitude is good, but radical honesty is better. Write about what stretched you, what scared you, what moments made you proud. A 2018 study from *JMIR Mental Health* found that emotional journaling improves self-awareness, stress regulation, and confidence tracking. This isn't about venting—it's about data. And data drives identity.

Visual anchors keep your subconscious aligned. Your brain's reticular activating system (RAS) filters your reality based on what you've declared as important. When you place vision boards, declarations, and empowering images where you can see them daily, you activate the RAS to search for opportunities and proof that your identity is real. That's not delusion. That's programming.

How you end the day matters just as much as how you start it. Before bed, ask yourself: "Did I live from truth today? Where can I adjust without shame?" This nightly debrief isn't about guilt—it's about refinement. Ending your day with ownership teaches your subconscious that growth is safe, reflection is power, and your evolution is always in motion.

Confidence is not the absence of fear—it's the presence of rituals that keep you moving despite it. The most effective leaders don't wait to feel ready. They build readiness into their bodies and minds with deliberate, daily action. They're not wired differently. They're trained differently. And the good news is—you can train, too.

You don't wake up confident. You build it before the world opens its mouth. You repeat power until it becomes presence. You practice truth until it becomes tone. You stand tall so often, your spine remembers how leadership feels. And when that happens, the world doesn't ask if you're ready—it starts responding to the version of you that's already arrived.

Journal: Your Confidence Origin Story

You didn't enter this world questioning your worth. You didn't second-guess your laugh or shrink your brilliance. As a child, you were loud, expressive, curious, and free. Confidence wasn't something you had to earn—it was who you were. You danced before you knew how. You spoke before you understood fear. And if that confidence faded, it means it was conditioned out of you—not that it's gone forever.

Your first lessons in confidence came not from your victories, but from the reactions to your vulnerability. Developmental psychology research confirms that self-perception begins forming as early as age three, shaped not by our failures, but by how others respond to our expressions, emotions, and autonomy. If your early expressions were met with shame or silence, your nervous system made a simple but powerful decision: "It's not safe to be fully me."

Confidence doesn't disappear because you're weak. It dissolves when you associate visibility with pain. Maybe you were told to tone it down. Maybe your voice was too loud, your ideas too weird, your joy too much. And so you began to shrink—not because you lacked value, but because you learned it was safer to be invisible. That's not a flaw. That's survival. But now, it's time to unlearn that.

Shame is the thief of self-expression. According to research from Dr. Brené Brown, shame is "the fear of disconnection"—the fear that if we are truly seen, we'll be rejected. When your confidence is built on external validation, it becomes brittle. But when it's rooted in your wholeness—your ability to accept yourself regardless of the room—you become unstoppable.

So go back. Reclaim the story. Ask yourself: When was the first time I doubted myself? Whose voice made me question my own? What lie did I believe to stay safe, accepted, and small? Don't sugarcoat it. Don't spiritualize it. Write it raw. Neuroscience shows that expressive writing actually reduces the brain's fear response and activates clarity by increasing prefrontal cortex activity. This isn't just healing—it's rewiring.

Now reconnect with the version of you that existed before the world edited you. That child who didn't know self-doubt. Who lit up every room without wondering if they were too much. What were you always good at before someone told you not to be? What part of you is still waiting to speak? That's not a memory. That's a message.

There's always a turning point. A moment when you chose courage. When you said "no" to a lie. When you let truth come out of your mouth before you had time to filter it. That's the moment your original confidence cracked through the conditioning. Don't overlook it. Honor it. Document it. According to narrative psychology, people who reframe their life stories around resilience and strength report significantly higher self-worth and emotional stability over time.

You don't have to invent a new version of yourself. You have to return to the original blueprint. Your confidence doesn't need to be manufactured. It needs to be remembered. You were always powerful. You just got distracted by fear and trained to forget. But fear isn't fact. And memory isn't identity. You are allowed to return.

This isn't about becoming something new. It's about becoming true. Your story of shrinking isn't a sign of weakness—it's a map back to your power. The version of you that was silenced is still alive, waiting to be chosen again. And that choice doesn't need to be loud. It just needs to be consistent. Every time you choose self-trust over self-doubt, you reclaim ground.

Write it down. Own your evolution. This is not just journaling. It's activation. It's the ritual of remembering who you were before you were trained to abandon yourself. When you put your power back on paper, it becomes real again. It becomes proof. Not that you're becoming someone. But that you've always been that someone.

Say it out loud. Say it to the mirror. Say it until it feels natural again. "This is who I was before the world told me otherwise." "This is who I choose to become again." "And this time, I don't need permission."

Confidence is not performance. It's not a trick or a costume. It is the quiet decision to no longer apologize for your essence. It's remembering who you were before you learned to shrink—and deciding, once and for all, to never forget again.

Now that you've seen what's truly possible when you begin rewiring your mind for clarity and confidence, the only real question is—are you ready to go deeper? Because knowing this information is one thing… but living it, embodying it, and turning it into unstoppable momentum? That's where the real power is unlocked. The *Clarity Confidence Code Course* is your next step—it's the full immersion experience that takes everything you've read and hardwires it into your subconscious for life-changing results. You'll discover the exact tools, techniques, and guided exercises that high performers, visionary leaders, and unstoppable creators use to shift their identity and operate at a whole new level. Don't stop here. Go all in. Visit https://clarityconfidencecode.com and step into the version of you that doesn't just dream… but *dominates*.

Now, let's move forward—and unlock the next level of your power.

CHAPTER 5

BREAKING THE FEAR LOOP — HOW TO MOVE EVEN WHEN YOU'RE SCARED

Understanding the Fear Loop

You don't overcome fear by avoiding it. You overcome it by facing it, naming it, and choosing to move anyway. Most people misinterpret fear as a warning to stop, when in reality, it's often a compass guiding you toward your next level. When fear shows up, it means you're standing at the threshold of growth. It's not a wall—it's a door. And those who learn to walk through it are the ones who rise.

The body knows fear before the mind does. The trigger could be anything—a risk, a new challenge, a moment of visibility—and instantly, the amygdala fires. Cortisol floods your bloodstream. Your breath shortens. Your muscles tighten. Your vision narrows. The prefrontal cortex—the seat of logic and executive function—goes offline. You're no longer thinking from wisdom. You're reacting from survival. This is the fear loop (source).

That loop is not weakness. It's biology. Your brain was wired to protect you, not to promote you. It evolved to detect threats, not to push you into greatness. A study published in *Neuron* confirms that many fear responses are based on past memories, not current danger (source). So when fear rises, it's not always because you're unsafe—it's often because you're unfamiliar.

And what's unfamiliar often feels dangerous—even when it's exactly what you need. That's why fear isn't just personal—it's generational. It can be inherited through trauma, social learning, or childhood imprinting. You might be responding to someone else's script. But if you never question the fear, you'll follow it. And when you follow fear blindly, you mistake staying small for staying safe.

The first step out of the loop is awareness. Naming what's happening shifts brain activity from the fear center to the executive center. It's a technique called affect labeling. Neuroscience proves that when you say, "This is fear, not fact," the amygdala calms and the prefrontal cortex activates (source). You can't change what you won't name. But once it's named, it can be navigated.

Next comes the body. A deep, slow breath. A reset of posture. A return to your senses. Breath isn't just calming—it's chemical. It communicates safety to the nervous system. A 2017 study in *Frontiers in Psychology* shows that even five minutes of breathwork can reduce stress hormones and re-engage clarity centers in the brain (source). It's not just emotional. It's biological.

Once you've interrupted the pattern, it's time to reframe the story. Ask: "What is this fear trying to protect?" Most fear isn't about failure—it's about exposure. It's the fear of being seen trying. Of being judged. Of not living up to an internal standard set by your inner critic. But courage is not the absence of this fear—it's the decision to act anyway. That decision rewires your nervous system. It builds what researchers call "courage conditioning."

According to *Scientific American*, courage is not just a character trait—it's a trainable state. Just like fear can be programmed through trauma, courage can be cultivated through action ([source](#)). Every time you step through fear, even in micro-movements, you retrain your body to associate growth with safety. Over time, the fear loop gets weaker—and your confidence gets stronger.

Confidence doesn't arrive when fear disappears. It arrives when you prove to yourself that fear can't stop you. That proof becomes identity. That identity becomes presence. And that presence becomes magnetism. People feel it when you've walked through fire and chose truth anyway. They trust what you've embodied—not what you've avoided.

You will never eliminate fear completely—and that's okay. You're not supposed to. Fear isn't the enemy. It's the messenger. It reminds you that you're stretching, growing, evolving. It's not asking you to quit. It's asking you to listen. But once you've received the message, you have a choice: stay in the loop or step into the learning.

You break the loop when you take the action anyway. When you speak even though your voice trembles. When you stand even though your knees shake. When you breathe and choose your truth over your trigger. That's what ends the cycle—not perfection, but presence. Not fearlessness, but alignment.

Fear isn't the end. It's the edge. And when you cross it, you're not just freeing yourself—you're liberating every version of you that ever stayed quiet, compliant, or safe. You are teaching your nervous system that you are trustworthy. That your truth is stronger than your past. And that you no longer serve fear—you lead it.

Fight, Flight, Freeze — and Fawn

There's a version of fear that hides behind a smile. It doesn't scream or shake or run. It blends. It pleases. It nods in agreement even when your soul is screaming "no." It's called fawning—and it's one of the most misunderstood responses to fear. Most people know about fight, flight, and freeze. But fawn is the silent survival pattern that masquerades as kindness while erasing your authenticity.

Fawning is not weakness. It's a nervous system adaptation. When your brain perceives danger—especially emotional threat—it doesn't consult logic. It reacts. The autonomic nervous system kicks in, and if fighting, fleeing, or freezing won't keep you safe, your body may choose appeasement. You begin to over-accommodate, over-agree, and over-function just to maintain a sense of safety. This isn't being polite. It's being programmed.

Trauma specialists have confirmed that fawning is especially common in people with histories of emotional neglect or abandonment. In these cases, survival meant becoming what others needed—at the cost of who you were. According to research from the *Neurobiology of Stress*, this pattern shows up in the brain as increased prefrontal activity (overthinking, hyper-awareness) and suppressed amygdala response (repressed emotion). It's not that you don't feel—it's that you were trained to ignore those feelings to avoid conflict (source).

The danger is that fawning looks like love. It's rewarded by society. People applaud your helpfulness, your patience, your selflessness. But what they're really cheering for is your self-abandonment. You've made everyone else comfortable while quietly dissolving your own boundaries. And the cost? Chronic exhaustion, resentment, identity loss. Because survival is not the same as wholeness.

Your body remembers what your mind tries to forget. That moment you swallowed your voice. That time you laughed when you were hurting. The countless yesses you gave when your entire being said no. These aren't personality quirks. They're survival strategies encoded deep in your nervous system. And if you don't bring awareness to them, they will keep running the show long after the threat is gone.

To break this pattern, you don't need to become aggressive. You need to become honest. It starts with noticing—when does your body contract in a conversation? When do your words feel like armor instead of expression? Somatic awareness is the beginning of reclamation. Your breath is your anchor. Your tension is your teacher. Your silence is not peace—it's data.

Then, begin the smallest revolution: the micro-boundary. Pause before you answer. Take one breath before you say yes. Ask yourself, "Is this true for me?" These may seem insignificant, but they retrain your nervous system to choose authenticity over appeasement. A study published in *The Journal of Experimental Psychology* showed that people who practiced setting minor boundaries over time experienced measurable increases in self-trust and psychological safety (source).

This is not just behavioral. It's biochemical. Every time you choose self-loyalty over self-abandonment, your brain forms new neural pathways. That's neuroplasticity. That's healing. You don't have to change your personality. You just need to stop leaving yourself behind. Because your truth doesn't have to be loud to be real. It just has to be yours.

And yes, it will feel scary. Your nervous system may interpret honesty as danger at first. But that's not a sign to stop—it's a sign to soothe. Speak to your inner child. Affirm: "I am safe to be real." "My needs are not a burden." "I do not need to earn love through sacrifice." These aren't just affirmations. They are corrections to a lifetime of misbeliefs.

You don't heal from fawning by becoming hard. You heal by becoming whole. By remembering that your kindness is a gift, but not a currency. You can be compassionate without being compliant. You can be generous without abandoning yourself. You can serve others without sacrificing your soul.

This is not about rebellion—it's about restoration. You are not here to be palatable. You are here to be powerful. And power doesn't come from pleasing. It comes from presence. It comes from choosing yourself in a world that benefits from your silence. That's not selfish. That's sacred.

You are not too much. You were just never meant to shrink. So the next time you feel the urge to please instead of speak, remember: you are not here to keep the peace by losing yours. You are here to take up space. To tell the truth. To love out loud. And to never again mistake your survival patterns for your identity.

Fear as a Feedback System

Fear isn't failure. It isn't weakness. It's not your enemy. Fear is data. It's feedback. It's a signal, not a sentence. Most people stop at fear because they misread its purpose. They treat it like a stop sign when it was always meant to be a compass. The brain isn't trying to scare you away from growth—it's scanning for anything unfamiliar, anything outside your comfort zone. Your amygdala doesn't ask if your goal is meaningful—it only asks if it's safe, if it's known, if it's been survived before. That's why fear often shows up precisely when you're on the edge of a breakthrough.

Understanding the science behind fear gives you the power to work with it instead of against it. The limbic system runs 24/7 threat detection and will trigger fear even if the only danger is to your identity—not your life. According to research from the National Institutes of Health, your brain's fear circuits are predictive. They fire based not just on present danger, but on what your mind believes might happen based on past experience. That means most of the fear you feel isn't about now—it's about a story your brain wrote years ago.

This makes fear one of the most powerful tools for transformation—if you know how to read it. High performers don't avoid fear. They lean into it. They know that what scares them often marks the edge of their next expansion. Fear becomes a north star, not a barrier. They've trained themselves to pause and ask, "What's the lesson here?" instead of defaulting to retreat. Because the presence of fear isn't a warning that you're off track—it's often a signal that you're about to grow.

This is where the power of cognitive reappraisal comes in. It's a scientifically proven method for reinterpreting fear. When you question the story fear is telling, your brain literally changes. Studies from the American Psychological

Association show that reframing emotions rewires your brain by decreasing activity in the amygdala and increasing resilience to future stress. That's not positive thinking—that's neuroscience.

Fear is a master storyteller. It speaks in exaggerations. It says, "What if they reject you?" "What if you fail publicly?" "What if you're not ready?" But when you slow down and ask questions like, "Is that actually true?" or "What would I do if I trusted myself right now?"—you shift from being the character in fear's story to the author of your own. That single pivot reclaims your power.

One of the most liberating truths about fear is this: most of it isn't even yours. It was installed. It was inherited. It was modeled by people who didn't know better. You absorbed it from culture, family, school—systems designed more for compliance than expansion. And if you don't challenge it, you'll obey it. You'll shrink your dreams to the size of your nervous system, instead of expanding your nervous system to hold your dreams.

According to Dr. Lisa Feldman Barrett, emotions are not fixed reactions. They are predictions shaped by your past experiences. That means fear isn't hardwired. It's a habit. A learned emotional reflex. And if it's learned, it can be unlearned. You can update the software. You can rewrite the script. Every time you act in alignment with your values despite the fear, you're installing new neural pathways that say, "It's safe to be seen. It's safe to speak. It's safe to stretch."

Reframing fear begins with language. Say, "This fear means I'm expanding." Say, "This fear means I'm alive." Say, "This fear means I'm not in a cage—I'm on the cusp." Use fear as an alert system, not a limitation system. It's not telling you to stop. It's telling you to pay attention. And often, it's pointing to a lie about your limitations. Wherever fear lives, a false belief about your power usually hides.

Fear reveals where your power is locked. It shows you the areas where your self-trust needs reinforcement. If you're afraid of speaking, it's because your voice matters. If you're afraid of being visible, it's because your presence is powerful. If you're afraid of rejection, it's because you're finally ready to stop abandoning yourself. Don't run from fear—interrogate it. Ask it what it's guarding. Ask it what it believes. And then show it who you are now.

Growth requires nervous system reconditioning. You can't expand if your body interprets visibility as danger. That's why breathwork, grounding, and somatic awareness are crucial. When you learn to calm the body, you create space for a new story. You restore your ability to choose. You activate your prefrontal cortex. And in that state, you don't just react to life—you respond with leadership.

Fear never really goes away. But it evolves. It stops being the loudest voice and starts becoming background noise. You don't eliminate fear. You outgrow its authority. You learn to hear it without obeying it. You learn to use it as fuel instead of a fence. And that's when the shift happens. Not when fear is gone—but when your courage becomes louder.

You were never meant to be fearless. You were meant to become fluent in the language of fear. To turn it from a barrier into a blueprint. To decode it, dance with it, and move through it. Because on the other side of every fear is not just freedom—but the real you. The one who stopped running. The one who listened. The one who led.

Naming and Normalizing Fear

Fear isn't a flaw—it's a function. It's not here to stop you. It's here to signal that you're standing at the threshold of something that matters. Most people spend their lives trying to silence fear, thinking that once it's gone, they'll be ready. But readiness doesn't come from the absence of fear. It comes from mastering your response to it. And that mastery begins the moment you decide to stop demonizing fear and start decoding it.

When you name your fear, you shift from reaction to awareness. That process is called affect labeling, and neuroscience confirms its power. A study from UCLA found that labeling emotions like fear actually reduces activity in the amygdala—the brain's fear center—while increasing activity in the prefrontal cortex, the part responsible for reasoning and decision-making (source). That means saying, "I feel anxious about this meeting" doesn't weaken you—it strengthens your brain's ability to lead through it.

Fear unspoken becomes shame. But fear acknowledged becomes strategy. The moment you say out loud, "I'm afraid of being judged," or "I'm nervous to fail publicly," you make the fear visible. And what's visible can be handled. It's not the fear that paralyzes—it's the secrecy. It's the belief that you shouldn't feel it. But every brave person you admire has felt fear. They've just trained themselves not to obey it.

Normalize it. That's the next move. Fear isn't a defect—it's a default. According to the American Psychological Association, fear is an evolutionary survival mechanism shared across every human nervous system. It's not a sign of weakness. It's a sign you're alive, conscious, and stepping into something that matters (source). You're not broken because you feel it. You're human because you do.

The real problem isn't fear—it's the belief that you shouldn't have it. When you personalize fear, you spiral. But when you normalize it, you reclaim power. Instead of saying, "Something's wrong with me," you say, "Of book this is here—I'm expanding." Fear doesn't mean "don't proceed." It means "prepare wisely." It means you've exited the comfort zone and entered the growth zone.

And in that zone, compassion is your anchor. Research from Dr. Kristin Neff shows that people who practice self-compassion in moments of fear experience greater emotional resilience and faster recovery from stress (source). When you meet fear with judgment, you compound the stress. When you meet it with understanding, you unlock clarity. Compassion is not softness. It's strategy.

Every bold decision will be accompanied by fear. Visibility. Vulnerability. Voice. These things will always trigger your nervous system. That doesn't mean you're unqualified. It means you're human—and it means you care. If you felt nothing, you wouldn't be growing. Fear is the friction that sharpens your edge. It's the signal that you're not coasting anymore. You're rising.

One of the fastest ways to move through fear is to speak it in a safe space. According to research published in *Social Cognitive and Affective Neuroscience*, verbalizing your fear to someone who listens without judgment can significantly reduce stress hormones and increase executive function (source). You don't need to vent. You need to name it. Claim it. And then act from clarity, not from contraction.

Write it down. Speak it out. Feel it through. Then move. Because fear that is normalized and expressed no longer controls you—it collaborates with you. You turn it into guidance, not governance. You use it as data, not definition. It becomes part of your process, not a reason to pause.

Most people wait for fear to go away before they act. But the most impactful people move while it's still present. They don't wait for the absence of doubt—they develop the presence of decision. They don't perform fearlessness—they practice alignment. They normalize the discomfort and move anyway.

Every time you feel fear and move forward, you're doing more than taking a step—you're rewriting your nervous system's script. You're telling your brain, "We can survive visibility. We can speak and still be safe. We can stretch and still be whole." That's how fear turns into freedom. Not when it disappears, but when it no longer drives.

So name the fear. Normalize the fear. Then walk into the room, the opportunity, the future—like your purpose is louder than your panic. You don't wait for fear to leave. You lead anyway. Because courage doesn't cancel fear. It converts it into fuel.

The Role of the Inner Protector

Inside every human being is a voice that whispers caution. It says, "Don't go there." "That's too risky." "You're not ready yet." It rises not when you're coasting, but when you're about to rise—when you're about to speak your truth, take the leap, or break an old pattern. That voice isn't sabotage. It's your Inner Protector. And its job isn't to ruin your life—it's to preserve it. But sometimes, preservation turns into paralysis.

The Inner Protector is not built to assess your greatness. It's designed to avoid pain. And that part of you, while protective, was formed in moments of emotional exposure. It took shape the first time honesty was punished, the first time ambition was mocked, or the first time vulnerability led to rejection. The nervous system coded those experiences as danger. And now, that protector activates whenever you move toward expansion.

The problem is, your Inner Protector is running old software. It's still trying to protect a version of you that no longer exists. A younger version. A hurt version. A you that didn't have the knowledge, tools, or support you now carry. What once helped you survive can now sabotage your potential—unless you update the system.

This part of you doesn't need to be crushed or silenced—it needs to be seen. Internal Family Systems (IFS) therapy teaches that every mind is made of parts. And the protector parts are often guarding younger, exiled parts that still carry pain. When you approach those parts with curiosity and compassion, integration begins. You don't reject the protector—you lead it.

Your Inner Protector gets loudest right before you do something big. Not because you're wrong—but because you're getting close to something meaningful. Close to visibility. Close to authenticity. Close to change. And because change feels like danger to the subconscious, the amygdala—the brain's threat detector—fires even in response to emotional risk, not just physical danger. It doesn't ask "Is this good?" It asks, "Is this familiar?"

So the goal is not to shut down the fear, but to re-educate the brain. Every time you speak your truth and remain safe, every time you take a bold step and nothing bad happens, you're feeding new evidence to your nervous system. You're saying, "This new version of me is capable. We can survive honesty now. We can handle success now." That's how you build embodied confidence—not by forcing courage, but by gently retraining safety.

Instead of battling fear, get curious about it. Ask your protector, "What are you trying to shield me from?" Ask, "How old is this fear?" Ask, "What did I believe back then that I no longer have to believe now?" According to a 2020 study in *Psychotherapy Research*, dialoguing with protector parts in a compassionate way reduces resistance and unlocks real change. The protector isn't the problem—it's your invitation.

You're not failing because you feel fear. You're succeeding because you see it. You're noticing the pattern. You're choosing leadership over autopilot. And that leadership doesn't always look loud or dramatic. Sometimes, it looks like pausing before you shrink. Breathing before you silence yourself. Saying yes to the truth even when your voice shakes.

You don't need to bypass the fear. You need to update the story. Because fear is often the voice of a child who didn't know how to protect themselves, who needed safety through silence, obedience, or invisibility. But you're not that child anymore. And your Inner Protector is waiting for proof that the adult version of you can now lead with love, not panic.

This is how healing becomes momentum. Not by eliminating fear, but by evolving the role it plays. Your protector stops being the gatekeeper of your past and becomes the guardian of your potential. It starts to say, "Yes, this is scary—but we're not alone anymore. We've got this. We can lead now."

You become unstoppable not when you stop feeling afraid—but when you stop letting fear decide. Mastery is not the absence of trembling. It's the presence of clarity. It's the decision to move forward even when that Inner Protector rises to its feet. You look it in the eyes and say, "Thank you. I know you're trying to help. But I've got this now."

And in that moment, the protector steps aside. Not because it's been defeated, but because it's been respected. And that respect turns fear into fuel. Doubt into data. Resistance into readiness. You're no longer reacting from old wounds. You're responding from new wisdom. And that's when your next level no longer feels like a threat. It feels like home.

How to Befriend Resistance

Resistance doesn't show up when you're stuck in the familiar. It rises when you're reaching toward expansion. It's not random, and it's not wrong. It's your brain's built-in alarm system, whispering, "This is new, this is different, this might change everything." And change—no matter how powerful—is processed first by your nervous system as a threat. That's biology, not brokenness.

When you feel resistance before a breakthrough, it's not a sign to retreat. It's confirmation that you're approaching a threshold. Neuroscientific research confirms that the amygdala, the brain's fear center, activates when you move toward anything unfamiliar—even if that unfamiliar thing is growth, success, or healing (source). So when resistance rises, don't ask, "What's wrong with me?" Ask, "What's trying to evolve in me?"

What makes resistance so deceptive is that it doesn't always scream. Sometimes, it shows up as perfectionism. Sometimes as fatigue. Sometimes as scrolling, cleaning, or endlessly tweaking your website instead of launching it. These aren't failures of discipline. They're signals of internal conflict. Your identity is trying to update, and your system is asking, "Are we sure we're safe doing this?"

Your brain doesn't resist effort. It resists identity change. A 2012 study in *Psychological Science* found that even positive changes—like pursuing a goal or adopting a new habit—can trigger resistance if they challenge your current sense of self (source). That means the resistance isn't against the task—it's against what the task represents: a version of you your brain hasn't fully met yet.

That's why befriending resistance is more powerful than fighting it. Internal Family Systems (IFS) therapy shows us that resistance is often a protective part—a younger, reactive version of you that once kept you safe by keeping you small. When you meet that part with curiosity instead of criticism, you open a doorway to transformation. You move from fear to leadership (source).

Naming the resistance brings it out of the shadows. Say it out loud: "I feel resistance toward launching this program." "I notice tension every time I prepare to speak." Labeling your emotional state calms your nervous system and reactivates the executive functions in your brain. This technique, known as affect labeling, is scientifically proven to reduce the intensity of emotional reactions (source).

Then take one small step. One email. One post. One sentence. Movement is medicine. A 2018 study in *Motivation and Emotion* showed that taking even the smallest action toward a feared goal increases dopamine and motivation, reducing future avoidance (source). You don't have to move fast. You just have to move forward.

Ritual is your ally. Systems are your structure. Willpower may start the engine, but ritual keeps it running. The most consistent people aren't the most motivated—they're the most supported. They've built internal and external systems that guide them through resistance when inspiration evaporates.

Resistance can also be a sign of alignment. Best-selling authors, top athletes, visionary leaders—they all feel it. Why? Because they're doing work that matters. Steven Pressfield calls it "Resistance with a capital R"—a force that rises in proportion to the importance of the calling (source). So if it scares you, it may be sacred. If it terrifies you, it may be your truth.

Ask deeper questions. Not "Why am I lazy?" but "What am I protecting?" Not "Why can't I finish?" but "What success might force me to confront?" Resistance is rarely about the task. It's about the transformation. And the more radical the transformation, the more fiercely the old version of you will cling to the comfort of what was.

Every time you meet resistance with presence instead of panic, you build nervous system resilience. You teach your body to stay in the room. You show your mind that visibility won't destroy you. You remind your protector parts that they're not in charge anymore—you are. And that shift from protector to leader is how you become unshakable.

Your next level isn't blocked by resistance—it's revealed through it. You don't need to crush it. You need to listen, lead, and keep moving. Because on the other side of resistance is not just your growth—it's the version of you that's been waiting all along. Ready. Aligned. And no longer ruled by the fear of who you were.

The "Micro-Courage" Principle

You don't have to wait for the perfect moment to act. That moment doesn't exist. What exists is now. And what creates the shift isn't some thunderous decision—it's micro-courage. That small, quiet bravery that whispers, "Do it anyway." It's not the grand leaps that transform your life. It's the little choices you make when no one else is watching. The moment you speak up even though your voice shakes. The second you hit send on that idea you've been sitting on. That's where your power lives—in the ordinary, repeated acts of inner boldness.

Science backs this up. According to Stanford's Behavior Design Lab, small, consistent actions are more powerful than rare, dramatic changes. It's known as "Tiny Habits," and it's not just about behavior. It's about identity. Because every time you choose the hard thing, even in a small way, you cast a vote for the future you. That version of you isn't built by force—it's built by frequency. Tiny wins compounded over time create massive change (source).

Every micro-act of courage floods your brain with dopamine. And dopamine isn't just the "feel-good" hormone—it's the motivation molecule. It rewards you for taking action and nudges you toward doing it again. This isn't fluff. It's neuroscience. The more often you choose courage, the more your brain wires for bravery. It builds a loop of internal reward that makes future boldness easier (source).

The brain is not naturally wired for growth—it's wired for survival. That's why new actions feel scary. When you try something unfamiliar, your amygdala—the brain's alarm system—lights up. It says, "Danger! Stay in the known." But when you take even one small step forward and survive, you disrupt the loop. You teach your brain that expansion doesn't equal death. You literally recondition your nervous system to hold more courage over time (source).

The more you move in the direction of your fear, the more you build something deeper than confidence—you build self-trust. Because trust isn't built in the big moments. It's built in the micro-decisions: the moments you want to retreat but move anyway. Every act of micro-courage becomes a vote for the identity of someone who follows through. As James Clear writes, "Every action you take is a vote for the person you wish to become" (source).

Courage isn't about feeling ready. It's about deciding anyway. So the question isn't, "What's the big move I need to make?" The real question is, "What small act of truth can I say yes to today?" Can you be 5% bolder in this moment? Can you take one action that aligns with your future self? That's how transformation begins—not with noise, but with a whisper that repeats itself daily.

And here's the magic—these small acts don't just change your life. They change your chemistry. They alter your physiology. Research in *Personality and Social Psychology Review* found that repeated small acts of courage measurably increase psychological capital—hope, resilience, optimism, and self-efficacy (source). This isn't about faking it till you make it. It's about facing it until you become it.

When you normalize micro-courage, you stop waiting for the fear to go away. You realize you can carry it and still move. That's how real confidence is born—not from the absence of fear, but from the presence of commitment. You don't need to roar. You just need to keep whispering "yes" to your truth until it becomes your new normal. It's a nervous system decision, not a motivational pep talk.

And the ripple effect is real. When you choose courage, you give others permission to do the same. Your family sees it. Your community feels it. Your energy becomes contagious. You don't just break your own ceiling—you create space for others to rise. Micro-courage becomes a quiet revolution.

You've been waiting for motivation when all you needed was movement. The version of you you're chasing isn't behind a wall of fear—it's one uncomfortable action away. Don't let the illusion of "more time" rob you of the moment you already have. Micro-courage doesn't need a stage. It needs a decision.

You were never meant to live in hesitation. You were built to move—even if it's slow, even if it's shaky. And the more often you move from truth, the more often life moves with you. Because the universe doesn't respond to potential. It responds to action. Action is your announcement. It says, "I'm serious about who I'm becoming."

It's not about being fearless. It's about being faithful in small moments. Because those small moments shape your nervous system, your identity, and your future. The version of you that's confident, grounded, and unstoppable isn't a fantasy. It's the reward for every micro-courage you stack today. So whisper "yes" now. Your transformation is already listening.

Movement Over Perfection

Perfection is a seductive lie. It dresses itself up as a high standard, a noble pursuit. But behind the curtain, it's fear in disguise. It tells you to wait. To overthink. To pause just a little longer until everything looks perfect. And while you wait, momentum slips through your fingers. Progress turns into procrastination. You don't need to be flawless—you need to be in motion. Because motion is what changes lives, not immaculate execution.

According to the American Psychological Association, perfectionism isn't a sign of excellence—it's a gateway to anxiety, burnout, and depression. It masquerades as ambition, but it's really avoidance. It's the ego's way of dodging judgment. You're not aiming higher—you're hiding. And every time you hold back your gift until it's polished, you rob the world of your presence and your potential (source).

There's nothing empowering about perfection. It doesn't strengthen you—it stalls you. Studies in the journal *Motivation and Emotion* show that people who take imperfect action are not only more likely to reach their goals, they also experience greater dopamine release and sustained motivation. The brain doesn't reward planning—it rewards progress. When you move, you feel alive. When you wait, you wither (source).

The difference between success and stagnation isn't talent—it's tempo. You don't need the best plan. You need the next step. And when you take it, even if it's messy, your body records it. Your nervous system whispers, "We did it." That's not just a mood shift—it's neuroplasticity in action. Every bold move reinforces the neural pathways of courage, of confidence, of capacity (source).

Confidence is built in motion. It doesn't come from thinking about action. It comes from taking it. Confidence is earned when you show up before you feel ready. When you speak before the words feel perfect. When you launch the project before the logo is finished. Movement builds belief because it gives your brain evidence that you're capable—even when the outcome isn't perfect.

What stops most people isn't failure. It's fear of looking foolish. But you can't rise while trying to manage everyone's perception of you. You'll either live for applause or live for alignment—but not both. And the more you choose motion over masking, the more your truth becomes magnetic. You stop performing and start leading. You stop proving and start becoming.

Harvard Business Review reports that action-oriented leaders are more respected, more trusted, and more likely to lead successful teams—even when they make mistakes. Why? Because people don't follow perfect—they follow real. They follow energy. They follow someone who moves with conviction, even if the path is unclear (source).

That's your new mission: progress over perfection. Replace "What's the best decision?" with "What's the next one?" Don't wait to be certain. Move and refine. Try and tweak. Let life meet you in motion. Feedback isn't failure. It's fuel. It's how you build agility, resilience, and creative power. The most confident people aren't always right—but they're always willing.

Let go of the idea that your first draft has to be your final masterpiece. Your message doesn't have to be polished to be powerful. Your business doesn't have to be perfect to make an impact. Your voice doesn't have to be rehearsed to be received. What matters is that you show up. Unfiltered. Unpolished. Unapologetic.

The trap of perfection will always whisper, "Wait a little longer." But the miracle lives in the messy middle. In the rough start. In the awkward launch. That's where breakthroughs are born. If you wait until you're ready, you'll never leave the dock. The wind doesn't show up for stationary ships—it finds the ones that set sail.

Progress isn't just a mindset—it's a nervous system reset. The more often you act, the more often you prove to your subconscious that you're a person who follows through. That self-trust is priceless. It becomes your compass when doubt creeps in. It becomes your anchor when storms hit. You don't need more motivation—you need more movement.

Because perfection isn't your standard—it's your stall. Movement is your breakthrough. The moment you stop worshipping polish and start choosing progress, you win. Not someday. Not when it's flawless. But now. Because now is where power lives. And now is all you need.

Fear Mapping & Emotional Safety

You can't conquer fear by running from it. You conquer it by facing it, feeling it, and decoding it. Because fear, when avoided, grows. It becomes louder, more convincing, more controlling. But when you stop running and start listening, it loses its power. You can't lead yourself or anyone else if fear is leading you. True power begins the moment you turn toward what you used to flee from—and say, "Let's talk."

Fear isn't random. It lives in your nervous system, shaped by patterns, pain, and past programming. According to Dr. Lisa Feldman Barrett's theory of constructed emotion, your brain doesn't just react—it predicts. Meaning your fear is often based on what your brain expects, not what's actually happening.

It's interpreting current events through old experiences, rehearsing survival before confirming danger. That's why you can feel fear even when there's no threat in sight (source).

The problem isn't fear—it's the lack of clarity around it. When you leave fear unnamed, it becomes a shadow that follows you. But when you map it, when you trace where it lives in your body, your thoughts, your habits—it becomes information. And information is power. Dr. Dan Siegel's "name it to tame it" model proves this. Simply labeling what you're feeling—naming the fear—deactivates your amygdala and engages your prefrontal cortex, restoring calm and clarity (source).

Fear mapping isn't therapy—it's leadership. You ask yourself, "Where does fear show up in my day-to-day?" "What do I do when I feel it?" "What does this fear say about my identity?" These questions turn fear into a mirror. And when fear becomes your mirror, you stop fighting it—you start learning from it. You stop making decisions out of panic and start moving with presence.

But fear doesn't loosen its grip unless your body feels safe. Emotional safety isn't optional—it's essential. Without it, your nervous system stays in defense mode, scanning for shame, rejection, or failure. Affirmations don't work if your body doesn't feel safe enough to believe them. According to research in *Neuroscience & Biobehavioral Reviews*, emotional safety enhances cognitive flexibility, resilience, and motivation (source).

So how do you build that safety? You start by refusing to abandon yourself when fear arises. Most people shame their fear. They call it weak. They try to push through it with force. But healing begins when you say, "You're allowed to be afraid—and I'm not going anywhere." When you bring compassion to your fear, your nervous system learns it doesn't have to fight, freeze, or flee. It can stay. It can breathe. It can lead.

Grounding becomes your daily ritual. Breathwork, gentle movement, somatic journaling—all of these practices calm your vagus nerve, the regulator of your body's stress response. Studies show that even 10 minutes of consistent vagal tone stimulation increases your ability to stay centered in the face of fear, building resilience instead of reactivity (source).

Fear mapping is not a one-time exercise—it's a weekly discipline. Set time aside to write down what scared you this week. What did you avoid? What did you overthink? What did you say no to that your soul wanted to say yes to? Research in *Behavior Research and Therapy* found that structured journaling about fear significantly reduced avoidance and boosted courageous action in people who previously felt stuck (source).

As you do this, your identity changes. You stop seeing fear as a threat. You begin to see it as a compass. It's no longer "I feel fear, so I retreat." It becomes "I feel fear, so I slow down. I ask questions. I move forward with intention instead of instinct." That's the essence of emotional mastery—not the absence of fear, but the integration of it.

Fear becomes your informant, not your enemy. You begin to decode its message instead of obeying its impulse. You realize it's not trying to ruin your life—it's trying to protect your past. But now, you're no longer living in that version of you. And the more you meet fear with presence and safety, the more that version fades away.

Every time you sit with your fear and don't flee, you send a message to your nervous system: "We are safe here. We are strong enough for this. We lead now." And that message rewires you. Over time, it builds an inner calm so stable, so grounded, that fear becomes just another voice in the room—not the one holding the microphone.

You don't need to eliminate fear. You need to elevate your relationship with it. Because once fear becomes your mirror instead of your master, your life no longer runs on survival. It runs on truth. And truth doesn't rush. It doesn't perform. It leads—with quiet, grounded power. And so will you.

Releasing Fear Through the Body

You can't outthink fear. It doesn't dissolve with logic. It doesn't surrender to affirmations alone. Because fear doesn't live in your head—it lives in your body. It's a physical imprint, not just a mental concept. Your shoulders remember what your voice won't say. Your breath carries the memory of every moment you froze. If you want to release fear, you don't just process it intellectually—you move it. You metabolize it. You feel it through.

Fear is not weakness—it's chemistry. When your nervous system senses a threat, real or perceived, it floods your body with cortisol, tightens your muscles, and restricts your breath. According to Harvard Medical School, even after the danger has passed, your body continues to hold the contraction. That means your body can live in a state of fear long after your mind has moved on (source).

This is why you can say, "I'm fine," but still feel anxious, restless, or frozen. Your body knows what your words deny. Somatic psychology teaches that every emotion has a motor pattern—a physical expression. Fear often manifests as clenched jaws, shallow breaths, hunched shoulders. These are not random—they are coded survival scripts. If you want to heal, you have to interrupt those patterns with movement and presence (source).

Somatic tools like shaking, breathwork, and trauma-informed movement don't just distract from fear—they help complete the stress cycle. A 2022 review in *Frontiers in Psychology* found that body-based trauma release reduces symptoms of PTSD and improves nervous system regulation. That's not just emotional—it's biological liberation (source).

Your breath is your first bridge. Practices like box breathing—inhale for 4, hold for 4, exhale for 4, hold for 4—activate your parasympathetic nervous system, which restores calm and signals to the brain, "We're safe." In a study published in *Cell Reports Medicine*, just five minutes a day of breathwork improved emotional regulation and reduced anxiety significantly (source).

Movement doesn't need choreography—it needs honesty. Let your spine roll, your hips sway, your limbs stretch. This isn't performance. It's expression. It's how your body speaks when words fall short. Research from *The Journal of Bodywork and Movement Therapies* confirms that expressive movement releases emotional tension and boosts psychological resilience (source).

Even your voice is a nervous system tool. The vagus nerve, which regulates emotional regulation and digestion, connects directly to your vocal cords. Practices like humming, toning, and sighing stimulate this nerve, release tension, and promote relaxation. A 2020 article in the *International Journal of Yoga* showed that humming increases nitric oxide, improving circulation and calm brainwave activity (source).

The point isn't to escape fear—it's to complete it. Let the body finish the emotional sentence it started years ago. Let it tremble, sigh, stretch, or weep if needed. These movements aren't regressions—they're releases. The trembling you fear isn't a breakdown. It's a breakthrough. It's your body finally letting go of the armor it no longer needs.

This isn't a one-time rescue. It's a daily return. A commitment to wholeness. You don't "cure" fear with a single session. You build a relationship with your body where fear is no longer an enemy but a signal. You become fluent in the language of sensation. And in doing so, you reclaim access to your full aliveness.

Your body is not betraying you. It's protecting you. Every flinch, every freeze, every contraction is a message—not a malfunction. When you stop shaming those signals and start responding to them with breath, movement, and love, you shift from reactivity to regulation. You become safe inside your own skin again.

And that safety becomes your superpower. Because a regulated body is a courageous body. One that can speak the truth, take the leap, and feel deeply without collapsing. That's not hype—it's neuroscience. Your ability to stay present with fear is what makes you unstoppable. It's not that fear disappears. It's that it stops running the show.

When you meet fear with movement instead of judgment, it becomes fuel. When you let your body finish the emotional story, you release power that no affirmation alone can access. The path isn't up or out—it's through. Through the breath. Through the shake. Through the sound. And on the other side is freedom. Not because the fear is gone—but because you've finally come home to your body.

Turning Fear into Fuel

Fear was never designed to stop you. It was designed to awaken you. The same signal that makes your heart race and your palms sweat can also sharpen your focus and ignite your resolve. Physiologically, fear and excitement are nearly indistinguishable—your heart rate rises, adrenaline surges, breath quickens. The only real difference is what your brain chooses to call it. When you reframe fear as readiness, you don't suppress it—you transmute it. That's not philosophy—it's neuroscience, proven by studies at Stanford and Harvard ([source](), [source]()).

That shift—labeling fear as energy—turns panic into power. It's the same principle that elite athletes use before championship games. They don't wait to feel calm. They train themselves to act under pressure. This is called "stress inoculation," and it conditions your nervous system to operate with clarity even in chaos. The point isn't to erase the fear. It's to build your capacity to carry it while moving forward with precision ([source]()).

The greatest mistake people make is waiting for fear to vanish before they act. But action itself rewires the fear. Every step you take toward what you fear signals courage to the brain, which triggers dopamine release—the very chemical of motivation. One decision. One move. That's all it takes to begin dismantling the loop. You don't need a breakthrough. You need momentum ([source]()).

You were never meant to cower in fear. You were meant to collaborate with it. Fear is not the enemy—it's information. It says, "You're at your edge." "You're stepping into the unknown." "You're about to level up." Most people misread that signal as danger when it's actually direction. When fear arises, ask, "What is this here to teach me?" "What growth is trying to happen right now?"

Use fear as a tool for introspection. Ask, "What identity is being threatened?" "What would I do if I trusted myself here?" These questions convert fear from a trigger into a teacher. According to Dr. Tara Brach, fear emerges most when we stretch beyond the borders of who we've been. It's not a warning—it's an invitation to evolve (source).

And you can't think your way through fear—you must move your way through it. Grounding techniques like deep breathing, gentle movement, or speaking out loud activate the parasympathetic nervous system and turn the energy of fear into fuel. The charge doesn't go away. It becomes usable. It powers your message, your mission, your momentum.

If you wait for fear to feel safe, you'll never begin. Because the moment is never perfect. But when you move in the presence of fear, you create safety through trust. Not trust in the outcome—but trust in your capacity to handle whatever comes. That trust is what turns ordinary people into extraordinary leaders. Not because they're fearless—but because they've made peace with the fire inside.

You're not being tested—you're being trained. Every challenge that rattles your nerves is preparing you for greater impact. Every tremble is a rehearsal for a bigger stage. Every doubt is a doorway to deeper truth. The path to mastery is not paved with ease—it's paved with decisions made in the middle of fear.

So don't shrink. Don't stall. Don't wait for clarity to come before you move. Clarity comes from movement. Feedback is your mentor. Failure is your tutor. Fear is your map. Your job is not to eliminate resistance—it's to rise through it. To say, "Yes, I'm scared—and I'm still showing up anyway."

The nervous system doesn't need perfection. It needs leadership. When you stabilize your body with breath and presence, you give fear a container. And inside that container, fear can't dominate. It has to obey. It becomes a tool—not a tyrant. You take the wheel. You let fear ride, but never drive.

You don't need less fear. You need a new relationship with it. One where fear becomes fuel. One where it becomes feedback. One where the energy that once stopped you now empowers you. You were born for this—not because you're fearless, but because you're willing. And that willingness, paired with action, is what transforms fear into fire.

So when fear says, "This is risky," you answer, "This is sacred." When fear whispers, "You're not ready," you reply, "Readiness is a decision." And when fear screams, "Stop," you calmly walk forward and say, "This is exactly where I rise." Because fear was never your ceiling—it was your invitation to fly.

Exercise: The Fear-Action Ladder

Fear isn't the end—it's the edge. And what you choose to do at the edge defines your entire trajectory. Most people stop there. They see fear as a wall. But what if fear isn't the barrier? What if it's the invitation? The threshold? That's where the Fear-Action Ladder comes in—not as a motivational slogan, but as a transformational system. It's built on science, structured around action, and designed to help you convert fear into forward motion.

Your mind loves clarity. When fear feels vague, it multiplies. It grows into stories, spirals into doubt, and loops through hesitation. But when you give fear structure—when you give it a ladder—it becomes climbable. That's the power of specificity. According to neuroscience, naming your emotion activates the prefrontal cortex and calms the amygdala, shrinking the emotional storm into something manageable ([source](#)).

Start with the truth. Identify your "fear target." That one thing you keep avoiding. Not because it's impossible—but because it's uncomfortable. Maybe it's launching your business. Maybe it's publishing your story. Maybe it's making the call that could change everything. Name it. Because when fear is named, it loses its mystery. And mystery is what gives it power.

Then, strip it down. Define your worst-case scenario. It sounds counterintuitive, but visualizing the worst helps. It clears the fog. Tim Ferriss's concept of "fear-setting" shows that when you walk your mind through the imagined consequences, you reduce the emotional charge and increase logical decision-making. When you see that the worst isn't as devastating as you feared, you stop giving fear the final vote (source).

Now, build your rungs. Break your fear target into micro-steps. This isn't about massive leaps—it's about measured movement. This strategy, known as "exposure hierarchy" in cognitive behavioral therapy, proves that gradual exposure to what you fear reduces stress and reconditions your nervous system over time (source). Each rung is a rehearsal for resilience.

These rungs might look like this: write the outline. Share it with a trusted friend. Record a short video—just for yourself. Post it in a private group. Then go public. Ask for feedback. Each step is a small challenge, but a big victory. Because every rung climbed builds proof—and proof becomes confidence. You're not hoping anymore. You're becoming.

Pause after each action. Reflect. Ask yourself: "What did I learn? What wasn't as scary as I expected? What strength did I activate?" According to research from the *Journal of Applied Psychology*, regular self-reflection enhances learning, emotional growth, and your belief in your own capabilities (source). This is how growth becomes sustainable.

And when fear rises again—because it will—you don't retreat. You return to the previous rung. This isn't regression. It's regulation. The nervous system doesn't respond to force. It responds to safety and repetition. Courage isn't a personality trait—it's a practice. And it must be repeated until it becomes reflex.

Every rung climbed becomes your new normal. Your comfort zone doesn't just stretch—it redefines itself. You evolve from someone who freezes to someone who rises. Your identity expands because you're no longer waiting for fear to leave—you're learning how to lead it. And that shift changes everything.

This process doesn't just get you moving—it rewires your identity. According to behavioral expert James Clear, every action is a vote for the kind of person you want to become. When you take micro-steps through fear, you're not just making progress. You're casting votes for the bold, powerful version of you that's always been waiting (source).

Fear loses its grip when you give it a map. The Fear-Action Ladder is that map. It doesn't ask you to leap. It asks you to climb. Slowly. Steadily. Strategically. One breath, one decision, one action at a time. This is how movement is made sacred. Not in grand declarations, but in small, consistent acts of courage.

You don't have to leap. Just climb. You don't have to be fearless. Just be willing. Because progress isn't born from perfection—it's born from presence. And the presence you bring to each rung of the ladder is what transforms your fear from the reason you paused into the reason you rise.

If what you've just read lit a fire inside you—if something deep down said *"Yes, this is what I've been waiting for"*—then you're already aligned with the breakthrough. But reading is only the spark. Real transformation happens when you *immerse* yourself in the frequency of it. That's why the **Clarity Confidence Code Course** exists—to take you from inspiration to embodiment. This is where you install the mindset, the belief system, and the emotional wiring of someone who lives with unshakable clarity and magnetic confidence—no more second guessing, no more playing small. If you're ready to hardwire this into your nervous system and finally become the person you were born to be, the full experience is waiting for you. Step in now at https://clarityconfidencecode.com

Now let's take everything you've awakened—and activate it fully in the next phase of your journey…

CHAPTER 6

DECISION MASTERY — HOW TO TRUST YOURSELF FULLY

Why Decision Fatigue Drains Your Power

Every morning, you begin with a full charge of mental energy. But each decision you make—what to wear, how to respond, when to speak—chips away at that reserve. It's not a lack of ambition that breaks people. It's decision fatigue. The slow erosion of clarity caused by too many choices. And it doesn't just drain your mind—it hijacks your future. When the mind is tired, it defaults to safety, hesitation, or avoidance. That's not failure—it's biology.

Science proves this. Research from Florida State University found that decision-making and willpower both draw from a shared pool of mental energy.

The more decisions you make, the lower the quality of those decisions becomes over time. That's why by 5 p.m., even high performers lose their edge. They're not weak. They're depleted. What you're calling procrastination might just be cognitive exhaustion (source).

This is why icons like Steve Jobs and Mark Zuckerberg wore the same outfit every day. Not because they lacked creativity—but because they understood energy economics. Every unimportant decision you remove from your day adds fuel to your mission. Mental minimalism isn't laziness. It's leadership. It's the art of saving your sharpest thinking for your most important goals.

The evidence goes deeper. A study published in *PNAS* showed that judges ruling on parole decisions were significantly more likely to grant parole early in the day than in the afternoon. By late afternoon, their approval rates dropped to near zero—not because of merit, but because of mental depletion. The decisions got harsher as energy declined. That's the cost of not managing cognitive load (source).

Your brain is not designed for decision chaos. It thrives on clarity, structure, and certainty. Every time you overthink a post, hesitate on a message, or debate what matters, you burn fuel that should be spent on execution. Action doesn't come from more information. It comes from reduced friction. That means fewer options. Clearer defaults. Systems over willpower.

According to Harvard Business Review, automating and batching low-impact tasks—like emails, meals, and even gym prep—can boost productivity by 25% or more. The brain's processing speed increases when it's not juggling dozens of micro-decisions. The more your day is systemized, the more your mind is liberated for bold, creative, decisive action (source).

But the real damage of decision fatigue isn't just lost time—it's lost trust. Every time you overanalyze or second-guess, your self-belief weakens. You start stalling where you used to soar. Not because you lost your edge—but because you drowned it in choices. The noise gets louder. The vision gets blurry. And clarity begins to feel like a luxury instead of a standard.

The solution isn't discipline—it's design. Pre-decide who you are. What you believe. What you act on. This is called heuristic decision-making—living by principle, not pressure. When your values are clear, your decisions are fast. It removes hesitation, aligns your action, and replaces complexity with certainty. When you decide in advance, you no longer waste energy in the moment.

Dr. Sheena Iyengar, a pioneer in decision science, once said, "The art of choosing begins with reducing the noise." That noise isn't always external—it's internal clutter. Thoughts you don't need. Doubts you've outgrown. Conversations that pull you away from conviction. Your job isn't to entertain every possibility. It's to elevate your priorities.

Ask yourself: "Where am I leaking energy on decisions that don't matter?" "What can I automate, simplify, or eliminate?" "What value can I use to filter my choices faster?" Because every decision you delay drains your direction. And every system you build protects your power. Your most aligned version doesn't live in confusion—it lives in commitment.

Decide once. Then act often. That's how leaders think. They don't negotiate with their goals daily—they align with them once, then build routines that repeat that commitment. Clarity is a decision. Simplicity is a superpower. And systems aren't restrictive—they're liberating.

Because the most powerful version of you isn't making 1,000 decisions a day. They're making a few powerful ones—and letting those decisions automate the rest. You don't need more hours. You need more alignment. That's how the world changes—one clear, courageous decision at a time.

The Illusion of "Right" Choices

You don't need the perfect decision—you need a committed one. The obsession with making the "right" choice is one of the most dangerous mental traps. It paralyzes progress and cloaks itself in wisdom. But in reality, perfectionism in decision-making is fear wearing a suit. It convinces you that waiting is intelligence, when what you're really doing is rehearsing regret. You don't move because you're scared of getting it wrong, but what you fail to realize is that no decision is final—only your inaction is.

Psychologists call it "maximizing"—anxiously evaluating every possible option for the best outcome. And it backfires. A study from Swarthmore College showed that people who overanalyze choices are less satisfied, more regretful, and more anxious—even when they make better choices on paper. The mental toll of endless evaluation drains confidence and fuels doubt. The more options you consider, the more afraid you become of missing the "best" one. But clarity doesn't come from overthinking—it comes from moving.

The secret most successful people understand is that choices aren't discovered—they're created. Neuroscience confirms this. Once you commit to a decision and begin taking action, your brain rewires itself to reinforce that path. Commitment triggers effort, and effort rewires perception. You don't wait for certainty—you generate it by walking. Momentum is your mentor.

If you want to feel powerful again, stop chasing perfection. Choose powerfully and follow through. Indecision is a silent leak—it drains your energy, your belief, your drive. But action builds clarity, sharpens awareness, and silences doubt. Even a messy decision made boldly is more effective than the perfect decision you never commit to.

Growth doesn't come from always choosing right. It comes from choosing with integrity and having your own back when things go sideways. Harvard research proves this. It's not the quality of the choice that determines long-term success—it's the quality of character applied after the choice. Resilience, ownership, adaptability—these traits matter more than precision.

So instead of asking, "What's the perfect next step?" ask, "What choice aligns with my values—even if it's uncertain?" "What decision expands my soul—even if it scares my mind?" That's how you move from stagnation into sovereignty. The goal isn't to eliminate risk—it's to elevate responsibility. Because you weren't meant to play small in the waiting room of indecision.

The antidote to overthinking is action with alignment. You don't need to be 100% sure. You need to be 80% aligned and 100% committed. That's the formula for power. Because progress is less about precision and more about momentum. One decision—made with courage—can change the direction of your entire life.

The mind loves certainty. But life rewards those who move with intention despite uncertainty. The Paradox of Choice teaches us that too many options create paralysis. The solution isn't to over-optimize—it's to simplify. Make one bold, growth-centered choice and let the path refine you along the way. You weren't meant to get it all right. You were meant to get moving.

Let go of the illusion that you'll find a perfect moment. It doesn't exist. What exists is your willingness to choose. To trust. To act. And in doing so, you shift from victim to visionary. From passive consumer of life to powerful creator of it. Decision is creation. Commitment is momentum. Action is liberation.

When you embrace movement over mastery, you become magnetic. People don't follow those who are always right—they follow those who lead boldly. Who move first. Who adjust with integrity. Your energy becomes contagious when it's fueled by ownership, not hesitation. Don't look for permission. Lead with conviction.

You don't need another opinion—you need a decision. You don't need another delay—you need direction. And the moment you choose from alignment instead of anxiety, your life shifts. Not because everything becomes easy, but because you stop being your own bottleneck. Your courage becomes your clarity.

You were never meant to live stuck in hesitation. You were born to lead—not by waiting for the perfect path, but by creating it with every bold step. The truth is, you don't find the way. You make it. You build it. You walk it. And with each move, you remind the world—and yourself—who you really are.

Understanding Inner Authority

You were not born with limits—you were taught them. Every belief you carry about what's possible was shaped by repetition, authority, and environment. And until you examine those beliefs, you will unknowingly obey them. Research from Stanford University shows that most people operate within "self-imposed boundaries" rooted not in fact, but in conditioning. These boundaries masquerade as truth, but they are simply inherited ideas we never questioned. And what you do not question, you will unconsciously live by.

The mind is programmable. Just like software, it can be installed, upgraded, or corrupted. Studies in neuroplasticity confirm that the brain physically changes in response to focused thoughts, repetitive behavior, and emotional intensity. That means your belief system is not fixed—it's flexible. When you repeat a new thought with conviction and emotion, you begin rewiring your neural pathways. You are not stuck—you are simply rehearsing the same mental code.

Your beliefs shape your perception, and your perception filters your entire world. If you believe life is hard, you will subconsciously filter out ease. If you believe money is scarce, you'll reject opportunities to receive. It's not that those opportunities aren't there—it's that your filter won't allow them in. Cognitive psychology calls this "confirmation bias," and it affects everything from your success to your self-worth. You don't see life as it is—you see it as you are.

This is why belief is not passive—it is the root of all action. You will never act beyond the identity you believe is yours. You might dream bigger, but you will sabotage or delay until your internal identity matches your external goal. According to the Journal of Experimental Social Psychology, people perform according to their self-concept, not just their ability. So if you want to expand your results, you must first expand your identity.

Identity isn't who you are—it's who you think you are. And that can be changed. Every time you affirm a new truth with feeling—"I am worthy," "I am capable," "I am ready"—you chip away at the old programming. But repetition is key. Just like a computer doesn't install a program with one click, the subconscious doesn't update with one affirmation. You need volume. You need emotional intensity. You need consistency.

It's not enough to think differently—you must feel differently. Emotion is the glue that makes a thought stick. The subconscious speaks the language of feeling. When you pair a new belief with elevated emotion—gratitude, excitement, certainty—you accelerate change. That's not hype. That's chemistry. Positive emotional states release dopamine and acetylcholine, which enhance learning and neural growth. When you feel it, you seal it.

Environment reinforces belief. You can't install new programming in a toxic atmosphere. Your surroundings, conversations, media, and mentors either support your expansion or sabotage it. Studies in behavioral psychology show that willpower is finite, but environment is constant. This means the fastest way to change your behavior is to change your setting. You need to immerse yourself in spaces where the new belief is normalized.

One of the most powerful tools for belief reprogramming is visualization. The brain doesn't distinguish well between real and vividly imagined experience. Mental rehearsal activates the same neural circuits as physical execution. Olympic athletes, Navy SEALs, and world-class performers all use this method to pre-install success before it happens. Visualization isn't fantasy—it's mental conditioning. When done consistently, it creates what neuroscientists call "automaticity"—where the desired behavior becomes instinct.

But belief alone is not enough. It must be followed by behavior. The subconscious accepts a belief faster when it sees you act as if it's already true. When you behave like the future version of yourself—before you feel fully ready—you compress time. You send a message to your brain: "This is who we are now." And that alignment between thought and action creates momentum.

Momentum dissolves fear. When you begin moving, even with uncertainty, you create feedback. Feedback sharpens your belief. Action builds evidence. And evidence becomes conviction. Suddenly, you no longer have to convince yourself—you have proof. That proof becomes your new baseline. You expand what you believe is possible because you've already done it.

But none of this works without decision. You must decide that your old story is no longer your truth. You must decide that your future will not be governed by your past. Decision doesn't require certainty—it requires clarity. The moment you decide, you activate the reticular activating system in your brain, which begins filtering reality to match that decision. It's not magic—it's biology. Life starts responding differently when you do.

You are not your thoughts—you are the thinker. You are not your past—you are the chooser. And at any moment, you can choose to rewrite the program. To question the rules. To override the script. Because your future is not dictated by your fear—it's shaped by your faith. And when that faith is directed inward, paired with action, and reinforced with truth—you don't just break free. You become unstoppable.

Tools for Cultivating Intuition

You don't need more information. You need deeper connection. That quiet whisper within you—the one you've often dismissed or second-guessed—is not fantasy. It's your greatest form of wisdom. Intuition isn't mystical or abstract. It's your nervous system's ability to process vast amounts of data in real time, faster than your conscious brain can keep up. According to research from the University of New South Wales, intuitive decision-makers outperform logical ones under pressure because intuition taps into a reservoir of nonconscious intelligence your body already holds (source).

Your body has been listening long before your mind was ready. That "gut feeling" you've ignored? It's rooted in biology. The enteric nervous system—a network of over 500 million neurons in your gut—sends messages directly to your brain via the vagus nerve. When something feels off, it isn't just emotional—it's electrical. Harvard Health confirms the gut-brain connection is powerful and real, shaping both instinct and emotion (source).

Intuition isn't loud. It doesn't shout over your distractions. That's why silence isn't luxury—it's a necessity. Mindfulness meditation, proven in Psychological Science, increases accuracy in pattern recognition by activating the insula—the brain's center for internal awareness. When the noise fades, the knowing surfaces (source).

Your dreams speak in the language of the soul. They bypass logic, offering messages through metaphor and symbol. The International Journal of Dream Research found that journaling your dreams not only improves emotional balance but strengthens your access to intuitive signals. What seems random in sleep may be wisdom in disguise (source).

Sometimes, your greatest truths emerge not when you think—but when you write. Free-flow, intuitive writing—what neuroscience calls activating the "default mode network"—allows access to deep self-knowledge and spontaneous insight. It's not about what you plan to say. It's about what's ready to be heard when the pen moves without permission (source).

Nature doesn't just restore your mood—it recalibrates your intuition. Forests, rivers, open skies—they return your body to its baseline. In a 2020 study published in *Frontiers in Psychology*, individuals who spent even 20 minutes immersed in nature displayed significantly greater intuitive clarity than those in urban settings. Nature reconnects you to the intelligence that's always been within (source).

You won't hear your intuition if your senses are numbed. Sensory presence—smelling your tea, feeling your heartbeat, truly tasting your food—activates the insular cortex, heightening your ability to perceive inner signals. According to research in neuroscience, this interoceptive ability is foundational to intuitive awareness. You can't feel what's next if you're not feeling what's now (source).

The quality of your questions dictates the clarity of your answers. Intuition thrives on specificity. Don't ask, "What should I do?" Ask, "Which path brings me peace?" "What next step feels alive?" Research in *Cognitive Processing* shows that emotionally focused, targeted questions amplify intuitive accuracy. Your inner knowing needs direction, not doubt (source).

Every time you say "yes" to what misaligns, you silence your intuition. Every time you say "no" without needing to justify it, you turn up its volume. Boundary-setting strengthens inner trust. A 2021 study found that assertiveness in personal choices increased intuitive clarity and long-term confidence. Saying no is not rejection—it's redirection toward your truth (source).

You've been taught to seek answers outside yourself. To gather more facts. More feedback. More permission. But true power begins when you turn inward. Your intuition has never been wrong—it's only been overridden. Not because it failed you, but because fear was louder. When you quiet the fear, the clarity comes through like a tuning fork ringing in the dark.

You don't develop intuition by waiting for it—you build it through use. Just like a muscle, it grows with every rep. Every time you follow it, even when it doesn't make sense, you create evidence that your inner voice is valid. The more proof you gather, the louder your inner guidance becomes. This isn't about belief. It's about trust earned through experience.

You were never meant to outsource your knowing. You are your own oracle. Your own compass. Your own highest authority. The truth you've been seeking lives in the still moments, the gut tugs, the electric yes that happens before your brain even speaks. Intuition is not irrational—it's ancient intelligence. It remembers what your mind forgot. And when you finally listen, your life realigns with the wisdom that's been waiting inside you all along.

How to Clear Noise and Distractions

You don't need to see the whole path before you begin—your intuition will guide you step by step. It's not magic; it's intelligence in motion, deeply embedded in your biology. According to research from the University of New South Wales, people who rely on intuition often make faster and more accurate decisions in high-pressure environments. Why? Because your nervous system is constantly processing data below the surface—data your logical mind can't always access in real time. What you feel in your gut is often truth before it becomes fact. (Source)

Your body is hardwired to perceive beyond logic. The enteric nervous system—often called the "second brain"—contains over 500 million neurons and communicates with your brain through the vagus nerve. This isn't a metaphor—it's a biological truth. Harvard Health confirms that those gut feelings are based on real-time sensory and emotional feedback. That tension in your stomach? That flutter of unease? That's your system decoding what words can't yet explain. (Source)

But you won't hear your inner voice if you're drowning in noise. Meditation becomes essential not just for peace, but for precision. A study in *Psychological Science* showed that mindfulness enhances intuitive accuracy by activating the insula—your brain's hub for internal awareness. In silence, the static clears. The knowing gets louder. You're not guessing anymore—you're remembering. (Source)

Your dreams are not distractions—they're encrypted messages from the subconscious. Journaling them first thing in the morning captures raw insight that logic often overrides. The International Journal of Dream Research found that dream recall improves emotional clarity and strengthens intuitive reasoning. What seems symbolic often contains solutions. Your subconscious speaks in metaphors—learn its language and you unlock another dimension of guidance. (Source)

When you sit down and let your pen move without planning—just letting it flow—you tap into what neuroscience calls the "default mode network." This part of your brain reveals deeper truths and creative insight you can't access through conscious planning. Intuitive writing isn't brainstorming—it's listening. Your hand knows things your mouth can't yet say. (Source)

The environment you choose matters. Nature doesn't just soothe—it sharpens. A 2020 study in *Frontiers in Psychology* revealed that people who spent just 20 minutes in nature had greater access to intuitive decision-making than those in urban settings. Forests, oceans, and sunlight recalibrate your inner compass. You don't have to retreat to the mountains—just step outside. Let the earth remind you of your original frequency. (Source)

When you slow down and actually feel your body—smell your coffee, feel your heartbeat, listen to the quiet—you activate the insular cortex. This is the part of your brain responsible for sensing internal signals. And according to neuroscience, this interoceptive awareness is the foundation of intuitive intelligence. You won't hear truth if you can't hear yourself. (Source)

The quality of your questions determines the clarity of your answers. Don't ask, "What should I do?" Ask, "What step brings me peace?" or "What feels alive right now?" A study in *Cognitive Processing* shows that emotionally charged, specific questions sharpen the brain's intuitive response. Intuition doesn't need perfect logic—it needs precision in feeling. (Source)

Every time you say "yes" to something misaligned, you say "no" to your soul. Practice saying no without explanation. A 2021 study found that assertive boundary-setting significantly increases self-trust and intuitive clarity. When you honor what doesn't feel right, you amplify what does. The world doesn't need your people-pleasing—it needs your presence. (Source)

Intuition is a muscle. And like any muscle, it grows through resistance and repetition. Every time you trust it—especially when logic disagrees—you gather evidence. That evidence becomes confidence. That confidence becomes momentum. And soon, you no longer wait for certainty—you walk in it.

You don't need to be psychic. You just need to be present. Intuition is not irrational—it's your most ancient intelligence. It remembers what your brain forgot. And the more you listen, the louder it gets. Eventually, it stops whispering and starts leading. And when you follow it, life no longer feels like guesswork—it feels like alignment.

You were never meant to outsource your knowing. You are the oracle. You are the guide. Your intuition has never been wrong—it's only been overridden by fear, doubt, and noise. But the moment you silence the world long enough to hear yourself, everything changes. Not because you find the answer—but because you remember it was already within you.

The Somatic Signal Method

Your body is speaking to you every moment, and yet most people have been trained to ignore it. That tightness in your chest, the knot in your stomach, the warmth or lightness in your limbs—those aren't random sensations. They are signals. Signals from the most advanced guidance system you'll ever have: your nervous system. And according to research from *The Journal of Neuroscience*, these bodily cues often influence your decisions before your conscious mind even knows what's happening. That means your body knows the truth before your brain does.

This isn't spiritual guesswork—it's scientific fact. The insula, a region deep within your brain, governs interoception—your awareness of internal bodily states. When you practice tuning into your body, that part of your brain lights up, enhancing your emotional clarity and intuitive accuracy. You don't need to analyze your way into a breakthrough. You need to feel your way into alignment. The data is already there—you've just been taught to ignore it.

That's where the Somatic Signal Method changes the game. Step one: pause and scan. Before you make that call, say yes to that deal, or push through something that feels off—stop. Ask yourself, "Where do I feel this in my body?" "Is it tight or loose?" "Heavy or light?" These aren't random questions. According to Polyvagal Theory, your nervous system responds to perceived safety or threat before logic even enters the picture. Safety feels like openness. Danger feels like constriction.

Next, name the signal. This process is called affect labeling. Neuroscience confirms that simply labeling your feeling—"I feel a tightness in my chest"—calms the emotional center of the brain and activates the logical side. You're not pushing the emotion away—you're integrating it. You're telling your body, "I hear you," and that acknowledgment alone reduces the emotional intensity of the moment.

Once the signal is clear, you ask the most important question: "What is this sensation protecting?" Sometimes the flutter in your chest is not fear—it's anticipation. Sometimes the contraction in your gut isn't intuition—it's an old trauma triggered by something that feels new. This is the moment of discernment. You don't run from discomfort—you decode it. Because hidden inside every reaction is a message waiting to become wisdom.

And that wisdom becomes more accessible when you move. Somatic signals are not meant to stay stuck—they are meant to be expressed. Movement—whether it's stretching, shaking, humming, or even walking—releases stored energy and helps regulate your nervous system. A 2021 study published in *Frontiers in Psychology* showed that physical movement increases vagal tone, which enhances your emotional resilience and your ability to return to clarity.

Then comes the most powerful step: choose from the body up—not the mind down. Once you're grounded, make your decision based on which option your body leans toward. You'll often find that the "logical" choice is the one that makes your body contract, while the "crazy" one feels like freedom. That's not irrationality—that's embodied truth. And over time, choosing from the body builds a level of confidence no external approval can match.

This is not about perfection. This is about power. Because when you start listening to your body, you stop outsourcing your decisions. You stop waiting for validation. You begin leading from a place of inner authority. You don't need to be told what to do—you already know. Your body holds the truth your mind was trained to doubt.

This practice isn't woo. It's wisdom backed by neuroscience and thousands of years of somatic intelligence. Dr. Peter Levine and Eugene Gendlin have shown that unresolved emotions live in the body—and by tapping into the "felt sense," you not only heal the past but access clarity in the present. When your mind spins, drop into the body. When confusion rises, return to sensation. Because that's where your truth lives.

When you stop resisting your body and start respecting it, everything shifts. Your relationships become more honest. Your work becomes more aligned. Your voice becomes more authentic. Not because you've found some magical blueprint—but because you've finally reconnected to the compass that was there all along.

This is your invitation to lead differently. Not from hustle, but from harmony. Not from anxiety, but from alignment. Because in a world screaming for direction, the most revolutionary thing you can do is follow the wisdom within. That wisdom is felt, not forced. And it begins the moment you choose to listen.

Your body isn't a barrier—it's a bridge. A bridge back to your soul, your strength, and your knowing. So the next time the world feels noisy, chaotic, or unclear—don't reach out. Reach in. Because when your mind is confused but your body is clear, that clarity is your calling. And it's time to answer.

Releasing Guilt Around Choices

Guilt is not always a warning sign—it's often a growth signal. It shows up not because you did something wrong, but because you did something new. You made a move that didn't match the old version of you that others were comfortable with. And if you don't decode that feeling, it will whisper lies to your mind and chain your progress to your past. According to research published in *The Journal of Personality and Social Psychology*, guilt can arise from violating someone else's expectations—not your own values. It's not always about ethics—it's often about conditioning. ([Source](#))

You were programmed before you were conscious. Family, culture, religion—they all taught you what was acceptable, lovable, and "right." But not all of those values were designed to empower you. Some were meant to control you. So when guilt shows up, the question is not "What did I do wrong?" but "Whose voice am I hearing in my head?" If it's not your voice, from your truth, aligned with your values, then that guilt isn't sacred—it's sabotage.

Unchecked guilt becomes a prison. It doesn't guide—it punishes. It makes you explain yourself too much. Apologize too often. Shrink your desires just to maintain peace. And peace without authenticity is not peace—it's performance. Dr. Brené Brown distinguishes guilt from shame: guilt says "I did something bad," while shame says "I am bad." But when guilt is chronic and unexamined, it leads to both. (Source)

To free yourself, you must interrogate the guilt. That process is called cognitive reappraisal. It's not mental gymnastics—it's mental maturity. Neuroscientific studies show that when people reframe their guilt and question its validity, their brain activity shifts in the medial prefrontal cortex—the area associated with self-awareness and emotional clarity. (Source)

Ask yourself, "Is this guilt about a true moral violation—or about stepping into a new identity?" "Am I betraying my values—or just someone else's comfort zone?" "Is this my conscience—or my conditioning?" The moment you get clear on that, guilt begins to dissolve. Clarity cuts the cord.

Then comes self-forgiveness. That doesn't mean you excuse past misalignment. It means you stop being the warden of your own prison. Research from UC Berkeley shows that self-forgiveness doesn't make you weaker—it makes you more productive, less anxious, and more emotionally resilient. (Source)

You don't grow by dragging your past behind you. You grow by integrating it, learning from it, and moving forward with power. True responsibility is not rooted in shame—it's rooted in love. You own your decisions. You make amends when necessary. But you do it from strength, not from self-punishment.

Sometimes guilt comes simply from choosing yourself. Saying no to what drains you. Walking away from what no longer fits. Letting go of people who preferred the version of you that abandoned your needs to please them. But you were not born to be small. You were born to be sovereign. Dr. Kristin Neff's research proves that self-compassion, not guilt, is what actually leads to responsible action and emotional bounce-back. (Source)

If you're growing, someone's going to be disappointed. But you are not responsible for their expectations—you are responsible for your alignment. And here's the truth most never say: the people who benefited from your silence, your sacrifice, or your self-betrayal will be the first to call your freedom "selfish." Don't let their discomfort dictate your destiny.

You don't owe anyone a version of yourself you've healed beyond. You don't have to water yourself down to keep old connections intact. Growth requires grieving, yes—but it also requires rising. And the only thing standing between you and your next level may be a guilt that was never yours to carry.

This is not the time to justify. This is the time to embody. Your future doesn't need you to explain your past. It needs you to own your power, release the guilt, and walk boldly into the version of you who no longer negotiates their worth.

Because guilt will always shrink you. But growth will expand you. And the moment you choose to honor growth over guilt, your life begins to bend toward freedom, power, and the future that's been waiting for your full permission.

Deciding in Alignment, Not Anxiety

You are one decision away from a new reality—but that decision must come from alignment, not anxiety. Most people confuse logic with safety, and safety with truth. But neuroscience reveals that when you're anxious, the amygdala takes over and suppresses your prefrontal cortex—the part of your brain responsible for planning, vision, and reason. So in moments of fear, what feels "rational" is often just your nervous system trying to avoid discomfort, not honor your destiny. (Source)

You can't create a future from fear. You'll end up choosing what is familiar, not what is fulfilling. The job that doesn't excite you. The relationship that keeps you small. The habit that keeps you in place. These aren't conscious choices—they're comfort loops. And the price of staying safe is the life you were meant to live. What you call "playing it smart" is often just rehearsing old fear in a new form.

True alignment isn't a mental checklist—it's a somatic experience. It's when your thoughts, your body, and your spirit all say yes. That's the power of coherence. And when you decide from that place, your path opens—even if it's uncertain. Research published in *Frontiers in Psychology* shows that values-based decision-making creates more confidence, resilience, and long-term satisfaction than fear-based logic. (Source)

Your body is your compass. Not your critic. When you ask, "Does this decision feel expanding or contracting?" you're tapping into the truth beneath the noise. That's not imagination—it's interoception. Studies confirm that people who are attuned to their internal signals consistently make better, more congruent life decisions. You don't need more data—you need more trust in your inner cues. (Source)

Anxiety doesn't mean stop. It means pause. Breathe. Regulate. Give your soul the mic instead of your fear. Stanford psychologist Dr. Kelly McGonigal says when you reframe anxiety as a prompt to ground—not react—you make wiser choices. So when the pressure rises, your job isn't to act—it's to align. (Source)

Certainty is a myth. But alignment is real. You may never feel "sure," but you can feel congruent. You can move forward not because everything makes sense—but because everything feels right in your nervous system. Your path doesn't require proof. It requires permission. And that permission begins the moment you stop waiting to feel safe and start choosing what feels true.

Powerful decisions are rarely dramatic. They're quiet. Subtle. They come in the stillness when the noise dies down and your soul finally speaks. They don't yell. They resonate. They say, "Yes, this is me," without needing to convince anyone else. And those are the choices that change lives. Because they come from ownership—not obligation.

You've been taught to seek peace after you act. But when you decide from alignment, you carry peace into the decision. You don't need the world to approve your path. When your values and your vision agree, that's the only validation you'll ever need. You stop asking for signs and start becoming one.

Let go of the idea that doubt disqualifies alignment. Doubt is the echo of old programming. It will always speak. Your job is to not let it lead. Let your breath lead. Let your body lead. Let your values lead. When those three line up, that's the signal. Even if your mind trembles, your spirit knows.

This isn't about perfect decisions—it's about powerful ones. A powerful decision is one that says, "I choose who I am becoming over who I've been." It's one that closes the gap between your current identity and your future self. And the more of those you make, the faster your reality recalibrates to match your truth.

If your nervous system is in chaos, your clarity will be compromised. That's why grounding rituals aren't luxuries—they're leadership. Movement, breath, journaling, meditation—these aren't soft skills. They are strategic tools to access the clearest part of you. When your system is calm, your choices become congruent.

So today, don't just make a decision. Make an aligned decision. One that moves you closer to your highest truth, not just your current comfort. One that feels like peace, even if it looks like risk. Because that is the decision that will open doors logic can't see—and create the life you know deep down you were meant to lead.

Building Self-Trust Through Action

Self-trust isn't an emotion—it's an agreement. An agreement that you'll stand by yourself, even when doubt shouts louder than courage. It isn't something you're born with. It's something you build—one promise, one action, one courageous moment at a time. And the truth is, you don't learn to trust yourself by thinking. You learn by doing. By moving while uncertain. By showing your nervous system that fear doesn't mean stop—it means step forward anyway. (Source)

Confidence is the result—not the requirement. So many people wait until they feel confident to act, not realizing that confidence is created by action, not the other way around. Every time you take even a small step toward what scares you, your brain logs evidence: "I did it. I didn't die. I moved forward." That's self-efficacy—the belief that you can influence your outcomes—and it's one of the most powerful predictors of long-term resilience. (Source)

But let's be clear: self-trust doesn't come from perfection. It comes from follow-through. You don't build it by doing things flawlessly—you build it by doing what you said you'd do, especially when it's hard. According to a 2019 study in the *Journal of Personality*, consistent small actions built stronger inner trust than isolated bursts of achievement. It's not about crushing it once. It's about showing up again and again. (Source)

You want to trust yourself more? Make micro-promises—and keep them. Set your alarm and get up when it rings. Drink your water when you said you would. Speak the truth when it would be easier to shrink. Every time you follow through, you cast a vote for the version of you who is dependable. Not to others—but to yourself. And as James Clear said, "Every action you take is a vote for the kind of person you want to become." (Source)

Emotional integrity is the hidden layer of self-trust. If you keep saying "yes" when your body screams "no," you're not being nice—you're being dishonest. And that dishonesty tears at your own inner foundation. A 2021 study in the *Journal of Contextual Behavioral Science* found that people who aligned their behavior with their values had higher well-being and less internal conflict. Trust isn't just about actions—it's about alignment. (Source)

Failure doesn't break self-trust—your reaction to it does. When you respond to setbacks with self-hate, your nervous system starts to see trying as dangerous. But when you respond with grace, you create space to try again. Dr. Kristin Neff's research on self-compassion shows that it's the missing ingredient in high performers. Because when you see mistakes as feedback, not as identity, you grow instead of freeze. (Source)

Stop waiting to feel ready. Ready is a myth. You will rarely feel ready to launch the business, end the relationship, ask for what you're worth, or speak your truth. But action rewires the mind. When you act before you're ready, you send a message to your system: "We are safe. We are moving. We can handle what's next." That is the moment self-trust is born.

When you keep choosing alignment over approval, something wild begins to happen. Your voice gets louder. Your clarity sharpens. You stop outsourcing decisions to others. You stop needing consensus. You start listening inward. Not because you're trying to be rebellious—but because you're finally remembering that you are your own authority.

This isn't about being flawless—it's about being faithful. Faithful to your growth. Faithful to your calling. Faithful to the version of you that keeps whispering, "We can do this," even when the world around you doesn't see it yet. That faith, backed by action, becomes the foundation of unshakable confidence.

You don't need more time. You don't need another plan. You need to make one promise to yourself—and keep it. That's how you begin. And from that one promise comes another. Then another. And suddenly, you're no longer hoping to become the person you want to be. You're living as them.

The greatest breakthroughs don't come from information. They come from embodiment. From the decision to show up, even shaking. To speak, even stuttering. To leap, even doubting. And every time you do, the world shifts— not because it changed, but because you did.

Because self-trust isn't about never falling. It's about knowing you'll rise. Not someday. Not when it's perfect. But today. In motion. In courage. In truth. And when you begin walking like that, your life begins listening. Your future starts bending. And your identity finally catches up with your calling.

When to Wait, When to Move

There is a difference between waiting with power and waiting in fear. One is rooted in alignment; the other is masked by anxiety. Success is not always about who moves the fastest—it's about who moves in rhythm with their higher knowing. A study published by Harvard Business Review found that leaders who paused intentionally before making key decisions experienced higher confidence and lower regret, proving that stillness isn't weakness—it's strategy (source).

What most people call hesitation is often avoidance. Not because the opportunity isn't real—but because the nervous system isn't regulated enough to act. When the brain is in a reactive state, the amygdala hijacks your vision, and your actions serve only to maintain safety, not to create success. But when you pause with purpose, you activate the brain's default mode network—the system responsible for introspection, creative solutions, and intuitive insight (source).

Stillness becomes sacred when it's intentional. But when it's driven by fear of failure, judgment, or being seen—it becomes spiritual stagnation. Chronic indecision, according to *The Journal of Behavioral Therapy and Experimental Psychiatry*, is less about discernment and more about low self-trust and the fear of future regret (source).

Your body knows the difference. When you are in avoidance, your body tenses, your breath shortens, and your chest tightens. When you are in aligned stillness, you feel rooted—even when uncomfortable. A 2021 study on somatic awareness showed that individuals who trust their bodily cues make faster, wiser decisions under stress (source).

When your soul says "wait," honor the pause. But give that pause structure. Reflect. Prepare. Connect. Allow insight to crystallize. Because the stillness isn't emptiness—it's gestation. Something is forming beneath the surface. Don't dig up in doubt what you planted in faith. Wait not with passivity, but with power.

But if you've been circling the same decision for weeks, months—or even years—then what you need isn't more reflection. It's movement. According to the research behind the 5 Second Rule, the brain starts talking you out of decisions after just five seconds of hesitation. Which means if you don't move quickly, your fear will have time to craft the perfect excuse (source).

Aligned action often carries fear—but it's not the fear of danger. It's the fear of growth. That flutter in your chest, the forward pull—that's your body preparing for elevation. That's not panic—it's preparation. That's not anxiety—it's anticipation. You must learn to tell the difference. Because your destiny doesn't always come wrapped in certainty. Sometimes, it's cloaked in butterflies.

Don't wait for clarity to begin. Begin, and clarity will meet you. A study from *Organizational Behavior and Human Decision Processes* found that taking small, tangible steps reduces fear more effectively than journaling or visualization. Action, not analysis, is what builds momentum—and momentum is what sharpens direction (source).

You were never meant to force the rhythm of your breakthrough. You were meant to feel it. Trust it. Move with it. There is a timing to every transformation. And your job isn't to control the clock—it's to honor the cues. That means moving not just when it's convenient—but when your soul says, "Now."

Sometimes you're called to wait, not because it's not yours—but because you're not yet ready to carry it. And sometimes, you're called to leap, not because it's time—but because your faith needs to grow into it. The timing of your expansion will always challenge your comfort—but it will never violate your truth.

So ask yourself: is my waiting wisdom… or is it fear disguised as discernment? Is my pause sacred… or is it my old self delaying my new self's arrival? The answer lives in your nervous system. In your body. In your breath. It's not mental—it's felt.

You don't need more signs. You need to listen to the ones already showing up inside of you. Because timing isn't external—it's energetic. When your soul says pause, listen. When your soul says prepare, act. When your soul says leap—leap, even if your fear hasn't caught up. That's how you walk into the life you were destined for—not by watching the clock, but by following your calling.

Creating a Personal Decision Framework

You are not here to live by default—you are here to live by design. The most powerful people don't move faster because they're reckless. They move faster because they're clear. They don't consult their fear before making a move—they consult their framework. When life throws uncertainty, they don't panic. They align. Because clarity is not something you wait for. It's something you create through structure.

A personal decision framework isn't rigid—it's liberating. It frees you from the mental exhaustion of re-deciding your values every time you're triggered. According to research from Harvard Business Review, people with a pre-built decision model report less stress, greater follow-through, and quicker execution, even in high-pressure environments. It's not about having the right answer. It's about having the right foundation to decide from it with confidence (source).

When you don't have a framework, you default to emotion or pressure. You delay decisions that matter. You say yes to things that drain you. You overthink, second-guess, and call it "being responsible." But that's not responsibility—it's self-abandonment disguised as logic. Your soul doesn't need more pros and cons lists. It needs principles. It needs clarity. It needs you to remember what matters when life gets loud.

That's why it starts with values. Not borrowed ones. Not ones that sound good. Your real, raw, non-negotiable core values. A study in *Motivation and Emotion* found that people who filter decisions through their values have significantly higher life satisfaction and reduced long-term regret. That's not idealism. That's integrity in action (source).

Once you know your values, you need a filter. Use the "3-Filter Test": Does this feel right in my body? Does it align with my vision—not just my past? Does it reflect what I value, even if no one claps? If the answer is yes to all three, move. If not, pause. That isn't indecision. That's maturity.

Your boundaries must be built into your decision process. Neuroscience shows that when you define non-negotiables ahead of time, your brain conserves energy and avoids decision fatigue. Boundaries are not walls. They're gates for power to flow. They tell the world, "This is how I honor myself—even when I'm under pressure." (source)

Next, set a maximum decision window. The longer you linger, the louder your fear gets. Research in *Organizational Behavior and Human Decision Processes* proves that decision stress rises when thinking drags on. But when you set a time cap—24 hours, 3 days, a week—you move from avoidance to activation. Your brain thrives on constraint. Deadlines aren't stress—they're structure (source).

Don't forget the body check-in. Your nervous system is your compass. When you imagine saying "yes," do you feel expansion—or contraction? Peace—or pressure? Studies show that tuning into interoceptive signals enhances decision accuracy. Your body won't lie to you—but you've got to pause long enough to hear it (source).

And always evaluate for long-term impact. Fear makes you pick short-term comfort over future fulfillment. But wisdom asks: "What will I wish I chose 12 months from now?" Discomfort isn't a sign to stop. It's a sign you're growing. As recent research confirms, leaning into short-term challenge often leads to the most meaningful gains (source).

Anchoring all of this is your decision mantra. Not a slogan—an identity anchor. Say it aloud: "I make aligned choices, not anxious ones." "I don't need certainty—I need integrity." "Peace is my signal. Expansion is my yes." These phrases turn your nervous system into your guide—not your saboteur. Your words shape your chemistry. Speak alignment until your mind believes it.

You don't have to always get it right. You just have to be real. When you build your choices on clarity, values, and trust, the outcome matters less—because you were in your power. You weren't negotiating with fear. You were responding with wisdom. That's the difference between surviving and leading.

You were never meant to figure it out every time from scratch. You were meant to build a framework that makes your next move obvious. Because when you've pre-decided who you are, how you choose becomes simple. And when that's in place, indecision can't live in the presence of alignment. Create your framework. Trust your values. And watch clarity turn your hesitation into certainty.

Practice: Embodied Decision-Making

You were never meant to figure everything out in your head. The mind is a powerful servant, but a poor master. It will rationalize fear as logic and disguise avoidance as strategy. But your body—it never lies. Neuroscience confirms this: the body often registers truth faster than conscious thought. Somatic markers—bodily cues like tension or openness—play a critical role in intuitive decision-making under pressure. The body knows first, and it speaks clearly—if you're willing to listen (source).

The problem is, most people have been taught to distrust that wisdom. Society rewards intellect and punishes intuition. You were told to "think it through," "be rational," and "not get emotional." But this well-meaning advice has disconnected you from your own source of clarity. When you make decisions without involving your body, you cut yourself off from the most ancient and accurate guidance system you possess.

That's why embodied decision-making is not a trend—it's a return to truth. It brings you back to your original intelligence, before the conditioning, before the performance, before the paralysis. Research on Focusing Therapy by Eugene Gendlin proves that when people make choices from their felt sense—tuning into what their body feels—they report fewer regrets and deeper satisfaction (source).

The first step is stillness. Before you rush into strategy or pros-and-cons lists, pause. Sit. Breathe. Ask yourself: "What happens in me when I consider this path?" And then listen. Your body will answer. Not in words, but in tension, in breath, in posture. You'll feel it. Tightness is usually avoidance. Expansion is often alignment. You're not making things up—you're reading your own internal compass.

This isn't mysticism—it's interoception. It's your brain's ability to read and interpret internal bodily signals. The insular cortex, the part of your brain responsible for interoception, is directly linked to intuitive clarity and decision-making. A study in *Trends in Cognitive Sciences* found that the more aware someone is of their internal states, the better their choices under pressure (source).

Then comes the spoken test. Say it out loud: "I'm going to accept this opportunity." Then, "I'm going to decline this opportunity." Which one feels lighter? Which one feels like exhale, like ease, like truth? Which one stirs a quiet "yes" before the noise of logic kicks in? The nervous system knows before the ego decides. Your job is to catch the signal before the noise takes over.

Once you feel it—move with it. Literally. Don't just sit and journal about what your body said. Stand up. Walk it out. Stretch. Breathe. Shake. Move in a way that integrates the message. Movement regulates the vagus nerve, which governs your body's response to stress and trust. According to *Frontiers in Psychology*, physical movement aligned with inner awareness helps you encode the decision in your nervous system (source).

When you move your body, you move the story. What once felt confusing becomes crystal clear. What felt risky becomes rooted. That's why some of your clearest answers come during a walk, a run, or even in the shower—when your brain isn't trying to perform, but your body is finally allowed to speak.

Don't overstay the clarity window. Once the body gives you a green light, act before the ego finds a reason to retreat. You don't need the full plan. You just need the next aligned move. This builds neural confidence. Your nervous system begins to associate intuitive decisions with safety and forward momentum. That's how you rewire fear into flow.

Embodied decision-making doesn't promise comfort—it promises congruence. You may still feel fear. But it won't be the paralyzing kind. It'll be the kind that comes with flight before lift-off. And that sensation isn't a warning sign—it's a signal that you're about to become someone new. Expansion always comes with sensation. Learn to welcome it.

Your body is not a backup system. It is the original operating system. It's not a vessel to carry your mind—it's a guide to carry your soul. Every time you feel, pause, trust, and move, you reclaim a piece of yourself the world told you to outsource. And every time you move in truth, you build a life that doesn't just look good—but feels right.

You don't need to think your way to your next breakthrough. You need to feel your way. You need to breathe it. Speak it. Move it. Trust it. Because your greatest alignment is not found in a spreadsheet—it's already alive in your chest, your breath, your spine. And once you trust that wisdom, your life will stop repeating—and start rising.

What you've just uncovered is more than insight—it's ignition. But the truth is, knowing isn't enough. You must *install* this clarity and confidence into your subconscious so deeply that it becomes who you are. That's exactly what the **Clarity Confidence Code Course** is designed to do. It's the missing link—the immersive system that takes these teachings and hardwires them into your identity so that you naturally think, act, and attract from a place of power. No more hoping. No more hesitation. Just results. If you're ready to master the inner game and finally live from the version of you that *already knows*, step into the full experience now at https://clarityconfidencecode.com

Because the next chapter isn't just about learning—it's about *living* the code. Let's go.

CHAPTER 7

MAGNETIZING OPPORTUNITIES — ALIGNING WITH YOUR HIGHEST TIMELINE

What It Means to Be Magnetic

You don't attract what you want—you attract what you are. This isn't a motivational slogan. It's a physiological and psychological reality. Your entire being emits signals—energetic, emotional, and behavioral—that shape how others respond to you. The HeartMath Institute confirms that the human heart generates an electromagnetic field that can be measured several feet from the body, broadcasting your emotional coherence or chaos like a radio tower. When you're aligned internally, people feel it—even if they can't explain why (source).

Magnetism is not manipulation. It's integrity. It's when your thoughts, words, and actions are in such harmony that your presence becomes undeniable. Your nervous system is either resonant or repellent. People are neurologically wired to detect authenticity. A study in *Psychological Science* found that we can assess emotional sincerity in under a second. No script, no sales tactic—just vibration, frequency, and congruence (source).

You've been told to fake it till you make it. But fake confidence is loud and hollow. Real confidence is rooted and calm. It's the energy of someone who has nothing to prove because they already know their worth. That confidence doesn't repel—it attracts. It says, "I'm not here to be chosen. I'm here because I've already chosen myself." That's when life starts matching your frequency instead of your fears.

If you want to become magnetic, start with your identity. Who are you when no one's watching? What values do you hold when validation isn't in the room? According to *The Journal of Positive Psychology*, individuals with a well-defined sense of self exhibit greater influence, confidence, and resilience in social environments (source).

Then own your emotions. Don't bypass them. Don't package them for approval. When you feel your emotions in real time and express them with clarity—not chaos—you emit coherence. A 2016 neuroimaging study showed that emotional congruence directly improves social connection and reduces stress in interpersonal relationships (source).

Magnetic people lead with value, not validation. They don't chase applause. They show up with contribution. And that energy triggers a psychological principle called reciprocity—people feel compelled to give back. According to the work of social psychologist Dr. Robert Cialdini, those who give first—without strings—are consistently rated as more likable and influential (source).

Speak with boldness. Not volume—vibration. A 2022 study in *Journal of Personality and Social Psychology* found that conviction, tone, and emotional transparency increased trustworthiness and charisma—even when the speaker's views were unconventional. Don't dilute your truth for comfort. When your voice carries your full presence, people lean in (source).

And walk in that truth. Don't explain your alignment. Don't negotiate your peace. Confidence isn't a performance—it's a posture. And when that posture comes from embodied alignment, you start pulling in relationships, opportunities, and abundance that match your energy—not your excuses.

Your nervous system is a tuning fork. When it's dysregulated by shame, guilt, or fear, you send mixed signals—and repel what you say you want. But when you're clean in your emotions, decisions, and energy, your frequency becomes magnetic. Life doesn't respond to effort—it responds to resonance.

Stop chasing and start becoming. Stop hustling for connection and start embodying your truth. You don't magnetize what you mimic—you magnetize what you live. When your inner life becomes congruent, your outer world becomes miraculous.

The people who change rooms don't do it with noise. They do it with alignment. You know them when they walk in—not because they demand attention, but because their frequency shifts the atmosphere. That's not charisma. That's coherence. That's the power of a regulated, rooted, and radiant human being.

You're not here to be liked—you're here to be lit. To be so full of your own truth, clarity, and alignment that your presence becomes permission for others to rise. When you activate that energy, you don't just create impact—you become inevitable.

How You're Pushing Away What You Want

You're not unlucky. You're not forgotten. And you're certainly not cursed. What you're experiencing is not rejection—it's misalignment. Most people aren't being denied the life they desire; they're energetically contradicting it. The moment your inner belief says "I'm not worthy," but your mouth says "I want more," the universe receives two different signals—and the stronger one always wins. According to psychophysiological research, inner conflict triggers the sympathetic nervous system, keeping you in survival mode and blocking receptivity to joy, creativity, and aligned opportunity (source).

This is why people can work endlessly hard and still feel stuck. They hustle, affirm, meditate—and yet the breakthrough doesn't come. Why? Because the subconscious blueprint hasn't changed. If deep down you believe success equals burnout, or that money comes with shame, or that love will hurt you, then no matter how much you want it, you'll subconsciously repel it. Dr. Gay Hendricks calls this the "Upper Limit Problem"—an internal thermostat that sabotages joy the moment it exceeds your identity's safety zone (source).

The harder you grasp, the more you choke the flow. Neuroscience shows that desperation activates a narrowed field of awareness and hypervigilance, which makes you blind to options and solutions right in front of you. But when you're in a state of joy or gratitude, the prefrontal cortex lights up, broadening your perception and allowing inspiration and synchronicity to enter. You stop forcing—and start receiving (source).

That's the paradox of attraction: it's not about begging the universe to deliver. It's about preparing yourself to receive. The law of vibration makes it clear—you don't attract what you say, you attract what you are. Every thought, every action, every emotion is casting a vote for the kind of energy you're broadcasting. And the universe always responds to consistency, not desperation.

So how do you shift from resistance to resonance? First, you get radically honest. What part of you still believes it's unsafe to rise? What emotion are you secretly clinging to that contradicts your desires? Studies on Cognitive Behavioral Therapy reveal that identifying and restructuring distorted thought patterns produces not just emotional relief, but tangible life changes (source).

Next, you stop chasing—and start choosing. Wanting isn't enough. You must embody readiness. According to behavioral science, when your identity shifts, your habits follow. And when your habits change, your results compound. You don't get what you want. You get what you prepare for by becoming it in action and attitude, every single day (source).

Then, you surrender the "how." Manifestation dies in the grip of control. The more you cling to a timeline or a specific path, the more you block the flow. Research in Acceptance and Commitment Therapy proves that releasing rigid control leads to greater well-being, adaptability, and manifestation success (source).

You align your frequency not through perfection—but through congruence. You speak like someone who believes. You act like someone who belongs. You make peace-driven decisions instead of fear-based ones. When your energy stops pleading and starts proclaiming, life rearranges to reflect it. That's not magic—it's physics. The external must mirror the internal. It always does.

So no, you're not blocked. You're just out of sync. But the moment you align—everything shifts. Doors open that logic never could. People appear who resonate with your truth, not your performance. Opportunities land, not because you chased them—but because you were finally a vibrational match.

The version of you who's aligned doesn't ask, "Is it working yet?" They walk like it's done. They speak like it's done. Because in their reality—it already is. And when you embody that energy, the gap between desire and manifestation collapses. You don't just attract success. You become the environment where it thrives.

That's the secret the world doesn't tell you: The path isn't found. It's remembered. And when you become internally congruent, the external path lights up beneath your feet. You're not waiting for permission. You are the permission. The magnetism. The miracle. So stop asking the world to believe in you. It's your turn to believe in yourself—with a frequency too powerful to be denied.

The Energetics of Deserving

Deserving isn't something you earn—it's something you embody. And until you believe you deserve what you're asking for, you will keep creating barriers disguised as "being realistic." This isn't just a motivational idea—it's a measurable truth. According to neuroscience, people with low self-worth show heightened activity in the amygdala—the brain's fear center—and reduced function in the prefrontal cortex, which governs rational action and risk-taking. In other words, doubt doesn't just slow you down—it biologically blocks your ability to move forward with power (source).

You can't attract from a place of unworthiness. You might say the right words. You might take the right steps. But if your identity still whispers "I'm not good enough," your results will echo that belief. The universe doesn't respond to what you want—it responds to what you believe you're allowed to have. Subconsciously, you're always voting for your limits or your liberation. Not with your wishes—but with your alignment.

There's a hidden pattern to sabotage: guilt. Guilt for receiving. Guilt for rising. Guilt for leaving others behind. But you are not here to shrink for the comfort of others. You are here to model expansion. According to The Lancet Psychiatry, trauma survivors often associate joy and ease with danger—triggering discomfort even in the presence of goodness. So if abundance feels "unsafe," it's not your dream that's broken—it's your nervous system still healing (source).

That's why healing isn't just emotional—it's energetic. Deserving is a frequency. The Journal of Experimental Social Psychology found that self-affirmations based on worthiness significantly increased persistence and success in goal pursuit. Why? Because when your identity upgrades, your life follows. You don't need to force results. You need to calibrate to them (source).

Your worth was never up for negotiation. You don't earn it by doing more, proving more, or pleasing others. You claim it by being. By remembering who you were before the world taught you to beg for your birthright. That's not arrogance. That's alignment. It's saying, "I am no longer performing for what I already deserve."

Still think this is too "soft" to create change? Then understand this: neuroplasticity, the brain's ability to rewire itself, is activated through repetition and belief. When you affirm your value and act accordingly, you strengthen the insula and prefrontal cortex—two regions responsible for emotional stability, decision-making, and behavioral change. Worthiness isn't a vibe. It's a neurological state (source).

Want to know your real self-worth? Look at your boundaries. Do you say yes when you mean no? Do you lower your rates, your standards, or your needs to "keep the peace"? These aren't habits. They're reflections of your internal thermostat. Raise that thermostat, and you'll start tolerating only what matches your truth. And life will follow suit.

High self-worth isn't loud. It's not about being flashy or superior. It's quiet. It's a calm certainty that says, "I don't need to chase—I choose." "I don't need to beg—I belong." "I'm not hoping—I'm aligned." And when you move from that place, the right people, the right opportunities, and the right abundance can finally find you.

When you start believing you're worthy, everything changes. You stop settling. You stop self-abandoning. You stop asking for permission. You begin walking with presence. You begin speaking with clarity. You become magnetic—not because you're trying to be—but because you've stopped trying to hide.

This is the real shift. It's not about doing more. It's about becoming more of who you already are—without apology. Your worth doesn't increase with hustle. It expands with alignment. And when you drop the performance, the proving, and the pleasing, you step into a power that needs no validation.

You don't have to earn the love. You don't have to hustle for the blessing. You don't have to be perfect to receive the promise. You simply have to stop arguing with your own value. That's when you stop chasing success—and start receiving it. Not because it suddenly appeared. But because you finally stopped blocking it.

This is your moment to embody it. To feel it in your bones. To declare it without shrinking. You are not behind. You are not broken. You are not too late. You are worthy now. And the moment you believe that—the world will start reflecting it back to you in ways your logic could never have planned.

Magnetic Energy vs. Hustle Energy

You don't become magnetic by doing more. You become magnetic by being more of who you truly are. Not the conditioned self that hustles for validation—but the aligned self that trusts their worth, walks in their power, and radiates from the inside out. Research in neurocardiology shows that the heart emits an electromagnetic field 60 times greater than the brain, and people can physiologically sense your emotional state before you even speak. You're already broadcasting something—so the question is, are you broadcasting fear or certainty? (source)

Magnetic energy is about coherence—when your heart, mind, and body are in agreement. It's not loud. It doesn't need applause. It feels like peace that can't be shaken. That kind of coherence is measurable: a regulated nervous system with high heart rate variability is scientifically linked to resilience, clarity, and attraction. Not metaphorically—but biologically. When your system is calm, your presence becomes compelling. (source)

We've been taught to grind. To hustle. To earn everything with exhaustion. But hustle born from fear creates more resistance than results. Stress hormones like cortisol, when chronically elevated, reduce creativity, lower cognitive performance, and even impair intuition. When you operate from survival mode, your very biology fights against your desires. Magnetic energy, on the other hand, relaxes the system and sharpens perception. It's not lazy—it's strategic. (source)

Magnetic people aren't lucky. They're regulated. They've trained themselves to stay grounded in chaos, to act from clarity, and to release outcomes. A

Harvard study on successful leaders found that emotional self-regulation—not intelligence or skill—was the number one predictor of sustained influence. That's not charm. That's nervous system mastery. ([source](#))

Magnetism is quiet power. You feel it in someone who speaks slowly, confidently, and intentionally. You see it in someone who doesn't need the spotlight—but owns it when it finds them. This isn't arrogance. It's alignment. And alignment is the greatest force multiplier on Earth. It makes small actions create massive impact—because there's no resistance, only resonance.

This kind of power can't be faked. People know when you're congruent. Studies show we can detect inauthenticity in body language and tone within milliseconds. You don't attract trust by sounding good. You attract it by being real. That's why magnetic leaders don't perform—they embody. They don't pitch—they invite. And that's why people lean in when they speak.

Magnetism doesn't chase. It allows. It doesn't need to convince or force or beg. It trusts that what aligns will arrive. That's not passivity. That's precision. It means moving only when movement is aligned, and resting when rest is required. It's a level of self-trust that says, "I know I'm the source—not the seeker."

That doesn't mean magnetic people don't take action. They do. But their action is sourced from overflow—not urgency. They give because they're full—not because they're empty and desperate for validation. Their presence becomes their pitch. Their peace becomes their proof. And their energy becomes their filter.

In a world obsessed with visibility, magnetism teaches you the power of presence. It's the frequency you carry into the room that makes people turn their heads—not the volume of your voice. Presence is felt before words are spoken. And the science backs this up: mirror neurons in the brain pick up emotional states instantly. That's why some people shift the room just by walking in.

You stop being magnetic the moment you start outsourcing your worth. The moment you base your value on results or applause, you enter the frequency of neediness—and people feel it. Need repels. Certainty attracts. And that certainty doesn't come from knowing everything. It comes from knowing yourself.

So you can keep running after opportunity—or you can become the kind of person opportunity runs toward. You can keep tweaking your strategy—or you can tweak your frequency. Because when your inner world is clean, clear, and coherent, the outer world responds in kind. Not because it changed. But because you did.

You weren't born to chase. You were born to radiate. To embody such deep alignment that miracles feel logical, timing feels divine, and attraction becomes inevitable. You don't get there by pushing harder. You get there by letting go of everything that told you your worth had to be earned. Because you're not here to hustle your way into power—you're here to remember you always had it. And once you do, the world can't help but mirror it back.

Becoming a Vibrational Match

Becoming a vibrational match means tuning your inner world so powerfully that what you desire no longer feels like a fantasy—it feels inevitable. It's not about forcing, chasing, or performing. It's about shifting your energy, your beliefs, and your emotional baseline until your external reality has no choice but to rise to meet your frequency. Your energy introduces you before your words ever will, and when that energy is clean, clear, and congruent with your desires, manifestation becomes a natural byproduct—not a struggle.

Everything in the universe operates on frequency. Your thoughts carry frequency. Your emotions emit frequency. Even your expectations create a vibrational ripple that interacts with the field around you. This isn't mysticism—it's quantum physics. Just like a tuning fork causes another fork to vibrate in resonance, your internal state calls in what matches its rhythm. The people who get what they want without desperation aren't "lucky"—they're aligned.

The truth is, you're already manifesting all the time. The question isn't whether you're attracting—it's whether you're attracting what you *want*, or what you *are unconsciously embodying*. If you say you want love, but you constantly feel unworthy, guess what gets reflected back? If you want wealth, but your dominant emotion is fear or lack, that's what you'll keep recreating. Your vibrational signal doesn't respond to what you say—it responds to what you *feel and expect*.

This is why inner work is the real secret weapon. You don't need more willpower—you need more alignment. You don't need more strategies—you need a new emotional set point. When you raise your baseline frequency to match the energy of your desires, reality bends. Synchronicities multiply. Right people show up. Doors swing open without force. It feels like magic, but it's really **resonance** at work.

To become a vibrational match, you must first feel it *now*. Most people delay good feelings until they get results. But that creates a loop of postponement. The people who manifest with power are the ones who **generate the emotion first.** They feel abundant before the money. They feel joy before the breakthrough. They feel loved before the relationship. Emotion is the attractor, not the reward.

This is where gratitude becomes a supercharger. Gratitude isn't just a nice idea—it literally rewires your brain for abundance. Studies in neuroplasticity show that daily gratitude practice strengthens pathways associated with reward and optimism. It raises your emotional frequency and primes your mind to recognize opportunities that align with your desires. When you're grateful for what you haven't even received yet, you become a beacon for it.

Another key is emotional congruence. You can't affirm abundance and embody lack. You can't visualize success while vibrating with self-doubt. The subconscious always wins, and it doesn't respond to your affirmations—it responds to your *emotional truth*. When your thoughts, feelings, and actions are saying the same thing, your energy becomes unstoppable. The more coherent your frequency, the faster reality organizes around you.

Embodiment matters more than effort. Who are you being *now*? Are you living like someone who knows they're worthy of that vision, or someone hoping to earn it someday? Every decision, every boundary, every interaction either affirms your alignment or leaks your power. When you carry yourself like it's already yours—not arrogantly, but confidently—you collapse the gap between you and what you want.

Becoming a vibrational match is not about perfection. It's about **emotional responsibility.** Catch yourself when you drift into fear. Interrupt the old identity when it resurfaces. Re-center. Choose again. The people who live extraordinary lives aren't immune to doubt—they're just faster at realignment. Their discipline isn't in action alone—it's in *energy stewardship*.

There's a reason joy, peace, and love are called high-frequency emotions. They unlock creativity. They expand vision. They amplify magnetism. The more time you spend in those states, the more momentum you build. That's why mindset is just the start—*state* is where the transformation happens. Your state is your signal. Your signal is your power.

You weren't meant to fight for your blessings. You were meant to align with them. The universe is not holding back—it's waiting on you to rise. Not through more hustle, but through more harmony. Not by striving harder, but by becoming the kind of person for whom the thing you want is **normal.**

You are not chasing the dream—you are *matching* it. And when you become a vibrational match, the dream doesn't feel distant anymore. It feels natural. Familiar. Expected. That's when you know you've arrived—not when the thing shows up, but when you no longer question that it will.

The Role of Joy, Play, and Presence

Joy isn't a luxury. It's a frequency. A doorway. A divine shortcut to alignment. In a world that idolizes hustle and overachievement, joy can feel like rebellion—but it's actually the most magnetic state you can live in. Joy recalibrates your nervous system, restores emotional clarity, and amplifies your power. When you're in joy, you're not just happy—you're *in sync* with the version of you that already has what you want.

Play isn't childish—it's sacred. It is the energetic signature of flow. When you engage in play, you tap into a deep state of presence that bypasses resistance and ignites creativity. That's why some of your best ideas don't come when you're grinding—they come when you're laughing, walking, dancing, or doing something that has no outcome attached. It's because your ego takes a step back, and your higher intelligence steps in.

Presence is the foundation of all power. You cannot access your intuition, your courage, or your inner wisdom without it. When you're present, you stop living in the past and predicting doom from the future. You breathe into what *is*, and from that grounded place, real decisions can be made. Presence silences the noise so that clarity can rise. And clarity is the launching pad for aligned action.

Joy expands your heart. It increases coherence between the brain and the body. When you feel good, your physiology shifts—your immune system strengthens, your hormones balance, and your perception sharpens. That's not just emotional benefit—that's *biological intelligence*. Your body was designed to thrive in elevated states.

But many people are afraid of joy. They've linked it to vulnerability. They fear that if they let themselves feel too good, the other shoe will drop. That kind of conditional joy is not true joy—it's emotional bargaining. And that fear-based thinking shrinks your capacity to receive. You don't protect your power by numbing your joy. You *amplify* it by embracing it unapologetically.

When you give yourself permission to play, you rewire your beliefs about work, worth, and what's required. Play teaches your nervous system that you can feel safe in pleasure, not just in pressure. That you can create from joy, not just pain. That you are allowed to *enjoy* the life you are building—not just survive it.

Presence doesn't mean passivity. It means showing up fully, with all your senses, emotions, and truth intact. When you are present, you stop reacting and start *responding*. You break the addiction to urgency and tune into divine timing. And that's when manifestation becomes less about controlling outcomes and more about trusting alignment.

Joy raises your baseline vibration. That's why when you feel good for no reason, everything around you begins to change. Opportunities seem to appear. People light up in your presence. Solutions unfold. This isn't coincidence—it's resonance. Your state becomes a signal. And when that signal is joy, the response is always elevation.

Play reconnects you to your essence. It unhooks you from performance and returns you to presence. That's why some of the most magnetic, successful, and creative people make time for art, movement, humor, or adventure. Not as a reward after achievement—but as a gateway to it. Joy doesn't come after success. It *creates* it.

When you prioritize joy, you stop operating from emptiness. You stop measuring your worth by your output. You shift from "What do I need to fix?" to "What would feel delicious to create?" And from that space, you access your genius—not because you're trying harder, but because you're tuned in to truth.

There is divine intelligence in delight. There is courage in play. There is healing in presence. When you commit to these states—not occasionally, but as a way of being—you don't just live more freely. You *attract* more freely. Because the version of you that knows how to celebrate life is the same version that's ready to receive more of it.

You are not here to grind your way to greatness. You are here to remember that joy is your natural frequency, play is your soul's language, and presence is your personal portal to everything you've been trying to manifest. Let joy be your strategy. Let presence be your power. Let play be your permission slip to rise.

Magnetic Morning Routine

Your morning is not just the start of your day—it's the stage where your energy, intentions, and subconscious direction are set. From the moment you wake up, you are either stepping into alignment or reactivating autopilot. The most magnetic people on the planet don't leave their energy to chance—they craft it deliberately, especially in the first hour. Because how you start your day isn't about productivity. It's about *frequency alignment*.

The first 20 minutes of your morning are when your subconscious mind is the most impressionable. Brainwave studies show that during this window, your mind is in a theta-to-alpha state, meaning it absorbs suggestions and emotional input like a sponge. This is why consuming fear-driven news or social media drama first thing can hijack your vibration and shape your entire emotional tone for the day. You think you're just scrolling—but you're actually *programming*.

Magnetic energy begins in stillness, not stimulation. Instead of checking messages or reacting to the world, start by anchoring into your body and your breath. Your breath is the remote control for your nervous system. When you consciously breathe with intention, you shift from stress to regulation, from chaos to clarity. A calm nervous system is a *magnetic* nervous system. It radiates trust, presence, and embodied leadership.

The most powerful people in the world often start their day with silence, visualization, gratitude, and movement. These aren't self-help clichés—they're neural priming techniques. When you visualize the outcomes you desire while feeling the emotion of already having them, your brain begins creating new pathways to match that vision. This isn't fantasy—it's neuroscience. The mind doesn't distinguish between imagination and reality. It responds to what's rehearsed emotionally.

Gratitude is one of the fastest ways to elevate your emotional frequency. It shifts your focus from what's missing to what's already working. When you start your morning by giving thanks—not just mentally, but with your whole emotional body—you tune your frequency to abundance. Gratitude isn't a mood—it's a muscle. And the more you flex it, the more magnetic you become.

Movement is another magnetic amplifier. Whether it's stretching, walking, dancing, or working out, physical activity boosts dopamine, serotonin, and endorphins—your natural feel-good chemicals. More than that, it shakes off the stagnation of yesterday. It signals to your body, *"We are moving forward."* You don't have to run a marathon. You just have to move your body with *intention*.

Affirmations are not about saying pretty words—they're about reprogramming the identity that leads your choices. When you speak out loud who you choose to be—boldly, unapologetically, and consistently—you reinforce the version of yourself that naturally attracts the life you're calling in. The key is feeling the *truth* in those words, not just reciting them from your head. Emotion is what makes it stick.

The most magnetic morning routines are not about tasks. They're about tuning. You're tuning your frequency like an instrument. You're setting the tone for how you will walk, talk, lead, love, and respond throughout the day. And when you tune into clarity, purpose, and power first thing, the rest of your day bends to that energy.

This is why reactionary mornings kill momentum. When your first action is reacting to emails, messages, or notifications, you hand over your energy before you've anchored it. You begin your day in a frequency of *reception*, not creation. And that energy follows you. On the other hand, when you own your first hour, the rest of the day feels like a reflection of your *intention*, not a fight against interruptions.

Creating a magnetic morning routine is not about perfection—it's about presence. It's not about doing everything. It's about choosing *what tunes you in*. Maybe it's prayer. Maybe it's journaling. Maybe it's looking at your vision board and saying, "Yes. That's mine." Whatever pulls you into the version of you that's already aligned—that's your power source.

You become magnetic by choosing yourself first thing every morning. Before you check the world's demands, check your alignment. Before you serve others, serve your own frequency. Because the most powerful version of you isn't someone who's constantly doing more—it's someone who starts their day deeply *centered* in who they truly are.

You don't need a perfect plan. You need a consistent intention. Start small. Anchor deep. Choose joy, presence, and embodiment at sunrise—and watch how the universe responds by matching your energy before noon. Your morning is your miracle portal. Step into it like you know what you're calling in. Because when your energy is right, everything else becomes a matter of *when*, not *if*.

Removing Hidden Blocks to Receiving

Receiving isn't just about being open. It's about being *available*. And most people are unknowingly unavailable to the very things they're praying for. You can want something deeply—love, abundance, recognition—but if there's a hidden block in your energy, your beliefs, or your body, it won't land. It's not that the universe is denying you. It's that your nervous system is saying, "I'm not safe with this yet."

One of the biggest hidden blocks to receiving is unworthiness. It often disguises itself as humility, selflessness, or "not needing too much." But underneath is a subconscious script that says, "I haven't done enough. I'm not enough. I can't hold that." These beliefs were usually formed early, through childhood programming, trauma, or religious conditioning. And until you rewrite them, you'll keep deflecting the very breakthroughs you desire.

Another block is guilt. Guilt for wanting more. Guilt for outgrowing your environment. Guilt for succeeding when others are struggling. Guilt is sticky energy. It creates a ceiling on how much joy, wealth, and ease you'll allow yourself to feel before you unconsciously sabotage it. You think you're protecting others—but you're actually punishing yourself.

Control is another barrier. When you obsess over "how" something will come, you're signaling a lack of trust. You're trying to micromanage what only surrender can deliver. The energy of control is constriction. It chokes flow. Receiving requires openness. Spaciousness. A willingness to let go of timing, form, and logic—and make room for miracles.

Unprocessed grief also blocks receiving. The parts of you that are still grieving past failures, betrayals, or losses may quietly whisper, "I don't want to feel that again." So you stay safe by staying small. But safety isn't the same as peace. Peace comes from healing. And once you tend to the wounds, your system can finally breathe—and receive—again.

Old identity is one of the sneakiest blocks. You've outgrown who you were, but part of you still clings to that version. Why? Because it's familiar. Because it's been with you for years. But here's the truth: your next level won't feel safe to the old you. You have to let that outdated identity die in order for the new one to emerge. That's not loss—that's liberation.

Busyness is another disguise for avoidance. If your calendar is packed with tasks but your soul feels empty, ask yourself: What am I avoiding feeling by staying busy? What gift is trying to reach me that I don't have space for? Often, slowing down is the most courageous thing you can do. Because stillness reveals what motion hides.

Energetically, your body needs to feel safe with more. More attention. More money. More responsibility. More intimacy. And if your nervous system is stuck in survival mode, "more" won't feel exciting—it will feel threatening. This is why somatic work is crucial. When you teach your body that expansion is safe, receiving becomes a natural next step, not a nervous leap.

Language reveals hidden blocks. Listen to yourself: Do you deflect compliments? Downplay your desires? Use words like "hopefully" instead of "certainly"? Your vocabulary mirrors your vibration. And if your language is softening your truth, you're unconsciously signaling that you're not fully anchored in your worth.

Receiving is an act of power—not passivity. It's not about waiting. It's about *welcoming*. It's about saying, "I'm ready. I'm open. I trust myself to hold what's next." It's not needy. It's noble. And when you show up with that energy, the world responds accordingly.

The most magnetic people aren't the ones who ask for more—they're the ones who *allow* more. They're not perfect. They're not unafraid. But they've made a decision: to stop blocking the blessings meant for them. And that choice alone shifts everything.

You don't have to force your next level. You simply have to remove what's in the way. Peel back the guilt. Loosen the grip of control. Let go of the old story. Make space for the version of you who doesn't chase—but *receives with grace*. Because the life you want isn't far away. It's just waiting for a "yes" that lives deeper than your mind. It's waiting for you to open.

Living in Your "Yes Frequency"

Living in your "Yes Frequency" is about embodying a state of energetic agreement with your highest self. It's not just about positive thinking—it's about becoming a living, breathing invitation to the life you desire. It's the vibration you carry when you stop negotiating with doubt and start aligning with truth. When your thoughts, words, emotions, and actions all say "yes" to your purpose, the universe doesn't hesitate—it responds.

You were never meant to live in hesitation. That murky middle space between commitment and confusion is where dreams go to die. The "yes frequency" is a declaration. It's not loud or frantic—it's calm, clear, and powerful. It says, "I choose expansion. I choose alignment. I choose now." It doesn't beg. It doesn't plead. It commands, through conviction and consistency.

Science confirms that the emotions we cultivate influence our perception and physiology. When you live in states like joy, certainty, love, and confidence, your brain enters a more coherent state. Your heart rate becomes more rhythmic. Your immune system strengthens. Your decision-making sharpens.

You literally become more magnetic, more focused, more creative. It's not metaphysical—it's measurable.

Most people live in a default frequency of "maybe." They want the breakthrough, but they doubt. They desire love, but they fear rejection. They ask for abundance, but expect struggle. That vibrational contradiction cancels the signal. The universe doesn't respond to partial energy—it matches your dominant frequency. When you live in "maybe," your results reflect uncertainty. But when you shift to "yes," the doors start opening.

"Living in your yes" doesn't mean everything feels easy. It means you're no longer outsourcing permission. You're no longer waiting for proof before you believe. You *decide* that it's already yours in energy. From that state, you move differently. You speak differently. You invest, create, and show up like it's inevitable—not optional.

Your nervous system is the transmitter. If your body is constantly in fight, flight, or freeze, "yes" won't feel safe—it'll feel threatening. That's why embodiment practices like breathwork, movement, and stillness are critical. You're not just thinking your "yes"—you're **becoming** it. You're teaching your system that it's safe to expand, to shine, to succeed.

Language is a powerful mirror. When you live in "yes," your vocabulary changes. You stop saying "I hope" and start saying "I trust." You stop asking "What if it doesn't work?" and start asking "What if it does?" Your words become spells. And every time you speak with conviction, you reinforce the frequency you've chosen to live in.

Yes isn't reckless—it's resolute. You can still be strategic. You can still be discerning. But your baseline becomes belief, not doubt. You don't wait for clarity to fall into your lap—you create it with every courageous step. The most aligned opportunities rarely show up when you're passive. They meet you in motion, in momentum, in the embodied signal of your yes.

Relationships shift when you live in your yes. People feel your energy. They know you're no longer wavering. And that certainty either draws them closer or filters them out. That's not rejection—it's alignment doing its job. Your yes repels what isn't meant and attracts what is. That's how resonance works.

Living in yes doesn't mean you never feel fear. It means you don't let fear vote anymore. You acknowledge it. You thank it for trying to protect you. And then you choose differently. Over time, the more you honor your yes, the quieter fear becomes. Not because you silenced it—but because you proved it wrong.

Everything changes when your baseline becomes "I'm available for miracles. I'm worthy of more. I trust the unfolding." From that state, you move into creation—not compensation. You stop living for approval and start living from alignment. You become less reactive and more receptive. Less forceful, more faithful.

This is what it means to live in your yes frequency: to stand in full energetic congruence with the life that's been waiting on the other side of your permission. Not someday. Not when it's convenient. But now. Because the universe is always listening—and when it hears the full-body yes, it answers without delay.

Attraction Through Authenticity

Attraction doesn't come from perfection—it comes from presence. And presence is the result of authenticity. When you are fully yourself, unapologetically and consistently, you transmit a frequency that is both rare and irresistible. People are magnetized by truth, even if they don't consciously know why. Your authenticity gives others permission to be real, and that is the deepest form of connection.

In a world saturated with filters, facades, and performance personas, authenticity stands out like a lighthouse in a storm. It cuts through noise. It pierces through skepticism. It reaches past logic and lands in the heart. When you show up as you—flaws, quirks, and all—you're saying to the world, "This is who I am, and I am safe to be seen." That energy is pure power.

True authenticity isn't about oversharing or being messy for attention. It's about being rooted. It's about knowing your values, your vision, and your voice—and living from that center no matter who's watching. People can feel when someone's energy is congruent. It creates trust. And trust is the foundation of influence, intimacy, and impact.

Psychologically, authenticity builds rapport faster than any scripted pitch. Studies show that people are drawn to those who display emotional congruence—where what they say matches what they feel and do. It creates coherence in the brain of the observer, triggering safety and resonance. Simply put: when you are real, people relax. And relaxed people are open people.

But authenticity requires courage. It means releasing the need to be liked by everyone. It means risking rejection to remain in integrity. It means no longer morphing to fit into rooms that weren't built for your truth. You stop shrinking, shape-shifting, or softening your edges just to gain approval. Because the moment you abandon yourself to be accepted, you disconnect from the very frequency that makes you magnetic.

Attraction through authenticity means leading with alignment instead of image. You no longer market a mask—you embody your message. You don't try to be the smartest, flashiest, or loudest in the room. You're simply the most *you*. And that confidence—rooted in self-awareness, not ego—draws in the right people, opportunities, and experiences.

Authenticity doesn't guarantee immediate applause. In fact, it often triggers resistance at first. Because truth confronts comfort. It challenges the status quo. But over time, it builds unshakable credibility. While others exhaust themselves trying to maintain appearances, the authentic stand tall, grounded, and resilient—because they're not performing, they're *being*.

There is deep freedom in no longer needing to be "on." When you live authentically, you conserve energy. You stop managing perceptions and start creating from purpose. And that shift in energy is felt. People lean in. They remember how you made them feel. Because authenticity doesn't need to persuade—it simply resonates.

Your greatest asset isn't your script, your resume, or your strategy. It's your essence. It's your lived truth. It's the clarity in your eyes when you speak from the heart. When your story is unfiltered and your energy is clean, you don't have to chase anything. You attract what's meant because your frequency has nothing to hide.

When you operate from authenticity, rejection becomes redirection. You're no longer shattered by a "no" because you know that what's truly aligned will never require self-abandonment. You stop needing to convince, control, or chase. You trust that the people and paths who recognize your truth will feel it—and come closer.

The irony is that the more you try to be what others want, the more invisible you become. But the moment you show up fully, something shifts. You stop blending. You start standing out—not because you're trying to—but because you're *real*. And in a world starving for real, that's what magnetizes.

Authenticity isn't a strategy. It's a frequency. A decision. A lifestyle. And the more you live in that truth, the more the universe aligns in your favor—not because you manipulated it, but because you finally had the courage to let yourself be seen. Unmasked. Unfiltered. Unapologetic. And unforgettable.

Quantum Leaps Through Alignment

Quantum leaps don't happen by working harder. They happen when your energy, intention, and actions lock into alignment so tightly that reality reorganizes itself around your clarity. Alignment isn't about perfection—it's about coherence. It's when your desires stop fighting your beliefs, and your inner world stops contradicting your outer expression. That's when things shift fast. Not incrementally. Not gradually. But *exponentially*.

In quantum physics, everything is energy. Everything vibrates. And what we perceive as "solid" reality is simply a reflection of frequency patterns. When your internal frequency matches the result you're aiming for, you collapse the time between desire and manifestation. It's not magic—it's mechanics. You're not attracting the outcome—you're *matching* it.

The problem is most people are working against themselves. They're taking aligned actions with unaligned beliefs. They're setting powerful intentions but waking up with self-doubt, fear, and internal contradiction. That's why the results stall. Energy first. Action second. When both are in sync, you don't just move forward—you *quantum leap.*

Quantum leaps require identity upgrades. You don't get to the next level with the same self-concept. You must become the version of you who already lives there—before the evidence shows up. That means thinking, feeling, and acting from your desired reality, not your current one. The nervous system learns through repetition and emotion. The more you practice being "her" or "him" now, the faster you rewire the default identity.

Emotional alignment is key. It's not just what you think—it's what you *feel.* If you affirm abundance but feel unworthy, you won't receive the breakthrough. Emotion is the true language of the subconscious mind. It doesn't speak in goals—it speaks in vibration. So if your dominant emotional state is stress, scarcity, or survival, your subconscious will work overtime to maintain what's familiar—even if it contradicts what you say you want.

Time is not linear when you're aligned. What once took years can take weeks. What required struggle suddenly shows up with ease. Alignment shortcuts the process—not because you bypass effort, but because you remove resistance. The universe doesn't withhold—it responds to readiness. And readiness isn't about hustle—it's about *energetic clarity.*

Faith plays a massive role in alignment. Not blind faith—but embodied trust. When you deeply believe it's already done, you stop leaking energy. You stop checking the clock, comparing timelines, or micromanaging the outcome. You show up, speak up, take the next bold step—and let the laws of the universe do the rest.

Every quantum leap begins with a decision. A moment where you say, "I'm no longer available for half-truths, half-efforts, or half-alignment." That decision shifts everything. Your body begins to calibrate. Your energy sharpens. Your actions gain weight. And what used to feel far suddenly feels inevitable.

You can't fake alignment. You can't fake belief. You either live it or you don't. That's why self-honesty is vital. Where are you out of alignment? What habits, thoughts, or relationships are pulling you off frequency? Quantum leaps are blocked by subtle misalignments. Clean those up, and what's been delayed often rushes in.

Clarity accelerates. The clearer you are on who you are, what you want, and why it matters, the faster the path unfolds. Vagueness creates static. But precision—emotional, energetic, and strategic—creates momentum. That's why aligned clarity is more potent than years of busywork. Because it channels your focus into laser-pointed action.

Quantum leaps also require nervous system capacity. If your body doesn't feel safe holding more—more visibility, more income, more responsibility—it will sabotage the expansion. That's why breathwork, grounding, movement, and emotional regulation aren't extras—they're essential. You don't just prepare mentally—you calibrate somatically.

You don't need a miracle to leap. You *become* the miracle by aligning so powerfully with your next level that life bends around your decision. That's what quantum alignment does—it doesn't wait for permission. It declares. It aligns. It moves. And the universe, without fail, moves in return.

Ritual: Step Into Your Magnetic Self

Ritual isn't routine—it's reverence in motion. It's how you remind the universe of who you are and what you're available for. When you step into your magnetic self, you're not becoming someone new—you're stripping away the layers that blocked your radiance. This ritual isn't about performance. It's about *presence*. It's the daily embodiment of your power, your truth, and your readiness to receive.

Every time you step into this version of you, you're creating a neural and energetic imprint. The body learns through repetition. When you repeatedly choose alignment, your nervous system begins to trust it. The mind begins to expect it. The world starts to reflect it. That's how identity upgrades happen—not by force, but through consistent acts of remembrance.

Begin with your body. Movement is a doorway. When you walk, stretch, dance, or breathe with intention, you shift your frequency. You tell your cells, "We are not surviving today—we are expanding." You override the familiar contractions of fear, and you invite flow. Motion dissolves stagnation. It activates the magnetism that lives in your posture, your breath, and your rhythm.

Use your voice. Speak your truth out loud. Recite declarations that make you stand taller. Say the words you've been waiting to hear from the world. Let them come from *you*. When you speak with conviction, your vocal vibration reprograms your subconscious. Your tone becomes your testimony. And people don't just hear it—they *feel* it.

Dress like your highest self. Not to impress, but to express. The clothes you wear can be armor or art. When you intentionally embody the energy of who you are becoming, your confidence rises. You carry yourself differently. It's not vanity—it's vibration. You are showing yourself and the universe that you are no longer hiding.

Light a candle, play a song, burn incense—engage your senses. Rituals ground us in the present. They mark the shift from ordinary to intentional. They anchor your energy and make your frequency tangible. The brain anchors memory through sensory experience. When your ritual involves sight, sound, scent, and sensation, it becomes embedded in your identity.

Hold stillness. Even for just a few minutes. Let your breath become your guide. In silence, you hear the whispers of your intuition. In stillness, you realign with your center. This is where the ego softens and the soul steps forward. You remember that your worth isn't based on doing—it's encoded in your *being*.

Visualize with emotion. Don't just see the outcome—*feel* it. Step into the scene. Walk through your future. Smell the room. Hear the applause. Feel the freedom. The brain doesn't know the difference between real and vividly imagined experiences. When you combine visualization with elevated emotion, you condition your body for success.

Gratitude is the energetic amplifier. End every ritual with a full-body thank you—not just for what is, but for what's becoming. Gratitude shifts you from craving to receiving. It turns waiting into welcoming. It calibrates your frequency to abundance, and abundance always responds to those who already feel full.

Let this ritual evolve. Let it be alive. Some days it might be 20 minutes, others it's 2—but the consistency is what counts. The message you send yourself is: "This is who I am now. I am available for more. I am magnetic by nature, not by luck."

You are not performing for the world—you're aligning with the truth. Your ritual isn't for validation—it's for calibration. And when you show up consistently, the gap between who you've been and who you're becoming starts to disappear.

The version of you that attracts effortlessly, speaks powerfully, walks boldly, and receives fully—that version isn't in the future. It's here. And every time you step into your ritual, you remind the universe, "I remember who I am. I am magnetic. I am ready. Let it begin."

What you've just read isn't theory—it's truth. But here's the secret: transformation doesn't happen just by knowing… it happens by *installing*. If you're serious about unlocking unstoppable clarity, next-level confidence, and the inner certainty to move through life like a force of nature, then the next step is simple. The **Clarity Confidence Code Course** is the full blueprint—designed to rewire your subconscious, activate your higher self, and lock in the identity of someone who always wins. This isn't hype. It's a system. And if you apply it, your results won't just improve—they'll multiply. Ready to stop circling the edges of your breakthrough and finally live it fully? Go here now 👉 https://clarityconfidencecode.com

Because the next chapter isn't just words—it's your transformation in motion. Let's keep going.

CHAPTER 8

ENERGETIC BOUNDARIES — PROTECTING YOUR PEACE WITHOUT GUILT

What Boundaries Actually Are

Boundaries are not walls that keep people out—they are bridges that keep your truth intact. They are not barriers to connection; they are the conditions that make healthy connection *possible*. Boundaries are the energetic contracts you create with the world, declaring what is acceptable, what is sacred, and what is non-negotiable in your life.

Many people confuse boundaries with rejection or selfishness, but the truth is, boundaries are an act of deep self-respect. They communicate, "I love you, and I love me too." Without boundaries, resentment builds. And where resentment grows, authenticity dies. That's why people pleasers often feel invisible—because in abandoning their own needs, they disappear from themselves.

At their core, boundaries are about energy management. Your time, attention, and emotional bandwidth are not infinite resources. They are currency. And how you spend them determines the quality of your life. Boundaries help you spend wisely. They help you stop bleeding energy into people, places, and problems that don't serve your evolution.

Science backs this up. Psychological studies have shown that individuals with strong personal boundaries experience less stress, fewer symptoms of anxiety and depression, and greater relationship satisfaction. That's because boundaries reduce chaos and increase clarity. When people know where you stand, they can meet you there—or they naturally fall away. Either outcome creates peace.

Boundaries are not static. They evolve with you. What was okay last year might no longer fit your new level of self-awareness. That doesn't mean you're rigid—it means you're *growing*. Every version of you will require new standards, new expectations, and new energetic agreements. Growth requires recalibration.

Saying no is not an attack—it's an alignment. It doesn't mean you're cruel. It means you're clear. And clarity is kind. It allows others to adjust, respond, or redirect without confusion. When you say yes out of guilt, fear, or obligation, you're not being generous—you're being dishonest. Boundaries restore your truth to the surface.

People who don't respect your boundaries are revealing their relationship to control, not your worth. Let that sink in. Your limits don't hurt healthy relationships—they *protect* them. In fact, the most soul-nourishing relationships thrive on mutual respect, not endless access. Love is not proven through tolerance. It is deepened through trust—and trust is built through honoring limits.

Energetically, boundaries also protect your nervous system. When you consistently override your own needs to avoid conflict, you activate a stress response that becomes your baseline. Over time, this leads to burnout, resentment, and emotional numbness. Boundaries are how you regulate not just your schedule, but your *state*.

What you allow teaches people how to engage with you. Your boundaries are your curriculum. Every time you reinforce them with grace and consistency, you teach the world how to love, respect, and support you. And every time you abandon them, you send the opposite message: "I don't matter." The work is to reverse that.

Boundaries are not always about others. They're often about you. The boundaries you keep with your own distractions, your own patterns, your own inner critic—those are the ones that transform your life from the inside out. When you stop betraying yourself for comfort or approval, you begin to build a reality that reflects your worth.

You are not responsible for how others feel about your truth. You are responsible for honoring it. And the moment you do, you reclaim the energy that's been scattered, the voice that's been silenced, and the self-respect that's been deferred for too long. Boundaries don't push people away—they pull your power back.

So let the new standard be peace. Let the new normal be reciprocity. Let the new agreement be this: "If it costs me my authenticity, it's too expensive." Because what you protect grows. And when you protect your energy, your voice, and your value, the world learns to treat you accordingly. Not because you demanded it—but because you *embodied* it.

Why People-Pleasing Drains Confidence

People-pleasing is often mistaken for kindness, but in truth, it's a quiet form of self-abandonment. It's not generosity—it's performance. When you shape-shift to avoid conflict, say "yes" to avoid guilt, or silence your needs to stay liked, you're sending a dangerous message to your subconscious: that your voice, value, and truth are negotiable. Over time, this erodes confidence at the deepest level—because you've trained yourself to betray who you are to be accepted.

Confidence doesn't come from how others see you. It comes from how deeply you honor what you see in yourself. And every time you override your inner "no" for someone else's comfort, you reinforce the belief that other people's approval is more important than your alignment. That belief creates anxiety, self-doubt, and exhaustion—not peace. You might look polished on the outside, but inside, you're living under constant pressure to perform.

Neuroscience shows that when you suppress your truth repeatedly, the brain's stress circuits remain active. Your body starts to associate authenticity with danger. So even when you're safe, you feel on edge. You second-guess yourself. You question your worth. That's not weakness—it's wiring. But the good news is: it can be reprogrammed.

People-pleasing is rooted in fear: fear of being rejected, misunderstood, abandoned, or alone. It often comes from childhood environments where love was conditional, or where you were rewarded for being "easy," "helpful," or "nice." But as you grow, what once kept you safe starts to keep you small. You become emotionally depleted, constantly anticipating other people's needs while your own remain unmet.

Over time, this creates a false identity—one that looks agreeable but feels hollow. You forget what *you* want. You lose clarity. You become disconnected from your desires, your intuition, and your inner guidance. And without that connection, confidence can't survive. Because confidence doesn't come from being liked—it comes from being *aligned*.

Authenticity is the foundation of true confidence. When you know who you are and act from that place—without apology—you walk differently. You speak with clarity. You attract people who resonate with your truth instead of being addicted to your performance. You don't need to chase approval because you've given yourself *permission*.

Letting go of people-pleasing doesn't mean becoming rude, cold, or dismissive. It means learning how to disappoint others to remain true to yourself. It means setting boundaries without guilt. It means trusting that the right people will not only respect your limits—they'll rise to meet them. And those who don't? They were never aligned to begin with.

Studies on assertiveness show that people who practice clear, respectful communication without over-explaining or justifying themselves experience higher levels of confidence and lower levels of anxiety. It's not about being aggressive—it's about being grounded in your truth. And that truth has weight. It teaches the world how to treat you.

Confidence grows every time you choose yourself without shame. Every time you say no and don't rush to apologize. Every time you express a need and don't shrink when someone doesn't like it. That's not ego—that's embodiment. You're not asking for permission to be you—you're owning it.

People-pleasing is a survival pattern, not a personality trait. And anything that was learned can be unlearned. You are not here to be agreeable—you're here to be *authentic*. Your role in this world isn't to keep the peace at the expense of your voice. It's to speak, live, and lead in a way that honors who you are.

When you start honoring your truth, your energy changes. You don't just reclaim your time—you reclaim your *frequency*. You stop walking on eggshells and start walking in purpose. You stop dimming and start radiating. Because the version of you that no longer needs to be liked by everyone is the version that's ready to be respected by the right ones.

You don't build confidence by pleasing others. You build it by pleasing your *soul*. And when your soul feels seen, heard, and honored by you—you no longer need external validation to feel powerful. Because you've finally remembered: your truth was never too much. It was your power source all along.

Signs You Have Leaky Boundaries

Leaky boundaries aren't always obvious. They don't always show up as blatant disrespect or outright violation. Sometimes, they look like exhaustion you can't explain. Chronic guilt you can't shake. Saying "yes" when everything in your body screams "no." These aren't personality flaws—they're symptoms of energetic leakage, where your time, attention, and emotional resources are seeping out in places you haven't consciously authorized.

One of the clearest signs of leaky boundaries is emotional burnout. You find yourself constantly overwhelmed, yet unable to say no. You're everyone's sounding board, everyone's fixer, everyone's emergency contact—but no one is refilling *you*. That's because you've set the pattern that your energy is always available, regardless of your capacity. And people respond to the access you grant, not the needs you silently suppress.

Another subtle sign is over-explaining. When you feel the need to justify your no, to soften your truth, or to convince others to understand your decision, it's often because you don't feel safe standing in it. True boundaries are clear, not contorted. When your "no" requires a paragraph of disclaimers, your subconscious is asking for permission instead of giving direction.

Constantly rescuing others at the cost of your own peace is another red flag. This kind of "helping" often comes from a subconscious belief that your worth is tied to how useful you are. But when you become addicted to solving everyone's problems, you unconsciously communicate that your needs come last. That's not compassion—it's co-dependence dressed as care.

Leaky boundaries also manifest as resentment. You feel angry, unappreciated, or taken for granted—but instead of addressing it, you suppress it. This buried frustration becomes a toxin. It turns your energy bitter and brittle. And while you smile on the outside, your body carries the weight of unspoken truths and unmet needs.

You may also find yourself constantly doubting your decisions. You say yes, then regret it. You agree to plans, then dread them. You bend your time, budget, or energy to accommodate others, then feel drained for days. This pattern isn't about poor time management—it's a signal that you're prioritizing peace *for others* at the cost of internal chaos *for yourself.*

Another leak shows up through chronic availability. You're answering texts at midnight, jumping on calls with no notice, and rearranging your calendar to accommodate everyone but you. In doing so, you train people to see you as a resource, not a sovereign being. Your time is sacred—but until you treat it that way, no one else will.

Physical symptoms can also emerge. Headaches, muscle tension, fatigue, and even digestive issues are often linked to prolonged stress from boundary violations. Your body knows when you're living out of alignment, even when your words say otherwise. Chronic stress isn't always from external pressure—it's often from internal dissonance.

You may also find that you attract the same types of draining relationships again and again. That's not coincidence—it's repetition. When your boundaries are porous, your energy becomes a match for people who thrive on access without accountability. Until you recalibrate your standards, your experiences will keep reflecting the same imbalance.

One powerful sign of boundary leakage is self-betrayal. You abandon your own routines, ignore your own intuition, and quiet your voice to maintain harmony. But harmony built on self-erasure is a false peace. Eventually, your soul begins to rebel—not through loud resistance, but through subtle withdrawal from joy, passion, and purpose.

Perhaps most damaging of all is the erosion of self-trust. When you don't honor your own limits, you teach yourself that your needs are negotiable. And confidence can't thrive in a system where you constantly override your own guidance. Rebuilding trust starts with one decision: to stop leaking energy into places where your presence is tolerated but not cherished.

Boundaries don't just protect your time—they preserve your power. They tell the world, "I honor my energy. I respect my intuition. I value my peace."

And when your boundaries are strong, your energy stops scattering—and starts speaking for you. That's when people don't just hear your no—they *feel* your worth. Without a word. Without apology. With complete, embodied authority.

How to Identify Energy Drains

Energy doesn't just disappear. It leaks. It scatters. It gets drained by invisible commitments, emotional noise, unspoken obligations, and unconscious agreements that were never yours to begin with. When your energy is drained, it's not just about sleep or calories—it's about *clarity*. And clarity starts with knowing where your power is going and why.

One of the clearest signs of energy drain is chronic fatigue that rest doesn't fix. You might sleep, but still wake up exhausted. That's not laziness—it's leakage. Emotional labor, unresolved tension, and constant people-pleasing consume energy at a cellular level. Your body knows when your boundaries are being violated—even when your mouth stays silent.

Look at your calendar. If your days are filled with obligations you dread, that's not just time being wasted—it's *life force*. Every "yes" that came from guilt, fear, or obligation is a withdrawal from your energy account. And when you consistently spend your time on what doesn't feed you, burnout becomes inevitable.

Pay attention to your conversations. Do you leave certain interactions feeling depleted instead of uplifted? Energy vampires aren't just in movies—they're real, and they often don't know they're draining you. But it's your responsibility to notice the impact and adjust accordingly. Not everyone deserves unlimited access to your attention, your empathy, or your presence.

Digital energy drains are equally potent. Every scroll, click, notification, and dopamine hit creates cognitive load. Studies in neuropsychology show that constant digital stimulation decreases focus, increases anxiety, and taxes your prefrontal cortex—the part of your brain responsible for executive function and emotional regulation. If your mind feels foggy or overwhelmed, look at your screen time.

Emotional avoidance is another massive drain. When you avoid difficult conversations, suppress how you really feel, or ignore intuitive nudges, you're spending energy to maintain a façade. That internal conflict creates a low-level tension that robs you of clarity. And clarity is the true currency of power. You can't act with precision if you're emotionally tangled.

Physical clutter creates energetic clutter. Your environment reflects your mental state. A chaotic space contributes to decision fatigue and cortisol spikes. You may think the mess is harmless, but your brain is constantly scanning your environment for threats and unfinished tasks. A cluttered room is a silent to-do list—draining you with every glance.

Unfinished tasks also bleed energy. Every unresolved commitment, unpaid bill, or unread message lingers in the background like a tab open in your mind. Psychologists call this the Zeigarnik Effect—your brain keeps reminding you of incomplete tasks, pulling energy even when you're not actively thinking about them. Closing loops creates *relief* and restores your focus.

Relationships without reciprocity are heavy. If you're constantly giving, listening, supporting, and adjusting while receiving little in return, you're not in connection—you're in consumption. True relationships are mutual refueling stations, not one-way energy highways. Take note of where you feel consistently unseen, unheard, or undervalued.

Your own inner critic can be one of the biggest energy thieves. That voice that questions your every move, rehearses every mistake, and doubts every decision isn't motivating—it's *draining*. And the more you listen to it, the more you shrink. Self-compassion isn't indulgent. It's protective. It seals the leaks that self-judgment creates.

Tolerations—those small annoyances you've accepted—are stealth energy drains. The broken cabinet, the friend who always crosses the line, the task you've put off for months. Each one whispers, "You don't matter enough to fix this." And that message chips away at your confidence. When you handle what you've been tolerating, you reclaim energy *and* self-respect.

Energy is your most precious currency. Protect it like royalty. Audit your time, your space, your habits, your thoughts, and your connections. Don't just ask, "What do I need to do?" Ask, "What's draining me that I need to release?" Because when your energy is clean, your vision sharpens, your magnetism rises, and your capacity to create becomes unstoppable. That's not just how you protect your power—it's how you *amplify* it.

The Link Between Worth and Boundaries

Boundaries are not just about what you allow from others—they are a mirror reflecting what you believe about yourself. Every boundary you hold, stretch, or abandon reveals the internal story you carry about your worth. When your sense of worth is high, boundaries become non-negotiable. They're not a defense mechanism—they're a declaration: "I matter. My energy matters. My voice matters."

People with strong self-worth don't tolerate disrespect, not because they're rigid, but because they're rooted. They understand that saying no to what drains them is a yes to what grows them. When you're clear on your value, compromise doesn't feel like compassion—it feels like self-betrayal. You stop shrinking for validation and start expanding in truth.

Self-worth is shaped by experience, yes—but it's maintained through decision. You may have learned as a child that love was earned through compliance, or that your needs were too much. But at some point, healing becomes a choice. And that choice gets reinforced every time you honor a boundary instead of abandoning it to avoid discomfort.

There's a neurological connection between boundary setting and self-esteem. Studies have shown that individuals who consistently practice assertiveness—respectfully expressing their needs and limits—report higher levels of confidence and emotional regulation. It's because every time you uphold a boundary, your brain receives evidence: "I can trust myself." That trust is the foundation of real confidence.

When worth is low, boundaries feel threatening. You fear losing love, opportunity, or acceptance. So you say yes when you mean no. You stay silent when your truth is loud. You endure behavior that drains you just to maintain connection. But that connection is false—it's built on performance, not presence. And your soul feels the cost.

The moment you start believing that your needs aren't too much, everything changes. You no longer wait for others to validate your worth—you live from it. You stop asking for permission to take up space. You start protecting your peace, time, and truth as sacred. Because they are. And the more you protect them, the more magnetic you become.

Boundaries are the physical expression of internal alignment. When your energy is aligned with your worth, you don't need to explain your limits. They become a frequency. People feel them. And those who are in resonance with that frequency will honor it without resistance. Those who don't will fall away—and that's not loss, that's alignment doing its job.

Worth teaches you discernment. You stop saying yes to everything because you know not every opportunity is aligned. You stop engaging with chaos because you know peace is more profitable. You stop proving, pleasing, and performing because who you are is already enough. And boundaries become your sacred yes to that truth.

Your calendar, your inbox, your relationships—they all tell the story of your worth. Are they filled with urgency, obligation, and resentment? Or are they reflections of joy, alignment, and reciprocity? If not, boundaries are the path back—not to control others, but to reclaim yourself.

Healing your worth is a somatic process too. You don't just think your way into confidence—you embody it. Every time you say no with love, every time you express a need without guilt, every time you protect your peace over your popularity, you rewire your nervous system to feel safe in worthiness.

You don't raise your worth through hustle. You raise it through *honoring*. Honoring your energy. Honoring your voice. Honoring your values. When your actions reflect your worth, the world responds in kind. Not because you demanded more—but because you *embodied* more.

You teach the world how to treat you through the way you treat yourself. Boundaries are not barriers—they are invitations. Invitations for others to meet you at your level of self-respect. The higher that level rises, the more you attract what mirrors it. Not by force. By frequency. By choosing yourself without apology—and watching your life rise to meet you.

Loving Detachment vs. Disconnection

Loving detachment is not walking away—it's standing strong without clinging. It's the power to love fully without losing yourself. In contrast, disconnection is withdrawal rooted in pain, fear, or avoidance. Where detachment honors boundaries and self-respect, disconnection suppresses emotion and disconnects from both others and self. The key difference lies in energy: detachment keeps the heart open, while disconnection shuts it down.

Many people confuse detachment with coldness, but true detachment is warm, grounded, and deeply compassionate. It doesn't demand that someone change to earn your love. It allows space for growth without control. You're not stepping back out of resentment—you're stepping back out of clarity. Because trying to save someone who isn't ready is how you drown in their storm.

Psychologists describe emotional enmeshment as a lack of differentiation between two people—where one person's mood, decisions, and peace are dictated by the other's behavior. Loving detachment breaks this pattern. It's the decision to stop rescuing, fixing, or absorbing someone else's chaos. You can care deeply and still say, "This is not mine to carry."

Disconnection, on the other hand, stems from shutdown. It often follows unresolved trauma, betrayal, or years of emotional burnout. You stop responding, not out of peace—but out of numbness. The danger of disconnection is that it masquerades as peace, but it's really avoidance. It doesn't heal. It hardens. And what hardens can no longer receive.

In relationships, loving detachment sounds like, "I love you, and I trust your path—even when it's different from mine." It says, "I'm here, but I won't betray myself to be here." That energy creates safety and authenticity. People grow when they are loved without being controlled. And the space detachment creates often becomes the invitation for true connection.

Detachment restores sovereignty. It allows you to be fully present without being energetically entangled. You stop reacting and start observing. You stop over-explaining and start expressing. Your power returns because your peace is no longer dependent on someone else's decisions, moods, or growth pace. That's emotional freedom.

Neuroscience backs this up. The ability to self-regulate—calm your nervous system in moments of conflict—is linked to emotional intelligence and secure attachment. Loving detachment is a practice of this regulation. It says, "I can hold my center no matter how someone else chooses to move." And from that grounded place, you lead—not from fear—but from example.

Disconnection often masquerades as strength: silence, distance, coldness. But it leaves a residue of loneliness. You can feel it in the body—a tightening in the chest, a heaviness in the gut. Detachment, in contrast, feels like lightness. Not because you don't care, but because you're no longer trying to control what's beyond your reach.

You don't have to disconnect to protect yourself. You can remain connected to your own heart while setting clear boundaries with others. You can say, "This is my limit," with softness. You can release someone with love, not bitterness. Because loving detachment is rooted in trust—trust in your worth, in their journey, and in the greater timing of life.

When you practice loving detachment, you become magnetic. You're no longer chasing, fixing, or forcing. That energy is liberating—for you and for them. You model what it means to be whole, self-responsible, and aligned. And in doing so, you invite others to rise—not because they were pressured, but because they were inspired.

You can hold space without holding the weight. You can love without losing yourself. That is the essence of detachment. It's not the absence of emotion—it's the presence of boundaries. It's not about giving up—it's about letting go of control while keeping your heart open.

This is the shift: from rescuing to witnessing. From grasping to allowing. From fear-based attachment to soul-led freedom. When you embrace loving detachment, you're not stepping away from love—you're stepping deeper into it. Into a kind of love that honors *you* as much as it honors them. And that love, rooted in truth and trust, is unshakable.

Scripts for Saying No Powerfully

Saying no is not a rejection—it's a revelation of your values. Every no you speak with clarity is a yes to your peace, purpose, and priorities. But for many, saying no feels dangerous. It stirs guilt, fear, and anxiety because we were conditioned to associate "no" with confrontation or failure. The truth is, the inability to say no is the fastest path to burnout, resentment, and powerlessness.

Your voice is your boundary. And boundaries are most often tested through requests: invitations, demands, favors, expectations. How you respond sets the tone for how others engage with you. When your "no" is spoken with grounded authority—not apology or aggression—it recalibrates the energy of every interaction. You teach others how to treat you not just by what you allow, but by what you *decline*.

Clarity is kindness. A firm, respectful no doesn't bruise others—it honors them. It says, "I respect you enough to be honest." It allows others to trust your word, because they know you're not saying yes just to avoid discomfort. People may not like your no, but they will respect it if it's spoken from truth, not ego.

Powerful nos are anchored in self-awareness. They don't come from defensiveness—they come from alignment. Instead of over-explaining, a strong no sounds like: "I'm not available for that, but I appreciate you asking."

Or, "That doesn't work for me, but thank you for thinking of me." These aren't just scripts—they're signals of sovereignty.

The key to a powerful no is tone. Studies in communication psychology reveal that how something is said often carries more weight than what is said. A calm, firm tone signals emotional maturity. When you pair a grounded tone with brief clarity, you reduce the likelihood of pushback—because your energy already communicated that you're not uncertain.

Saying no to friends or family is often the hardest. But these are the moments where your growth deepens. You don't owe everyone access to every part of your time and energy. A simple, "I'm focusing on other commitments right now," or "That's not something I can support at this time," is enough. You are not responsible for how others feel about your truth—you are responsible for speaking it.

In the workplace, boundaries protect not just your time, but your creativity and sanity. Saying no to overwork, last-minute tasks, or energy-draining meetings doesn't make you unprofessional—it makes you clear. Phrases like, "I don't have the bandwidth for that right now," or "Let me check my capacity and get back to you," preserve respect without guilt.

Even social invitations can become boundary lessons. You don't have to attend every event, answer every call, or engage in every conversation. Saying, "I'm choosing rest right now," or "That's not aligned for me this weekend," is not selfish—it's self-sustaining. When you protect your energy, you show up more powerfully when you do say yes.

Every no reinforces your identity. It reminds you that your time is valuable. Your energy is sacred. Your priorities matter. And when others witness you standing in that truth, they either rise to meet your standards or exit your space. Either way, your alignment remains intact.

You can soften your language without softening your stance. Saying no doesn't require harshness. It requires honesty. "I'm honored you thought of me, but I'll have to pass." Or, "That doesn't feel right for me right now." These are boundary phrases that honor both you and them. Grace and truth can coexist.

Practicing your no in front of a mirror or writing it down builds muscle memory. The more you use it, the less shaky it feels. Over time, "no" stops feeling like rejection and starts feeling like *redirection*. Not away from others—but toward your higher self.

A powerful no is not the end of connection—it's the beginning of clarity. It invites authentic relationships built on truth, not tolerance. And when your no is anchored in self-respect, your yes becomes sacred. Because a yes from a person who honors their no is a yes you can *trust*. And trust is the foundation of everything.

Boundaries in Relationships, Work, and Self

Boundaries are not restrictions—they are the framework that supports your highest freedom. In relationships, at work, and within your own self-concept, boundaries act as sacred lines that protect your peace, sharpen your clarity, and amplify your power. Without boundaries, connection becomes confusion, productivity becomes pressure, and self-care becomes self-neglect. With boundaries, everything becomes *clearer*.

In relationships, boundaries are the invisible contracts that define respect. When they are healthy, love flows with more trust, more truth, and more authenticity. When they are absent, resentment builds in silence. The most loving relationships are not built on access to all of you at all times—they are built on mutual understanding of where each person ends and the other begins. That space between is not distance—it's where real intimacy lives.

Saying no in a relationship is not rejection—it's reflection. It says, "I care enough about this connection to be honest about my limits." Whether it's emotional boundaries like not absorbing someone else's moods, or time boundaries like protecting your solitude, you are not withholding love—you're refining how it is exchanged. And healthy love will always rise to meet that clarity.

In the workplace, boundaries determine whether you thrive or merely survive. Overextension is often praised in toxic environments, where "yes" is equated with value. But research shows that employees with clear boundaries are more productive, less stressed, and less likely to burn out. When you protect your work-life balance, your creativity increases, your confidence strengthens, and your leadership expands.

Boundaries at work also include the way you communicate. Setting expectations around your availability, asking for compensation aligned with your worth, and speaking up when tasks exceed your role are all ways you teach your environment how to value your time and talent. You are not just an employee—you are an *energy manager*, and your energy is currency.

Personal boundaries are the deepest layer. These are the boundaries you hold with yourself—what you tolerate in your own thinking, how you speak to yourself, what habits you maintain, and how you treat your physical body. If you constantly override your need for rest, silence, joy, or nourishment, you're not leading—you're leaking. These self-boundaries shape everything else.

When you honor boundaries within, you teach your nervous system that safety is not based on chaos or approval—it's built internally. This is how you heal from trauma patterns like people-pleasing, overworking, or emotional numbing. Boundaries bring you back into your body, your breath, and your truth. And from that place, power returns.

Many people fear that boundaries create separation. But in reality, they create *alignment*. When you show up clearly, you attract people, opportunities, and experiences that respect your clarity. You stop being a magnet for chaos, and you become a match for reciprocity. That's the shift from survival-based connection to soul-level communion.

Boundaries aren't just about others—they're a reflection of how deeply you've come to know and love yourself. They say, "This is what honors me. This is what doesn't." They turn your values into visible behavior. When your behavior mirrors your beliefs, confidence becomes inevitable. That's not arrogance—it's integrity.

You will be tested. Every new level of self-worth invites new boundary challenges. But every time you hold your line with love, you reinforce the truth that your needs are not negotiable for the sake of comfort. And the people, environments, and habits that don't align will fall away—not because you pushed them, but because your frequency no longer makes room for what drains you.

Boundaries are how you sustain your momentum. They're how you protect your expansion. Without them, even the greatest success becomes a burden. But with them, you don't just grow—you *glow*. Because nothing dims your light faster than saying yes when you mean no, and nothing expands your presence more than living in full alignment with your truth.

Your relationships thrive when they're rooted in respect. Your career excels when it's guided by clarity. Your self-trust deepens when your boundaries become promises you keep. So don't apologize for your lines—bless them. Don't fear being too much—fear shrinking into too little. Boundaries aren't the end of connection. They're the beginning of *real* ones. Ones that meet you where you *truly* are.

Releasing Guilt for Choosing Yourself

Choosing yourself isn't betrayal—it's alignment. Yet so many carry guilt like a shadow, believing that putting themselves first makes them selfish, unkind, or unloving. But guilt is not always a signal of wrongdoing—it's often the residue of outdated programming. When you've been conditioned to prioritize others to feel safe or worthy, choosing yourself can feel foreign, even wrong. But the truth is, your liberation begins the moment you stop apologizing for honoring your soul.

Guilt thrives in the gap between who you truly are and who you've been taught to be. If you were praised for being "easy," "helpful," or "selfless" at the expense of your truth, then self-abandonment became your strategy for love. But love built on sacrifice is not sustainable. And a life built on guilt will always shrink to fit the expectations of others. Choosing yourself is how you break that cycle—not by rejecting others, but by reclaiming *you*.

Your worth is not dependent on how much you give, how often you say yes, or how well you play small. Your worth is intrinsic, unshakable, and not earned through burnout. When you choose rest over productivity, silence over chaos, or clarity over people-pleasing, you are not taking anything from anyone—you are returning to yourself. And that return heals not just you, but everyone around you who is watching and learning what's possible.

Guilt is often tied to roles—mother, partner, employee, friend. Society wires us to believe that choosing ourselves means failing in these roles. But the truth is, you cannot give from an empty vessel. You cannot pour presence, patience, or purpose from depletion. When you choose yourself, you expand your capacity. You don't give less—you give *better*. With boundaries. With authenticity. With energy that is whole, not hollow.

Releasing guilt requires understanding that you're not rejecting love—you're redefining it. Love that demands self-erasure isn't love—it's control. True love celebrates your growth, your no, your evolution. If someone's connection to you depends on your compliance, that's not a relationship—it's a contract built on condition. And breaking that contract is not cruelty—it's courage.

Neuroscience confirms that guilt, when chronic and unresolved, activates the same neural circuits as physical pain. Your body feels guilt like injury. It creates inflammation, weakens immunity, and floods your system with cortisol. So this is not just emotional healing—it's biological restoration. Choosing yourself is not selfish—it's *self-preservation*.

Let go of the idea that you owe people your past self. Just because a version of you tolerated something doesn't mean the current you has to keep doing it. Growth is your birthright, and with growth comes change. Some people will celebrate it. Others won't. But your job is not to manage their comfort—it's to honor your truth.

You are allowed to disappoint others without being wrong. You are allowed to choose peace over performance. You are allowed to let go of expectations that never fit you to begin with. This isn't abandonment—it's arrival. Arrival in your power. In your voice. In your boundaries. Guilt will try to convince you otherwise—but guilt is not your guide. Your soul is.

When you stop living for applause and start living from alignment, the guilt begins to fade. Not because it disappears overnight, but because you no longer feed it with apology. Every time you choose yourself with love and firmness, you create a new neural pathway that says: *It's safe to honor me.* That's how you retrain your body to trust your worth.

Releasing guilt also invites grace. Grace for the version of you who didn't know better. Who stayed too long. Who said yes too often. Who kept peace at the cost of truth. That version of you was surviving. Now you're *thriving*. Forgive the survival strategies. Bless the journey. And choose again—from wholeness, not fear.

You are not responsible for managing other people's reactions to your self-respect. You are only responsible for staying loyal to the version of you that no longer seeks validation through sacrifice. You are not here to prove your worth by bleeding for everyone else's comfort. You are here to *become*—and becoming requires boundaries.

The moment you release guilt for choosing yourself is the moment you reclaim the energy you've scattered in the name of acceptance. That energy becomes clarity. Confidence. Creation. And from that space, you no longer chase love—you *embody* it. Because choosing yourself is not a detour from love. It's the doorway to the kind that finally includes you.

Protecting Energy from External Chaos

Protecting your energy is not avoidance—it's alignment. In a world overloaded with noise, drama, and distraction, your ability to preserve your inner clarity becomes your greatest asset. Chaos is everywhere: in news cycles designed to incite fear, in social media engineered to hook your attention, in conversations that spiral into complaints, gossip, and negativity. But chaos only enters where there is no boundary, no filter, and no conscious protection of your emotional, mental, and spiritual bandwidth.

You are not here to absorb every vibration in the room. You are here to *influence* the room with your presence. But you cannot do that if you are constantly letting your frequency be hijacked by what's happening outside of you. Protecting your energy is how you stay rooted in truth while the world sways in illusion. It's how you lead with intention instead of reacting from impulse. It's not selfish—it's essential.

Every time you wake up and immediately check your phone, you're handing your nervous system over to the external world. Studies from the University of Pennsylvania show that social media overstimulation increases anxiety, depression, and distractibility. This is not a minor leak—it's a full-on energetic drain. Protecting your energy starts with what you allow to enter your awareness in the first moments of the day. Start with breath, gratitude, or stillness—*not chaos*.

Boundaries are your energetic gatekeepers. You are allowed to say, "I'm not available for this conversation." You're allowed to leave group chats that drain you. You're allowed to take a social media detox, mute notifications, or set specific times to check email. Technology is a tool—but when you don't set limits, it becomes a trap that keeps your mind in a constant state of reaction.

Your environment affects your frequency. Clutter, noise, and disorganization all contribute to a scattered field. According to environmental psychology, a disordered space leads to increased cortisol levels and reduced cognitive performance. Clean, calm spaces nourish clarity. You don't have to live in a minimalist sanctuary—but the intentional design of your space can be a shield against chaos.

Protecting your energy also means being mindful of who has access to it. Some people don't just vent—they *transfer* their anxiety, fear, and scarcity mindset onto you. They call it "processing," but really, they're offloading. You can love people without being their dumping ground. You can support them without absorbing their emotional turbulence. Listening is powerful—but taking on what isn't yours is a betrayal of your boundaries.

Your body is your greatest feedback mechanism. When you leave a conversation and feel heavy, tight, or fatigued, pay attention. Your nervous system doesn't lie. If you consistently feel drained after interacting with certain people or spaces, it's a sign that your energy is not being protected. That doesn't mean blame—it means awareness. And with awareness comes the ability to choose differently.

What you consume is just as important as what you avoid. Uplifting content, soulful music, nature walks, nourishing foods, and deep conversations all strengthen your energetic field. When you surround yourself with beauty, truth, and inspiration, you fortify your internal world. This is not about toxic positivity—it's about intentional nourishment. Just like your body needs nutrients, your energy needs resonance.

Breathwork, meditation, and movement are not just "wellness trends"—they are recalibration tools. They anchor you in the now. They discharge the emotional static you pick up throughout the day. Neuroscience confirms that conscious breathing and mindfulness practices reduce amygdala activation and restore parasympathetic balance. In other words, these tools keep you from being hijacked by stress and reactivity.

Grounding rituals protect you from chaos by reminding you who you are. Morning declarations, journaling, or even a simple hand over heart while affirming, "I choose peace today," can shift your entire frequency. These aren't superstitions—they're signals. Signals that tell your subconscious: *we are safe, centered, and sovereign.*

When the world pulls at your attention, your job is to return to center. You can't always control what happens outside, but you can control what you internalize. Your inner world is your responsibility. Protecting it is not an act of isolation—it's an act of leadership. Because when you protect your energy, you show others what's possible. You become an anchor in the storm.

Chaos will always exist. But so will clarity. So will peace. So will truth. The question is: which one will you practice today? Which one will you guard like gold? Because your energy is sacred. Not everyone deserves access. Not everything deserves your reaction. Protecting your energy isn't about building walls—it's about building *wisdom*. And wisdom never wastes itself on what drains it. It invests in what *expands* it.

Repatterning Old Boundary Programs

Most people don't lack boundaries—they inherited boundary *programs* that taught them to survive, not to thrive. These programs were installed long before you were conscious of them. Maybe you were raised in a home where love was earned through performance. Maybe you learned that speaking up meant conflict. Or perhaps you saw adults who sacrificed themselves daily and called it noble. These early imprints became scripts. And until they're reprogrammed, they run silently in the background, dictating your limits, your voice, and your worth.

Repatterning begins with awareness. You must first see the script to rewrite it. Where do you default to "yes" when you mean "no"? Where do you over-explain to avoid judgment? Where do you abandon your truth for temporary peace? These aren't just habits—they're protective mechanisms built in childhood and reinforced by society. But just because something was programmed early doesn't mean it's permanent. Neuroplasticity proves your brain can rewire through intention and repetition.

The subconscious mind—the part of you responsible for over 90% of your behaviors—doesn't distinguish between truth and repetition. It believes what it hears most often, especially when emotion is attached. That's why old boundary programs feel so real—they were formed in emotionally charged environments. But that's also why new ones can be installed the same way: with consistency, clarity, and conviction.

The first shift is internal permission. You must give yourself full permission to matter. Not when everyone else is okay. Not when your to-do list is done. *Now.* Boundary strength is directly tied to self-worth. When you believe you deserve to be honored, your no stops sounding like rebellion and starts sounding like responsibility. Not responsibility to others—but to your own soul.

Repatterning also means examining the reward system. Every boundary you've broken in the past had a payoff—approval, connection, validation, temporary peace. To change the pattern, you must replace the old reward with a deeper one: inner peace, authenticity, sovereignty. When the new reward outweighs the old, the nervous system begins to release its grip on the outdated program.

This process isn't just mental—it's somatic. Your body remembers every time your boundaries were crossed. That memory lives in your posture, breath, and tone. You can't just think your way into new boundaries—you must *embody* them. Breathwork, movement, and voice activation are powerful tools. When you speak your truth with grounded breath and anchored presence, your entire system begins to trust that it's safe to stand tall.

You also need new language. Words shape worlds. Instead of "I'm sorry, I just can't," try "That doesn't work for me." Instead of "I feel bad saying no," try "I'm choosing to honor my capacity." These shifts may feel uncomfortable at first, but they create powerful new scripts. Over time, your voice becomes your anchor, not your apology.

Another key is healing the guilt loop. Guilt is the alarm bell of old programming. It flares up not because you're wrong—but because you're stepping outside of the familiar. When guilt arises after setting a boundary, don't silence it—examine it. Ask, "Whose voice is this? Whose rule am I breaking?" Often, it's not your truth—it's someone else's conditioning. And that's your cue to choose differently.

Community matters. When you surround yourself with people who respect your no, honor your time, and reflect your growth, your nervous system learns a new normal. You stop bracing for backlash and start expecting respect. This doesn't mean cutting everyone off—it means curating your environment to match your evolution.

Visualization is another rewiring tool. Picture yourself confidently holding a boundary. Imagine the conversation, your posture, your tone. Feel the emotion of self-respect. The brain doesn't know the difference between a vividly imagined scenario and reality. Every time you rehearse this mentally, you're installing a new program physically.

Celebrate every win. Every time you hold a boundary—even if your voice shakes—you're rewriting history. That moment becomes evidence that it's safe to be sovereign. And your subconscious thrives on evidence. The more you affirm, "I can honor myself and still be loved," the more true it becomes.

You're not just breaking patterns—you're building a legacy. A legacy where self-worth is the default, not the exception. Where truth is spoken without trembling. Where boundaries aren't defenses—they're declarations. And with every new choice, every new word, every new breath, you become the author of a program that no longer tolerates sacrifice as love. Instead, it chooses alignment. Every time. Without apology. With power.

Journal: Your Boundary Upgrade Plan

Upgrading your boundaries begins with upgrading your beliefs. You cannot set higher standards for others than you hold for yourself. Journaling isn't just reflection—it's recalibration. It gives you a sacred mirror to see where you've been, what you've accepted, and what you're no longer available for. This process turns your emotional clutter into clarity. Because what you name, you can shift. And what you write, you begin to own.

Begin by identifying the places where your energy leaks the most. Write about where you feel consistently drained, obligated, or resentful. These emotions aren't flaws—they're flags. They signal unmet needs and blurred lines. Often, the areas that frustrate you the most are the ones asking for a boundary you haven't yet voiced. Don't judge what you find—witness it with radical honesty.

Next, write out the stories you've inherited about boundaries. Did you learn that saying no is rude? That keeping others happy is your responsibility? That your value is tied to how much you give? These old scripts are not your truth—they're someone else's limitation. When you write them down, you separate the story from your identity. And that's where the breakthrough begins.

Map your current patterns. Where do you overextend? Who do you struggle to say no to? What types of situations cause your voice to shrink? This isn't about blame—it's about awareness. Awareness gives you choice. And when you can see the loop, you can exit it. Write with detail. The more specific you are, the easier it becomes to recognize the trigger in real time.

Now reimagine. Journal as the version of you who already honors their boundaries with grace and confidence. How does this version speak, walk, choose? What do they no longer tolerate? What do they now protect fiercely—time, energy, peace, creativity? Get vivid. Neuroscience shows that mental rehearsal activates the same neural pathways as real action. Writing it down is how you start rewiring.

Craft scripts. Write the exact sentences you'll use in high-stakes moments. Whether it's "That doesn't work for me," or "I need some time to think about it," or "I'm choosing to focus on my priorities right now," having your language ready makes boundary-setting feel less reactive and more empowered. You don't need to explain—clarity doesn't require justification. Practice your phrases until they become natural.

Document your wins. Every time you set a new boundary—no matter how small—write it down. Track how it felt, what the outcome was, and what you learned. This creates a personal blueprint for expansion. Success leaves clues. And your nervous system needs reminders that it's safe to stand tall. These entries will become evidence when doubt tries to creep back in.

Visualize your ideal boundaries across relationships, work, and self. Write what each area looks and feels like when it's healthy and whole. In your journal, clarity becomes strategy. Instead of vague intentions, you create emotional architecture. For instance, "I only take meetings during set hours," or "I don't respond to texts after 8 PM," or "I take time alone before saying yes to emotional labor." Turn ideas into action.

Affirm your worth. Use your journal to declare, daily if needed, "I am allowed to have needs. I am worthy of protection. I am safe to be seen, heard, and respected." Research in positive psychology shows that affirmation paired with action enhances confidence and decreases anxiety. This is not fluff—it's frequency. And frequency reshapes identity.

Use your journal to process guilt and fear. Write letters you'll never send to those who've crossed your lines. Let the truth spill out. This clears energetic residue and breaks trauma loops. Emotional suppression costs energy. Expression returns it. Your journal becomes the space where silence finds voice and wounds begin to mend.

Declare your new standards. Write out your boundary upgrade plan like a contract with your future self. Include what you're available for, what you're not, and what changes starting now. This is your energetic blueprint. A boundary is not a wall—it's a declaration. One that says, "I finally remember who I am. And from now on, I act like it."

Your journal isn't just a reflection tool—it's a manifestation device. Each entry is a signal to your subconscious and the universe that you're no longer playing small. That your peace, power, and purpose are non-negotiable. You're not just writing about boundaries—you're *becoming* someone who lives by them. And that shift changes everything. From the inside out. Permanently.

Now that you've begun unlocking the truth about your inner power, it's time to go beyond just reading about it—and actually *install it* at the subconscious level where all lasting transformation happens. The **Clarity Confidence Code Course** was built for that exact purpose. This isn't surface-level information. It's a proven, step-by-step system designed to reprogram your beliefs, recalibrate your self-image, and activate the version of you who creates results automatically. No more overthinking. No more hesitation. Just clarity, confidence, and momentum. If you've felt even a spark from what you've read so far, this course will ignite the full flame. Step into your next level now https://clarityconfidencecode.com

Let's continue this journey—and turn inner certainty into outer reality.

CHAPTER 9

FROM DOUBT TO CERTAINTY — REPROGRAMMING YOUR MIND FOR SUCCESS

The Root of Self-Doubt

Self-doubt doesn't begin in the mind—it begins in the body. It starts the moment your nervous system registers a signal that says, "It's not safe to be fully seen." That message gets encoded through early experiences—being criticized, ignored, compared, or punished for being too loud, too different, too sensitive, or too ambitious. These moments accumulate quietly and settle into your subconscious as a belief: "Maybe I'm not enough." And from that seed, self-doubt grows.

What most people call "self-doubt" is really a memory loop. The brain remembers past failures or pain and projects them onto future possibilities. It becomes less about what's real and more about what's *familiar*. Studies in cognitive neuroscience show that negative self-beliefs are often reinforced by the brain's default mode network, which thrives on repetition, not truth. That means self-doubt isn't fact—it's a practiced perspective.

Social conditioning deepens this pattern. From a young age, we're taught to seek approval, fit in, and follow rules that often require abandoning our uniqueness. School systems reward conformity. Media glorifies comparison. Family dynamics enforce silent contracts of "don't be too much." All of this trains your internal GPS to seek validation externally, which creates a dangerous dependency: you only feel worthy when you're approved of by others.

The problem is, external validation is never stable. It shifts with moods, opinions, and circumstances. And when your self-worth is tied to something that moves, confidence becomes conditional. You feel good when things go well and worthless when they don't. But real confidence comes from building an internal foundation—one that doesn't crumble every time someone misunderstands you, rejects you, or overlooks you.

The voice of self-doubt often sounds like your own, but it's not. It's a composite of every unhealed wound, every critical parent, every judgmental teacher, every friend who left, and every situation where your worth was questioned. The mistake isn't hearing that voice—the mistake is *believing* it. And belief is a choice. One that can be rewired with practice, evidence, and awareness.

To uproot self-doubt, you must first stop fighting it. Fighting makes it stronger because it keeps your focus on the fear. Instead, you observe it. Name it. Write down its patterns. Ask, "Whose voice is this really?" Often, you'll find that what feels like insecurity is actually a script someone else wrote. And you've just been rehearsing it too long.

One of the most powerful antidotes to self-doubt is action. Not perfection—*movement*. When you take aligned action, even in fear, you gather new data. You begin to prove to yourself that you are more capable than your doubts suggest. Neuroscientific research shows that each time you succeed at something you feared, the brain forms new neural pathways. Repetition of success becomes the blueprint for belief.

But action alone is not enough—it must be paired with compassion. Because you don't shame yourself out of self-doubt. You *heal* it through gentleness. Through asking, "What part of me still feels unsafe to be seen?" And then offering that part what it never had—safety, affirmation, and permission. Healing is the soil where confidence grows.

Surroundings matter. Environments that constantly reinforce your value, uplift your voice, and challenge your growth become mirrors that reflect your true capacity. But toxic spaces—where you're criticized, minimized, or consistently doubted—become echo chambers that reinforce old fear. You become like the people you spend time with, not because you copy them, but because energy is contagious.

Your body keeps the score. If you were silenced for expressing yourself, your throat may tighten before you speak. If you were rejected for being yourself, your stomach may twist in moments of vulnerability. These physical signals are not defects—they're indicators. And they can be rewired through breathwork, somatic practices, and nervous system regulation that teach your body it's finally safe to show up fully.

Affirmations work not because they sound good, but because they overwrite the mental grooves formed by doubt. When you say, "I trust myself. I am capable. I am worthy even when unproven," you're not lying—you're layering a new narrative over an old wound. With repetition and emotion, these words become muscle memory. And that memory becomes your momentum.

The root of self-doubt is never weakness—it's wounding. And your job is not to destroy it, but to transform it. To turn fear into fuel. Insecurity into inquiry. Doubt into data. Because every time you show up despite the tremble, you reclaim a piece of your power. Not by becoming someone new, but by remembering who you were before the world convinced you otherwise. And that remembrance—that return—is the beginning of unstoppable confidence.

Neural Pathways and Limiting Beliefs

Your beliefs aren't just thoughts—they are *structures* in your brain. They're etched into neural pathways, like grooves carved by years of repeated thought, emotion, and experience. When you believe something over and over—whether it's "I'm not good enough," "Success is hard," or "I always mess things up"—you're not just repeating a thought. You're reinforcing a *circuit*. And that circuit fires automatically until something interrupts it.

Neural pathways form through repetition and emotion. The more intense the emotion, the faster the pathway is formed. That's why trauma installs beliefs quickly and deeply—it's emotional intensity paired with survival focus. But the same mechanism can work in your favor. When you pair new empowering beliefs with emotion and repetition, the brain begins to lay down new tracks. Science calls this neuroplasticity: the brain's ability to rewire itself. You're not stuck with the wiring you inherited—you're the engineer now.

Limiting beliefs often masquerade as truth because they've been rehearsed for so long. "I'm just not that type of person," "That's not realistic," or "People like me don't succeed" feel like facts, not filters. But that's exactly what they are—filters. Every belief acts like a lens that distorts or directs what you notice, what you attract, and how you behave. If you believe opportunity is scarce, your brain will only highlight scarcity. If you believe you're capable, your brain will highlight possibility.

The reticular activating system (RAS), a network in your brainstem, is the reason you notice what you believe. It filters information based on what's important to you—usually defined by your beliefs. When you believe you're overlooked, your RAS will scan the environment to find proof. If you believe you're chosen, it will scan for evidence of favor. This is how beliefs shape your *reality*, not just your mindset.

Your subconscious mind—the part responsible for 95% of your behavior—doesn't argue with you. It accepts whatever you consistently feed it, especially when repeated with emotion. That means your inner critic isn't just being loud—it's being consistent. And the only way to override it is with *deliberate input*. Every affirmation, visualization, and decision that aligns with a new belief begins to weaken the old circuit.

Studies at Harvard and Stanford have shown that repeating positive self-statements activates the brain's reward systems and boosts self-regulation. But it's not just words that rewire the mind—it's embodied *evidence*. Every time you act in a way that contradicts a limiting belief, you destabilize that pathway. That means saying yes when fear says no, speaking up when doubt says stay quiet, and choosing expansion when comfort says retreat.

This is the science of transformation. Change doesn't happen by thinking differently once. It happens by thinking differently *until*. Until the new thought becomes a new habit. Until the new belief becomes the new default. Until the old voice fades not because you silenced it—but because you stopped *feeding* it.

Visualization plays a powerful role. When you mentally rehearse new outcomes—seeing, feeling, and believing them in vivid detail—the brain lights up as if the event is happening in real life. Olympic athletes have used this technique for decades, and neuroscience confirms that the same motor and sensory pathways are activated during visualization as during real performance. Your brain learns from *imagination*, not just reality.

But to shift beliefs at the deepest level, emotion must be involved. Emotion is the glue of memory. That's why breakthroughs happen in moments of deep gratitude, grief, or joy. When you *feel* the new belief in your body—when you weep with relief at the realization "I am not broken"—that's when the old circuitry begins to collapse. Emotion tells the brain: "This matters. Wire it in."

Your body will resist at first. Limiting beliefs are often paired with protective patterns. "Don't shine too brightly or you'll be attacked." "Don't ask for more or you'll be rejected." These beliefs once kept you safe. Now they keep you stuck. But when you thank them for trying to protect you—and then choose differently—you start to move from fear-based survival into soul-based expansion.

Changing your beliefs is not about delusion—it's about alignment. It's about choosing what's *useful*, not just what's familiar. Ask yourself: "Is this belief helping me become who I'm here to be?" If not, it's a lie. And you have the power to replace it. Not overnight, but over time. Through conscious practice. Through consistent input. Through soul-level *decisions*.

You are not your limiting beliefs—you are the awareness that can *recode* them. Your neural pathways are malleable. Your mind is moldable. Your future is programmable. And the more you fire a new belief, the more you wire a new identity. This isn't magic—it's biology. You're not just shifting your mindset. You're *reclaiming your power*. From the brain out. From the body up. From the soul first.

The Subconscious Mind Explained Simply

The subconscious mind is the operating system behind your life. It doesn't speak in logic—it speaks in patterns. While your conscious mind analyzes, judges, and filters, the subconscious accepts without question. It stores everything you've ever experienced, especially the emotionally charged moments that shaped who you believe you are. That's why you can read every self-help book in the world and still repeat the same cycles—because transformation happens not just in thought, but in *programming*.

Most people misunderstand the subconscious. They think it's passive, buried, or hard to reach. But in truth, it's active every second. It controls over 90% of your daily behavior—your habits, reactions, emotional responses, and even your posture. It's why you can drive a car without thinking about every movement. It's why you have a gut reaction before your mind can explain it. The subconscious is fast, reactive, and deeply loyal to the identity you've rehearsed the longest.

It operates through association, not reason. If you experienced rejection as a child after speaking up, your subconscious may now associate visibility with danger. Even if, logically, you know it's safe to be seen, your body will hesitate. You'll freeze before public speaking. You'll shrink in the presence of authority. That's not your mind failing—it's your subconscious *protecting* you based on outdated information.

Reprogramming the subconscious isn't about force—it's about frequency. The subconscious responds to repetition, emotion, and imagery. That's why affirmations work when they're paired with feeling and consistency. That's why visualization activates the same brain regions as real experience. And that's why trauma gets stored so deeply—because the emotional intensity burns the experience into your inner software.

The language of the subconscious is sensory. It remembers feelings, images, sounds, smells—anything vivid. This is why memories from decades ago can be triggered by a scent or a song. If you want to speak to your subconscious, stop trying to reason with it. Start *feeling* your new truth. Start imagining it in detail. Speak it aloud with conviction. Your subconscious doesn't respond to what's "true"—it responds to what's *repeated with belief.*

Children live primarily in a subconscious state until around age seven. During those years, their brains operate in theta waves—similar to a deep meditative or hypnotic state. That's when most core beliefs about love, money, safety, and worth are formed. If those beliefs weren't upgraded in adulthood, they're still running the show today. That's why you might be 40 years old, but still reacting like the 7-year-old who was scolded for wanting too much.

The subconscious is not your enemy—it's your ally. It's doing exactly what it was programmed to do: keep you safe, familiar, and consistent. But what was safe back then may now be sabotaging your growth. This is where awareness becomes power. When you realize your reactions are automated, you stop identifying with them. You stop saying "I am anxious," and start saying "A program of fear is running—but I get to choose differently."

One powerful tool to access and influence the subconscious is self-hypnosis or meditation. When your brain enters alpha or theta states—common during relaxed, focused awareness—you become more suggestible. That's the ideal time to plant new beliefs. Repeating, "I am safe. I am worthy. I am powerful," in this state embeds those beliefs where they can take root—beneath the surface, where real change begins.

Another key is emotional healing. The subconscious stores repressed emotions, not just thoughts. When you avoid grief, shame, or anger, you suppress the very energy that keeps the old programming intact. But when you feel it fully, without judgment, you release the charge. And without emotional fuel, the belief loses power. Emotional honesty is not weakness—it's transformation in action.

Dreams are also windows into your subconscious. They bypass your logical defenses and reveal what your inner mind is processing. Recurring dreams, symbols, or themes are messages—not random noise. Pay attention to what you're rehearsing in your sleep. It often mirrors what your soul is trying to resolve in waking life.

To reprogram your subconscious is to reclaim your reality. It means choosing your inputs with precision—what you watch, who you surround yourself with, what you speak, and how you move. Every input is an instruction. The music you play. The media you consume. The words you repeat. These are not trivial—they are code. And your subconscious is always listening.

You are not broken—you are programmed. And programs can be rewritten. Your job is not to fix yourself, but to *recode* yourself. With repetition. With vision. With emotional truth. The subconscious doesn't need perfection—it needs leadership. And the moment you decide to lead from your highest truth instead of your oldest wound, you stop surviving by default and start living by design. That's not wishful thinking—that's neurobiology in motion.

Tools for Subconscious Reprogramming

Reprogramming your subconscious is the difference between reacting from history and creating from destiny. The subconscious doesn't change through information alone—it changes through *tools that speak its language*: repetition, imagery, emotion, and ritual. Every limiting belief you hold was installed using these elements. So to shift them, you must reverse-engineer the process. Not by willpower alone, but by reconditioning your inner software with precision and practice.

One of the most accessible tools is affirmation, but not the hollow kind. For affirmations to work, they must be repeated with conviction, emotion, and alignment. Saying "I am confident" once with doubt in your voice won't shift anything. But declaring it with power, daily, in front of a mirror while breathing deeply sends a clear message to your subconscious: "This is our new truth." Studies in neuroplasticity confirm that when thoughts are repeated with strong emotional engagement, they begin to rewire the brain's neural architecture.

Visualization is another high-impact tool. Your brain doesn't distinguish between real and vividly imagined experiences. When Olympic athletes mentally rehearse winning races, their muscles activate as if they're actually competing. You can use this same principle to rehearse confidence, peace, abundance, and boundaries. Imagine the desired version of yourself—what you wear, how you move, how you speak—and *feel* it in your body. This primes your brain to act in alignment with that vision.

Hypnosis and guided meditation take reprogramming deeper. In relaxed states—alpha and theta brain waves—you become highly suggestible, and new beliefs can be installed more easily. Hypnosis bypasses the critical filter of the conscious mind and plants suggestions directly into the subconscious. Countless clinical trials have shown hypnosis is effective for changing habits, reducing anxiety, and overcoming self-sabotage.

Journaling, when done with emotional honesty, is a tool for both awareness and rewiring. Writing out your limiting beliefs, tracing them to their origin, and replacing them with intentional truth makes the abstract visible. Neuroscience confirms that expressive writing not only improves mental health but also enhances emotional regulation and cognitive clarity. It externalizes what's internal—and what you can see, you can change.

Breathwork is a somatic gateway to subconscious healing. Breath regulates your nervous system and releases emotional blocks stored in the body. Fast, intentional breathing patterns—such as those used in holotropic or transformational breathwork—can bring buried beliefs to the surface for release. The breath doesn't lie. It opens doors that thought alone cannot.

Subliminal audio is another powerful approach. When you listen to tracks embedded with positive affirmations below the threshold of conscious hearing, your subconscious absorbs them without resistance. Over time, this background programming begins to shift your internal dialogue. It's not magic—it's science. It's simply using repetition without the interference of conscious doubt.

Movement-based practices like dance, yoga, or even walking meditations allow the body to embody new energy. Emotion is stored in the body. When you move intentionally while anchoring affirmations or declarations, you integrate the new belief on a physical level. Embodiment turns theory into experience. It turns "I believe" into "I *am*."

Environment is also a tool—one of the most overlooked. Your surroundings reinforce your identity. Clutter, chaos, and toxic relationships all signal your subconscious that disorder is normal. On the other hand, organized spaces, uplifting environments, and aligned social circles signal safety, worth, and expansion. Every time you upgrade your environment, you send a message: "We're no longer living like we used to."

Language is a daily reprogramming device. The words you speak most often become your subconscious vocabulary. Replace "I'm trying" with "I'm choosing." Replace "I hope" with "I intend." Words shape perception, and perception shapes possibility. You're not just talking—you're *coding*.

Sleep is a window to subconscious recalibration. The final 20 minutes before sleep and the first 20 minutes upon waking are prime time for reprogramming. In these moments, your brain operates in alpha and theta waves. Use that space for affirmations, gratitude, visualization, or listening to empowering content. The last voice you hear before sleep should be the one building your future, not replaying your past.

You are not stuck—you are *conditioned*. And what's been conditioned can be reconditioned. These tools aren't temporary fixes—they are vehicles for permanent transformation. The subconscious is always listening. So make sure what it hears from you daily is intentional, empowering, and aligned with the life you were born to lead. When you become fluent in the language of the subconscious, you no longer react from old programming—you rise into your *true* potential. And that is the path to real, unshakable freedom.

Shifting Your Inner Dialogue

Your inner dialogue is the narrator of your life. It tells the story that shapes how you see yourself, how you show up, and what you believe is possible. And the most dangerous part? It often runs unnoticed, quietly feeding you thoughts that were never truly yours. The voice that says "You're not ready," "You always mess this up," or "They won't like you" is not a prophet—it's a *program*. One inherited, rehearsed, and repeated until it became your identity.

This inner voice was formed through years of experiences—some painful, some mundane, but all emotionally imprinted. It reflects the voices you heard most: parents, teachers, peers, and culture. If you heard encouragement, your inner dialogue likely mirrors belief. But if you heard criticism, comparison, or silence when you needed support, your mind internalized a voice of doubt and limitation. According to the National Science Foundation, humans average 60,000 thoughts per day—most of which are repetitive and negative. That means your inner dialogue is not only powerful, but persistent.

Shifting it starts with awareness. You cannot change what you cannot hear. Begin to notice your default tone. Is it supportive or cynical? Is it encouraging or condemning? Pay attention to how you talk to yourself in failure, in rest, in success. This self-talk is not harmless—it shapes your neural wiring. As Dr. Joe Dispenza often teaches, repeated thoughts combined with emotion create your personality—and your personality drives your personal reality.

Language is frequency. Every word you speak inside your mind carries energy. "I can't" drains power. "I choose to" returns it. "I'm terrible at this" builds neural proof of incompetence. "I'm learning this skill" reinforces growth. Shifting your inner dialogue doesn't mean lying to yourself—it means *leading* yourself with words that activate possibility instead of paralysis.

The subconscious mind doesn't know the difference between sarcasm and sincerity. When you say, "I'm so stupid," even jokingly, your subconscious listens without context. That repetition becomes wiring. That wiring becomes belief. And belief becomes behavior. It's not about becoming delusional—it's about becoming *deliberate*. Speak to yourself like someone you're responsible for elevating.

Affirmations are more than mantras—they are neural commands. But for them to work, they must feel believable and be repeated consistently. Saying "I am unstoppable" once won't override years of "I'm not enough." But repeating it, visualizing it, embodying it—especially in moments of emotional intensity—rewires the default. The more emotionally charged the affirmation, the more effectively it's coded into your subconscious.

Journaling is another tool to shift the inner dialogue. When you write out your limiting thoughts, you make the invisible visible. And once seen, you can question them. "Is this really true?" "Whose voice is this?" "What is a more empowering truth I can live from today?" Cognitive Behavioral Therapy (CBT) is rooted in this exact process: challenging automatic negative thoughts and replacing them with evidence-based alternatives.

Movement matters. The body speaks the language of the subconscious. When you move confidently—shoulders back, chest open, breath deep—you reinforce empowerment in your nervous system. That physical shift influences your thoughts. You don't wait for confidence to speak differently—you move like someone who already believes. And your inner dialogue begins to catch up.

Your environment reinforces your internal script. If you're surrounded by people who reflect negativity, drama, or doubt, your inner voice will struggle to find a new rhythm. But when you spend time with uplifting voices—books, mentors, communities, and even music—your internal soundtrack begins to shift. You don't just need new thoughts. You need new *inputs*.

Meditation creates space. It doesn't silence thoughts, but it creates distance between you and them. It teaches you to observe without attachment. In that space, you become the chooser—not the reactor. You start noticing which thoughts drain you and which thoughts expand you. From that place of observation, you can respond with intention instead of instinct.

Remember, your inner dialogue doesn't need to be perfect—it needs to be *patterned*. Patterned with compassion, with power, and with truth. You don't have to go from self-judgment to self-love overnight. You just need to interrupt the old script and begin writing a new one. Thought by thought. Word by word. Breath by breath.

Shifting your inner dialogue is not just mindset work—it's a spiritual commitment. A commitment to no longer using your voice against yourself. A decision to lead your thoughts instead of being led by them. When you reclaim your inner narrative, you don't just change how you feel—you change what becomes possible. Because the world will always echo what you say to yourself first. So speak greatness. Speak worth. Speak power. Until that voice becomes the only one that guides your steps.

Anchoring Belief Through Evidence

Belief without evidence often feels like fantasy. That's why anchoring your beliefs in *evidence* is the bridge between wishing and knowing. When you want to shift from insecurity to certainty, from hope to confidence, you must collect proof. Not the kind the world gives you—*the kind you give yourself*. Because the subconscious mind doesn't obey commands; it obeys *patterns*. And the pattern it trusts most is consistent proof that your new belief is true.

Every time you take action in alignment with your desired belief—no matter how small—you're gathering internal evidence. When you say, "I am capable," and then follow through on a commitment, you reinforce that belief in your body and brain. That micro-win becomes a data point. And the brain collects these points the way a courtroom builds a case. Eventually, the old belief collapses—not because you rejected it, but because it simply stopped holding up under the weight of new proof.

Neuroscience shows that the brain learns best through emotional experience. That means a single moment of courage—felt deeply—can rewire more than a thousand empty repetitions. When you say, "I am powerful," and then do something that used to scare you, your nervous system records that experience as fact. That's evidence. That's embodiment. You don't just *say* the belief—you *prove* it.

Most people try to change their beliefs from the top down—repeating mantras and affirmations without action. But belief is bottom-up. It starts in the body. It begins when your nervous system has an experience that contradicts the old programming. That experience can be as simple as speaking your truth in a conversation, setting a boundary without apology, or completing a task you've been avoiding. Each of those is a vote for the new identity you're stepping into.

Evidence doesn't have to be dramatic. It can be as quiet as consistency. Waking up and meditating. Writing your goals each day. Saying no when something doesn't align. These aren't small—they are foundational. The subconscious mind records them as reliability. And reliability builds self-trust. When you trust yourself, your belief system stabilizes. You stop needing outside permission to feel worthy or powerful. You've already *proven it* to yourself.

Tracking your wins creates a feedback loop of confidence. When you document your progress—whether in a journal, a voice memo, or a habit tracker—you give your subconscious something tangible to point to. Instead of defaulting to doubt, you remind it of the facts: "Here's what I've done. Here's who I've become." That's why elite athletes and high performers use performance logs. It's not ego—it's evidence. It's how champions stay grounded in the truth of their evolution.

The more senses involved in reinforcing belief, the stronger the neural encoding. Speak your wins aloud. Visualize them. Feel them in your body. Write them down. Celebrate them. Each layer reinforces the signal. This multisensory reinforcement builds what psychologists call "experiential belief"—the kind of belief that feels so real, it becomes your identity. And once something becomes identity, it's no longer effort—it's *natural*.

Don't wait until you "feel ready" to start collecting evidence. Readiness is a result, not a prerequisite. Most of the world waits for confidence to act. But confidence is built *through* action. Every step you take while scared tells your subconscious: "We're doing this now." And eventually, your internal system catches up. The fear fades. The voice changes. The belief settles.

Even setbacks are evidence—if you frame them correctly. Failure is proof that you had the courage to try. Every mistake teaches resilience. Every challenge reveals capacity. Reframing your losses as learning rewires your relationship with risk. Instead of fearing failure, you start mining it for gold. And that makes you unstoppable.

Anchored belief also requires intentional reflection. At the end of each week, ask: "What did I do this week that supports my vision?" Review your actions, your decisions, and your growth. This simple ritual reinforces the truth that you're evolving. That you're not the same person you were a month ago. That your results may be catching up—but your identity is already shifting.

When others doubt you, your evidence keeps you centered. You don't need their approval, because you've already built your own foundation. That doesn't mean arrogance—it means sovereignty. It means you're no longer outsourcing your worth. You've done the work. You've lived the proof. And belief rooted in evidence is unshakeable.

Belief is not magic. It's not a motivational high. It's muscle built through repetition, emotion, and real-world proof. And when your belief is anchored by daily evidence, your transformation becomes inevitable. You no longer hope for change—you *embody* it. Because the most powerful belief is not the one you repeat in your mind. It's the one your life reflects back to you, every single day. Through action. Through alignment. Through proof.

Daily Mental Conditioning

Your mind, like your body, needs daily conditioning to perform at its peak. Just as muscles weaken without use, your mindset defaults to old patterns when left untrained. Success, confidence, resilience, and peace are not accidental states—they are cultivated through consistent mental discipline. The most successful people in any field don't leave their mindset to chance. They *train it*. Every day. Without exception.

Mental conditioning is the art of priming your inner world before the outer world tries to program it for you. The moment you wake up, your brain enters a state of heightened suggestibility—operating in alpha and theta waves—making it the perfect time to feed it intentional thoughts. If you don't deliberately choose your thoughts, the world will hand you distractions, fear, and noise. But when you begin your day with intention, you shape your frequency before anyone else can.

One of the most effective practices is scripting. This involves writing your desired reality in the present tense, as if it's already happening. "I am a clear, confident leader." "I attract aligned opportunities with ease." When you write your goals as facts, you tell your subconscious: "This is who we are now." Neuroscience shows that this kind of self-directed writing increases the likelihood of behavioral change and goal achievement by strengthening the brain's belief pathways.

Gratitude is another cornerstone of mental conditioning. But not surface-level gratitude—*emotionalized gratitude*. When you close your eyes and deeply feel appreciation for what you already have, you shift your entire physiology. Your brain releases dopamine and serotonin, flooding your system with joy and stability. According to research from UC Davis, people who practice gratitude daily experience higher optimism, better sleep, and stronger immune systems. Gratitude isn't a soft skill—it's *mental armor*.

Declarations are verbal affirmations spoken aloud with emotional intensity. These aren't quiet hopes—they're *commands*. Speaking your truth out loud with certainty reprograms your neural pathways. When your ears hear your voice declare, "I create my reality," your subconscious listens. Your nervous system responds. Your identity starts to shift. Repetition turns into resonance. And resonance creates results.

Mental conditioning also involves *eliminating* mental toxins. This means reducing exposure to negative media, gossip, doubt-filled conversations, and toxic narratives. Just as you wouldn't feed your body garbage and expect energy, you can't feed your mind drama and expect clarity. Protect your inputs. Curate your mental environment as carefully as you would a sacred space—because it *is*.

Visualization is another powerful tool. When you vividly imagine your goals as already achieved, you activate the same neural networks that would fire if you were actually living them. This mental rehearsal creates emotional certainty before physical reality catches up. Athletes, CEOs, and creators alike use this technique because it works. The mind rehearses success, and the body follows suit.

Breathwork and meditation clear mental static and restore inner alignment. When you quiet the external noise and focus on your breath, you activate the parasympathetic nervous system, reducing cortisol and enhancing cognitive function. Even five minutes of deep breathing each morning can ground you in the present and increase your capacity to respond—not react—to life's challenges.

Your physical habits also influence your mental state. Movement is medicine for the mind. A 20-minute walk, stretch, or workout boosts endorphins, enhances brain function, and stabilizes mood. When you move your body, you move energy. You shake off old states and step into new ones. Mental conditioning isn't just mindset—it's full-body alignment.

Another key is *mental rehearsal of identity*. Don't just visualize outcomes—visualize *yourself* showing up as the version of you who lives those outcomes.

How do you stand? Speak? Choose? Dress? Decide? The brain responds to identity more than goals. When you become that version in your mind, you begin acting from it naturally. Identity precedes performance.

Evening reflection is the bookend to powerful mental conditioning. Before bed, review your wins. Acknowledge what went well. Release what didn't. Set intentions for tomorrow. This primes your subconscious overnight, allowing your mind to integrate lessons and solutions as you sleep. Research shows that focused intention before rest enhances memory consolidation and insight.

Daily mental conditioning isn't a luxury—it's a *requirement* for a conscious, intentional life. The world throws confusion, noise, and distraction at you every day. Without inner training, you'll be led by fear. But with daily conditioning, you become the architect of your state. The master of your focus. The driver of your destiny. Your life rises—or falls—on the strength of your daily mindset rituals. Build them like your future depends on it. Because it does.

Affirmations That Actually Work

Affirmations aren't just feel-good phrases—they are tools for rewiring the subconscious mind. But not all affirmations are created equal. Some bounce off the surface because they lack emotional resonance or contradict deeply rooted beliefs. Others sink in and begin to shift your inner landscape because they're spoken with conviction, repetition, and alignment. The difference lies not just in what you say, but how you *say it*, when you say it, and how much you *believe* it while saying it.

The subconscious mind doesn't respond to fluff. It responds to repetition paired with emotion. When an affirmation is repeated in a low emotional state, the impact is minimal. But when you speak it with intensity—eyes locked in the mirror, posture tall, voice unwavering—it becomes a command. Neuroscience confirms that when thoughts are paired with elevated emotional states, neural pathways form faster and stronger. That's how belief becomes biology.

Affirmations that work don't start with fantasy—they start with believability. If your subconscious instantly rejects "I am wildly successful" because it's too far from your current self-image, it creates resistance. Instead, use bridge affirmations that feel more true: "I am becoming more confident each day," or "I am learning to trust my voice." These statements signal progress, not perfection—and progress is something the brain can embrace.

Present-tense language is critical. Your subconscious operates in the now. Saying "I will be happy" keeps happiness always out of reach. Saying "I am feeling peace now" anchors that feeling in the present moment. This is why elite performers use affirmations like "I am focused," "I am resilient," and "I am capable," before walking into high-pressure environments. They're not waiting for permission—they're *programming* their reality in real time.

Pairing affirmations with visualization multiplies their power. When you say, "I am a confident speaker," close your eyes and *see* yourself commanding the room. Feel the energy of your voice. Hear the applause. Your brain can't distinguish between a real event and a vividly imagined one. When spoken and visualized consistently, affirmations train the body to experience the future as if it's already here.

Consistency beats intensity. Whispering your affirmations daily beats screaming them once a month. Repetition is how habits form. The more frequently your subconscious hears the new belief, the more normal it becomes. Over time, the voice of fear gets quieter, and the voice of truth gets louder—not because fear disappears, but because it no longer dominates the airwaves.

The environment matters. Your affirmations are more powerful when spoken in an empowered state—after exercise, meditation, or deep breathing. Your physiology amplifies your psychology. Standing in a power pose, breathing deeply, and speaking your affirmations aloud creates a full-body imprint. This is not just mental work—it's somatic anchoring.

Affirmations that work are also specific. "I am wealthy" is fine, but "I attract aligned, joyful financial opportunities with ease" gives the subconscious more direction. The more sensory and emotional detail you attach to the affirmation, the faster it sticks. Your brain loves clarity. When it knows what to look for, it filters out distractions and highlights supportive opportunities through the reticular activating system.

Another technique is using "I remember when..." affirmations. Saying "I remember when I used to feel stuck, and now I feel aligned and in flow," creates a subconscious bridge from old identity to new. This format is powerful because it allows your mind to accept the transition as already having occurred. It bypasses resistance and installs belief more easily than direct statements alone.

Writing your affirmations by hand deepens the impact. The physical act of writing engages more of the brain than typing or thinking. It signals commitment and imprints the statement more deeply into your subconscious. This is why journaling paired with spoken affirmations creates exponential shifts—each modality reinforces the other.

Track the evidence. Every time you live out an affirmation—when you speak up, follow through, or attract a new opportunity—write it down. These become your receipts, your proof. And with every documented win, your subconscious gathers the data it needs to accept the new belief as true. Confidence grows not just from repetition, but from *results*.

Affirmations that work are not about pretending—they're about *creating*. They are declarations of who you are becoming, backed by consistent thought, feeling, and action. You are not lying to yourself when you speak power into your life. You are *leading* yourself. You are choosing the voice that shapes your future. And when that voice becomes louder than doubt, nothing can stop the version of you that's been waiting to be activated. Speak it. Feel it. Become it. Daily. Relentlessly. Unapologetically.

The 3-Level Belief Shift

Belief doesn't shift all at once—it evolves through stages. Just as a seed grows into a tree, belief matures layer by layer. The first level is intellectual.

You *know* something is possible. You've heard the quotes. You've read the books. You've watched the videos. But knowing isn't owning. It's a spark, not a flame. At this stage, belief lives in your head, not your heart. It's theory, not embodiment. The danger here is mistaking inspiration for transformation.

The second level of belief is emotional. You don't just *know* the truth—you start to *feel* it. Something shifts inside. A lump rises in your throat when you speak your dream aloud. A fire ignites when you visualize your future self. Emotion gives belief power. Neuroscience shows that emotionally charged experiences create stronger neural pathways. When you begin to feel worthy, feel powerful, feel aligned, your subconscious starts to listen.

But the third level is behavioral. This is where belief becomes identity. It's no longer just a thought or a feeling—it's a choice you make daily. You speak differently. You walk with purpose. You set higher boundaries. You take bolder actions. And the world begins to reflect your shift. Real belief is not passive. It's not something you affirm once. It's something you *practice* until it becomes who you are without trying.

Too many people get stuck at the first level—gathering information but never applying it. They recite affirmations without aligning their energy. They visualize success but act from fear. This creates cognitive dissonance, where your mind and behavior contradict each other. And the subconscious doesn't follow contradiction. It follows congruence. You must bring all three levels—thought, feeling, and action—into harmony.

The power lies in *integration*. When your mind believes, your heart feels, and your body acts in alignment with your truth, you become unstoppable. This integration builds momentum. And momentum builds identity. You stop needing external validation because your very existence becomes the evidence. Your consistency becomes your credibility. And belief, once a fragile whisper, becomes a thunderous knowing.

To move from level one to level two, you must immerse yourself in new inputs. Surround yourself with stories, mentors, and environments that normalize your next level. Your brain learns by mirroring. When it sees what's possible repeatedly, the line between "them" and "me" begins to blur. That's when emotion enters. That's when desire awakens not from envy, but from *recognition*.

To move from level two to level three, action is non-negotiable. Even small, imperfect steps create proof. And proof dismantles doubt. Your nervous system learns that it's safe to expand. That you can show up, speak up, and still be okay. This is where self-trust is born—not from outcomes, but from alignment. The reward isn't just what you achieve—it's who you become in the process.

Belief must be lived to be real. You can't affirm abundance and continue operating in scarcity. You can't declare confidence while hiding your voice. The universe responds not to wishful thinking, but to embodied energy. When your actions back your words, you send a clear signal: "I believe. I'm ready. Let's go." And that signal attracts experiences that match your frequency.

This three-level framework is not just psychological—it's neurological. Studies in brain plasticity confirm that consistent action reinforces belief more effectively than passive repetition. When you pair intention with behavior, your brain rewires itself around a new identity. That's how people go from stuck to sovereign. From fear to freedom. Not overnight—but through layered embodiment.

You must also watch for sabotage at each level. At the intellectual stage, it's overthinking. At the emotional stage, it's fear of disappointment. At the behavioral stage, it's inconsistency. Awareness is key. When you know what stage you're in, you can support yourself properly. You stop judging the process and start trusting the progression.

The three-level belief shift is the roadmap to becoming who you were meant to be. It honors the truth that change is both internal and external. That what you think, feel, and do must align for the transformation to take root. It's not about perfection—it's about progression. Layer by layer. Brick by brick. Until you no longer chase belief. You *live* it.

Because belief that's lived becomes reality that's undeniable. It moves from being a hope to a habit. From an idea to an identity. From a wish to a *witnessed truth*. That's when your presence speaks louder than your words. That's when you walk into rooms and shift the energy. Not because you said the right thing—but because you *became* the right thing. Aligned. Anchored. Alive.

Tracking Your Confidence Wins

Confidence isn't something you either have or don't—it's something you *build*. Like a muscle, it strengthens through consistent training, daily repetition, and most importantly, acknowledgment of progress. One of the most powerful but overlooked tools for developing lasting self-confidence is tracking your wins. Not just the big, obvious victories—but the small, quiet moments where you chose growth over fear, truth over approval, and alignment over comfort. These wins are not just motivational—they're *evidence* that you're becoming who you were meant to be.

Your brain is wired to notice problems more than progress. It's a survival mechanism. Evolutionarily, scanning for danger kept us alive—but today, it often keeps us stuck. According to neuroscience research, the brain reacts more strongly to negative stimuli than positive ones, a phenomenon known as the "negativity bias." That's why your inner critic seems louder than your inner coach. But when you intentionally track your wins, you override that bias and begin to shift your default perspective from lack to abundance, from fear to capability.

Confidence is built on *reference points*. The subconscious mind doesn't follow motivation—it follows *evidence*. Every time you record a win, no matter how small, you create a reference that your mind can pull from the next time fear arises. When you're about to speak up in a meeting, launch a new project, or ask for what you're worth, your mind will whisper, "You've done this before. You've survived. You've succeeded."

Tracking your confidence wins creates momentum. Momentum isn't created by one massive leap—it's created by stringing together tiny, aligned actions over time. Saying "no" when you usually people-please. Holding eye contact instead of looking away. Publishing that blog post even when you felt nervous. These are all wins. And when you write them down, you honor the courage it took to override the old pattern.

There's also something neurologically powerful about *writing* your wins. Studies show that writing things down strengthens the memory trace and enhances cognitive processing. It makes the event more "real" in your nervous system. When you journal your wins at the end of each day, you're not just reflecting—you're reinforcing new identity patterns. You're telling your subconscious, "This is who we are now."

Wins tracked consistently become identity-shifting proof. Over time, you stop seeing yourself as someone who *wants* confidence and start seeing yourself as someone who *is* confident. This shift is crucial, because confidence doesn't come from outcomes—it comes from congruence. When your actions align with your highest self, confidence becomes the natural result.

Tracking also helps you detach confidence from external validation. Instead of waiting for applause, likes, or praise to feel good about yourself, you generate internal validation through self-awareness. You become your own witness. Your own coach. Your own evidence collector. And that kind of self-sourced confidence is *unshakable*.

You don't need to wait for perfect conditions or massive milestones to begin. Start where you are. Create a note in your phone. Keep a confidence journal on your nightstand. Every evening, ask: "Where did I show up today? Where did I stretch? Where did I stay in integrity with myself?" Even one sentence per day becomes a logbook of transformation over time.

Celebrate your wins, too. Celebration isn't arrogance—it's *activation*. When you celebrate a win, you release dopamine, the brain's reward chemical. This reinforces the behavior and increases the likelihood of repeating it. Celebration isn't just emotional—it's biological. It tells your brain: "Do this again." So dance, smile, breathe deeply, or speak a victory mantra every time you log a win.

Your wins are also a defense against impostor syndrome. When doubt creeps in and says, "Who do you think you are?"—you can flip through your own record of proof. These are your receipts. Your track record. Your truth. And no internal critic or external voice can argue with the facts of your own lived experience.

Confidence tracking creates a personal legacy. One day, you'll look back and see how far you've come—not because someone else validated you, but because you *documented* your own evolution. This practice becomes a time capsule of courage. A tangible reminder that you are capable, resilient, and growing in real time.

You are building something powerful with every tracked win. A mind that believes in itself. A nervous system that trusts you. A story that reflects your highest truth. Don't wait for confidence to find you. *Track it. Build it. Own it.* Let your own life become the most undeniable proof that you are rising—one courageous step at a time.

Certainty as an Identity

Certainty is not arrogance, and it's not the absence of doubt. It's an *identity*—a way of being that comes from deep alignment, repeated integrity, and lived experience. While confidence can fluctuate with emotions, certainty is stable. It's the internal knowing that says, "I trust myself no matter what happens." You don't wake up with this identity—you *build* it. Day by day. Decision by decision. Until it's no longer something you try on—it's simply who you are.

You don't become certain by waiting to feel ready. Readiness is a myth created by fear to keep you small. Certainty begins the moment you decide that your word is law. That you no longer break promises to yourself. That you're willing to be consistent even when it's inconvenient. Research from the University of Chicago confirms that self-discipline—not talent—is the number one predictor of success. And self-discipline, practiced daily, becomes certainty.

The nervous system plays a powerful role in anchoring identity. Certainty isn't just a thought—it's a *felt* state. It's how your body responds to challenges. Do you contract or expand? Panic or pause? When your body learns to stay steady under pressure, you embody certainty on a cellular level. Breathwork, posture, and daily somatic practices train your physiology to support your new identity—even when the world throws chaos your way.

Certainty thrives in clarity. You can't stand strong in your truth if you don't know what your truth is. That's why soul-based decision-making matters. When you know what you value, what you're building, and who you're becoming, you stop chasing every shiny object. You become *unshakable*. Not because you have all the answers, but because you've anchored into a vision bigger than your fear.

Doubt will always knock. But when certainty is your identity, you answer the door with discernment. You don't panic when things don't go as planned—you pivot. You don't crumble at criticism—you calibrate. This is the power of internal leadership. You no longer outsource your direction to external opinions or fleeting feelings. You've decided that *you* are the source. And that decision changes everything.

Certainty isn't loud. It's not about forcing your presence—it's about *embodying* it. You can walk into a room and shift the energy without saying a word, because your frequency speaks louder than performance. Identity is energy. When you fully believe in who you are, the world adjusts. People feel it. Opportunities align with it. Resistance begins to respect it.

Every time you follow through, you build certainty. Every time you trust your gut, honor your boundary, or act on your vision—you send a signal to your subconscious: "This is who we are now." These small acts of alignment are not insignificant—they're identity builders. Neuroscience confirms that behavior reinforces belief far more effectively than thought alone. You don't think your way into certainty—you *act* your way into it.

Your language must match your identity. Certainty doesn't say, "I'll try," "I hope," or "Maybe someday." It says, "I've decided." "It's done." "I'm already on the path." When your words align with your vision, your subconscious has no choice but to follow. Words are not just communication—they are creative tools. Every sentence you speak is either building your certainty or eroding it.

Certainty also comes from *evidence*. Track your wins. Document your progress. Collect your proof. This creates a foundation you can return to when the storms come. Because they *will* come. But a person rooted in identity doesn't get washed away—they get refined. Pressure reveals character. And if you've been consistent, what it reveals is gold.

Environment matters too. Spend time around people who *expect* you to show up as your highest self. Certainty is contagious. Being in rooms where boldness is normal rewires your baseline. What once felt like a stretch becomes your new standard. Your surroundings should remind you of who you're becoming—not who you've been.

Don't confuse perfection with certainty. They're not the same. You don't need to have it all figured out. You just need to stop abandoning yourself. To choose presence over panic. Faith over fear. Action over hesitation. You become certain when you realize that *you are the constant*. Regardless of what changes around you, your alignment doesn't waver.

Certainty as an identity is the most magnetic force you can carry. It's not taught in school. It's forged in fire. In decisions that defy your doubt. In showing up when it would be easier to hide. In leading yourself even when no one is watching. And when it becomes who you are—your life rises to meet it. Not because of luck. But because certainty always creates its own momentum. Always.

Exercise: Rewrite the Doubt Script

Doubt is not your enemy—it's a doorway. Every time it appears, it's pointing to a threshold you're meant to cross. But most people treat doubt like a stop sign instead of a signal. They let it dictate their pace, shrink their vision, and define their limits. What if, instead, doubt was your greatest coach? What if it revealed the very belief systems ready to be rewritten? The script you inherited doesn't have to be the one you perform. You can rewrite it. You *must* rewrite it if you want to live free.

The doubt script is sneaky because it sounds like logic. It says, "Be realistic." "Don't get your hopes up." "Who do you think you are?" It uses the language of safety to justify staying small. But safety isn't always sacred. Sometimes it's just familiar pain. And familiar pain feels safer than unfamiliar power. To change the script, you have to challenge the voice that says you're not enough. Not with force—but with *truth*.

The first step is to identify the exact words your doubt uses. What phrases play on repeat when you try to stretch, speak, or start something new? Write them down, word for word. Don't sanitize them. Get raw. Let the voice speak. This isn't about giving it power—it's about *unmasking* it. Because when you shine light on subconscious patterns, they start to lose their grip.

Now, separate from the doubt. Recognize it as a pattern, not a prophecy. It's not *you*—it's a program. And programs can be rewritten. This is the moment where emotional detachment becomes a tool for power. You are not broken. You are not your fear. You are the *observer* of your mind, and the author of your new story. That single shift in perspective opens the door to liberation.

Begin rewriting each phrase with power. If the doubt says, "You're not qualified," your rewrite might say, "Every step I take qualifies me more." If it whispers, "They'll judge you," rewrite it as, "Their opinion is not my permission." These new affirmations aren't fluff—they're *counter-scripts* grounded in courage. You are training your brain to expect something different, and expectation is the foundation of manifestation.

Say these new scripts aloud. Your voice is a transmitter. When you speak your truth, your body begins to believe it. The vibration of your words hits your nervous system before your logic kicks in. That's why spoken affirmations carry more weight than silent thoughts. You're not just thinking different—you're *embodying* different.

The next layer is to visualize acting from your new script. Close your eyes. See yourself in the situation where doubt used to rule. But this time, respond from power. Watch yourself speak boldly, move with confidence, hold your standard. Your brain cannot distinguish imagined success from real success—it codes both as experience. And experience rewires belief.

Track evidence of your new script in action. Each time you override fear with truth, write it down. "Today I said yes to the opportunity even though I was nervous." "Today I asked for what I deserved." These wins are data points for your subconscious. Over time, the evidence piles up, and the doubt script gets weaker—not because it disappears, but because your belief gets louder.

Your body will test you. You might feel shaky. Your voice might tremble. That's okay. Doubt lives in the nervous system as much as in the mind. Breathwork, grounding, and movement are tools to anchor the new identity. You can't logic your way out of fear—you have to *feel* your way into safety. This is why embodiment work is essential to script rewiring.

Be aware of who reinforces your old script. Environments are mirrors. If the people around you constantly doubt your dreams or feed your fears, you must either set boundaries or upgrade your circle. Your new script deserves a stage where it can thrive. Surround yourself with voices that echo your power, not your past.

There will be days you forget. Days when the old script creeps back in and feels loud again. That's not failure—it's feedback. Use it as a reminder to return to the truth. To reread your declarations. To breathe. To remember that rewiring isn't a one-time event—it's a daily practice. A devotion. A revolution in motion.

You are not here to live someone else's narrative. You are here to write your own. Line by line. Decision by decision. Until the old story fades like a shadow at sunrise. You don't silence doubt by denying it. You silence it by *drowning it in truth*. And when your new script becomes the loudest voice in the room, that's when the world will rise to meet you—not because you never doubted, but because you chose to believe anyway.

You've just taken in powerful truths—truths most people will never hear, let alone apply. But awareness alone doesn't create results. Integration does. And that's exactly what the **Clarity Confidence Code Course** is designed to do. It's not just more information—it's a complete identity upgrade. The course gives you the exact step-by-step formula to reprogram your subconscious, dissolve hidden resistance, and lock in the habits, mindset, and emotional frequency of someone who moves through life with unstoppable clarity and magnetic confidence. If you're ready to stop dabbling and finally step into the version of yourself that *wins automatically*, then it's time. Step into the full experience now at https://clarityconfidencecode.com

Because the next chapter isn't about what you know—it's about who you *become*. Let's go.

CHAPTER 10

ACTIVATED ACTION — TURNING CLARITY INTO ALIGNED RESULTS

Action vs. Overthinking

Overthinking is the silent killer of dreams. It's dressed up as preparation, caution, logic—but it's often just fear in disguise. Action, on the other hand, is what builds momentum. Action is clarity in motion. While overthinking spins in circles trying to find the perfect path, action carves the path with imperfect steps. The difference isn't intelligence—it's courage. Courage to start without knowing every detail. Courage to fail forward. Courage to trust that progress comes from motion, not from mental gymnastics.

Your brain is designed to keep you safe, not successful. The prefrontal cortex weighs risks, searches for patterns, and tries to avoid failure. It's a great tool—but when unchecked, it becomes a prison. The longer you stay in thought without action, the more your brain fills the gap with fear-based predictions. Studies from the University of Michigan show that chronic overthinking leads to increased anxiety, insomnia, and reduced decision-making ability. In short: thinking more doesn't lead to better results. Doing does.

The moment you start doing, the fear shrinks. Action engages your nervous system in a new way. It sends a signal that says, "We're not frozen—we're leading." Even small actions—sending the email, making the call, writing the outline—shift you from powerlessness to momentum. Momentum is a confidence generator. Each small win rewires your brain with proof that you can move forward, even in uncertainty.

People think they need confidence before they act, but confidence is built *through* action. It's a byproduct, not a prerequisite. You don't become a speaker by thinking about speaking—you speak. You don't become a writer by analyzing sentences in your mind—you write. The more you act, the more your identity changes. Action teaches your mind that you are someone who moves, not just someone who waits.

Overthinking often masquerades as intelligence. It convinces you that more data is better, that waiting means wisdom. But decision paralysis isn't wisdom—it's avoidance. Analysis paralysis keeps you trapped in the illusion of productivity while secretly stealing your time and self-trust. The fastest way to break the cycle is to *decide*. Even a "wrong" decision teaches more than endless hesitation ever will.

Your body keeps the score. When you stay in overthinking mode, your body contracts. Shoulders hunch, breath shortens, energy stagnates. When you act, your physiology shifts. Energy rises. Posture straightens. Dopamine kicks in, reinforcing the behavior. Neuroscientific studies confirm that taking initiative—even on small tasks—triggers the brain's reward circuits, making future action easier. The key isn't waiting for motivation. It's moving first and letting the motivation catch up.

There's no such thing as perfect timing. Waiting for the stars to align is often just fear pretending to be strategy. Life rewards movement. The opportunities that shape your life don't always come with a guarantee. They come when you're *in motion*. That's why successful people don't always know more—they *do* more. They test, refine, iterate. Clarity comes from creation, not contemplation.

The enemy of overthinking is experimentation. Treat life like a lab. Run the test. Make the offer. Launch the idea. Stop tying your worth to outcomes and start tying it to your *willingness to try*. Every experiment gives you feedback. Every feedback loop sharpens your intuition. That's how you become wise—not through more time in your head, but through more *engagement* with reality.

One of the most powerful ways to bypass overthinking is to set micro-deadlines. Give yourself 20 minutes to write the first draft, not the whole book. Commit to one sales call today, not the entire campaign. Create a 24-hour goal, not a 12-month plan. Small, fast wins break inertia and prove that momentum is always within reach. Speed doesn't mean rushing—it means *reducing resistance*.

Environment also matters. Surround yourself with action-takers, not overanalyzers. Energy is contagious. If the people around you spend their lives planning but never building, you'll subconsciously mirror that frequency. But if your environment celebrates movement, courage, and iteration, you'll find yourself acting before fear has time to negotiate.

Train yourself to default to action. When faced with a fork in the road, choose forward. When the doubt says "wait," choose "go." Create a new identity: one that chooses movement over mastery, progress over perfection, faith over fear. You'll stumble, sure—but you'll also learn, grow, and evolve faster than you ever imagined. Because life doesn't reward those who know the most. It rewards those who *move* the most.

Overthinking creates distance between you and your potential. Action collapses that distance. It makes you magnetic, powerful, present. Your dreams don't need more thought—they need more *traction*. You already have what it takes. The next step isn't in your mind—it's in your *movement*. So step. Speak. Build. Begin. Your breakthrough doesn't live in your thoughts. It lives on the other side of your next bold action.

The Motivation Myth

The world has been sold a lie—that motivation is the spark for greatness. That you must feel inspired before you act. That some magical surge of energy will suddenly lift you out of your chair and make everything easy. But the truth is this: motivation is not the cause of action—it's the result. It follows momentum. It rises after discipline. Waiting for motivation is like waiting for the sun to rise before you turn on the light. You have power right now, and it's called choice.

People who achieve great things aren't always "motivated." They're consistent. They show up when it's inconvenient. They act while others wait to feel ready. Studies from behavioral science show that habits—not emotion—drive most human behavior. Motivation is fleeting. Habits, however, are reliable. The secret isn't to wait for inspiration; it's to build routines that bypass the need for it. Routine becomes ritual. And ritual becomes identity.

Motivation, as sold in highlight reels and social media snippets, is often based on external hype. But sustainable drive doesn't come from YouTube clips or temporary highs—it comes from *purpose*. When you're connected to a deeper reason—something that matters to your soul—action becomes sacred. You move not because you feel like it, but because you refuse to betray your calling.

The myth of motivation keeps people stuck in cycles of guilt. They ask, "Why don't I feel motivated?" as if something is wrong with them. But nothing is wrong. The brain is wired for comfort. It's designed to conserve energy. What looks like laziness is often just biology. But you're not here to be ruled by your biology—you're here to *master* it. And mastery starts with understanding the difference between desire and discipline.

Waiting for motivation often masks fear. "I'll start when I feel ready" usually means "I'm afraid to fail." But fear doesn't go away before you act—it gets *disproved* by action. That's the paradox: the thing you're waiting for only comes *after* you move. As Mel Robbins teaches in her "5 Second Rule," if you don't act within five seconds of having an instinct to move, your mind will kill the idea. Action must become automatic. Relentless. Non-negotiable.

Real momentum begins with the smallest possible step. Not the whole project. Not the 5-year vision. Just the *next* movement. When you shrink the task to something manageable, you reduce resistance. And once you start, motivation begins to build like a fire catching wind. Every completed task releases dopamine, reinforcing the behavior and giving you a sense of progress. That chemical reward is more effective than any pep talk.

The myth of motivation also ignores the role of environment. You can't expect consistent drive in a space filled with chaos, distraction, or negativity. Your surroundings either support or sabotage your energy. Clean your space. Curate your inputs. Create a cue-rich environment where focus is the default. Make success easier than sabotage. Your external world must align with the internal identity you're building.

Your physiology affects your psychology. Motion creates emotion. When you move your body, your mind follows. That's why a workout shifts your state faster than a motivational speech. The body leads the brain. If you want more energy, breathe deeply, stretch, dance, walk, run—*move*. Change your posture, and you'll change your perspective.

Accountability is another antidote to the motivation myth. When you declare your goals publicly or to a trusted group, your likelihood of following through increases dramatically. Studies show that accountability partners increase goal achievement rates by up to 95%. Why? Because when you have something on the line, you move. When someone's watching, you rise. Not from pressure—but from *integrity*.

You can also borrow motivation from your future self. Close your eyes and imagine the version of you who's already done the work. What do they look like? How do they speak? What decisions did they make when you were at this very moment of hesitation? That version exists because of the choice you make *today*. Motivation becomes irrelevant when *identity* becomes your compass.

There will be days when you don't feel it. Days when everything inside you says, "Not today." And those are the most important days to act. Because those are the days that separate the committed from the casual. You don't need to feel like a champion to train like one. You don't need to feel worthy to choose powerfully. You just need to decide—again and again—that your vision matters more than your mood.

So forget motivation. Build a system. Set a standard. Honor your word. Move your body. Choose your environment. Take the smallest step. Not once in a while—but daily. Relentlessly. And when the world sees your results, they'll call you "motivated." But you'll know the truth. You were *disciplined*. You were *aligned*. You were *unstoppable*. Not because you felt like it—but because you chose it. That's real power. That's freedom. That's how legacies are made.

How to Build Flow into Your Day

Flow is not just a mystical state reserved for athletes, artists, or peak performers—it's a replicable, biological condition you can *engineer* into your daily life. It's the sweet spot where your mind, body, and spirit align in such harmony that time seems to disappear, self-doubt fades, and results become effortless. You don't stumble into flow by chance; you cultivate it by design. When you master the art of creating flow, your days stop draining you and start *elevating* you.

To experience flow, your tasks must sit right at the edge of your comfort zone—not too easy, not too hard. Researchers call this the "challenge-skills balance." When you engage in activities slightly beyond your current skill level, your brain produces dopamine, sharpening focus and increasing motivation. That's why tasks that stretch you just enough pull you into deep engagement.

If you're too comfortable, you get bored. If you're overwhelmed, you shut down. But when you hit the edge—that's when flow begins.

The most successful people in the world don't hope to get into flow—they *structure* their day around it. They create uninterrupted blocks of time to dive deep without distraction. Your brain takes 20–30 minutes to fully enter flow, but a single notification can snap you out in seconds. That's why setting boundaries with your phone, email, and interruptions is not a luxury—it's a necessity. Flow demands your full presence, and presence begins with *protection*.

Rituals act as doorways into flow. Morning routines, breathwork, music, movement—all these anchor the body and signal the brain: "It's time to focus." Whether it's lighting a candle, sipping a specific tea, or putting on noise-canceling headphones, these triggers create neural associations. Your mind begins to anticipate the state of deep work, just as a sprinter prepares for the gunshot. Rituals train your nervous system to enter flow faster and stay longer.

One of the most overlooked flow accelerators is *clear goals*. Your brain thrives on direction. When you start your day with vague intentions like "get stuff done," your energy scatters. But when you define *exactly* what success looks like—write 1,000 words, complete three outreach emails, finish client onboarding—your brain locks in. Specificity ignites clarity, and clarity fuels flow.

Minimize cognitive switching. Every time you jump from task to task—especially from a creative task to a reactive one—you burn mental fuel. Studies from the American Psychological Association show that multitasking can reduce productivity by up to 40%. To build flow into your day, batch similar tasks together. Create blocks for creative work, admin work, and meetings. Don't let your energy bleed out in constant transition.

Your physical state affects your flow capacity. Dehydration, poor nutrition, lack of movement—all of these dull the mind and disrupt focus. But when your body is energized—when you've had quality sleep, clean fuel, and even light movement—your brain becomes a fertile ground for creativity and momentum. The best ideas don't come from pressure—they come from *readiness*.

Flow is amplified by feedback. Whether you're editing your writing in real time, adjusting your pitch based on audience reaction, or tracking performance metrics—getting immediate feedback keeps you engaged. It creates a loop that tells the brain, "We're making progress." That's why video games are so addictive—they give you instant results. Your workday can do the same if you build in systems that show you your wins.

Don't underestimate the role of emotion. Positive emotions—like curiosity, excitement, gratitude—open the gates to flow. When you approach your day with joy instead of dread, your creative pathways light up. When you appreciate the opportunity to *create* instead of *grind*, your productivity multiplies. Flow doesn't come from stress. It comes from *state*. So tend to your emotional state like a sacred ritual.

Nature is one of the greatest flow activators. A short walk outdoors, even just 15 minutes, resets your nervous system and boosts cognitive function. Sunlight, greenery, and movement all reduce cortisol while increasing serotonin and endorphins. If you want to hit a second wave of flow later in the day, step outside. Breathe. Reset. Then return with clarity and power.

End your day with a "flow review." Ask yourself: When did I feel most engaged? What sparked energy? What drained it? This reflection not only helps you replicate what worked—it also signals to your subconscious, "We're committed to mastery." Flow isn't just a performance tool. It's a lifestyle. It's a rhythm. And reviewing your day with intention keeps that rhythm aligned.

You were never meant to hustle through life in chaos and depletion. You were built for flow—for days filled with purpose, energy, and meaningful creation. Flow isn't a gift for the few. It's the *birthright* of the intentional. Build it into your day with devotion, and watch your productivity rise, your fulfillment deepen, and your impact multiply. Because when you live in flow, success is no longer a struggle—it's *inevitable*.

Creating Aligned To-Do Systems

Most people don't lack time—they lack alignment. They fill their to-do lists with tasks that keep them busy but not effective, productive but not fulfilled. An aligned to-do system doesn't just track what needs to get done—it *prioritizes* what actually matters. It's not about doing more. It's about doing what moves the needle in your purpose, your mission, and your joy. When your daily actions align with your higher vision, you become unstoppable.

Alignment begins with clarity. Before writing down any tasks, ask yourself: "What outcome am I committed to?" Clarity is a filter. It helps you decide what deserves your attention and what's just noise. A 2021 study in the *Journal of Applied Psychology* revealed that goal clarity leads to greater motivation, persistence, and performance. When your to-do list is built around your *outcomes*, not your overwhelm, you move from reaction to intention.

An aligned to-do system differentiates between *urgent* and *important*. Urgency screams. Importance whispers. The most meaningful work rarely shouts for your attention, but it changes everything when prioritized. That's why so many people end the day exhausted but unfulfilled—they answered emails, ran errands, stayed "on top of things," but never touched what actually builds their legacy. Stop letting the loudest task win. Let your vision decide.

Break your tasks into three categories: strategic, supportive, and draining. Strategic tasks move your mission forward. Supportive tasks maintain your life systems. Draining tasks can often be delegated, delayed, or deleted. When your day starts with strategic work—instead of chores or admin—you claim your power first. You train your mind to focus on *building*, not just maintaining. The result? Compounded momentum and clarity.

Energy mapping is another layer of alignment. Not all hours are created equal. Track when you feel most alert, creative, and decisive. Then place your most critical tasks in those windows. Don't schedule deep work when you're low-energy and reactive. Protect your peak state like sacred ground. This isn't about being rigid. It's about being *efficient with your genius*. Energy-aligned work delivers exponential results with less burnout.

Use visual planning tools that speak to your brain's natural processing style. For some, a digital app like Notion or ClickUp helps organize everything into dashboards and priorities. For others, pen and paper create deeper commitment. What matters most is that your system doesn't overwhelm—it *focuses*. When your system feels like a prison, you'll rebel. When it feels like a launchpad, you'll thrive.

Batching and theming your days is a powerful tactic for mental clarity. Assign certain days or blocks to specific types of work—creation, calls, admin, learning. This reduces decision fatigue and cognitive switching, which studies show can reduce efficiency by up to 40%. Batching turns chaos into rhythm. It gives each task a home, so it doesn't live rent-free in your head all week.

Include non-negotiables that fuel your well-being. Your to-do list isn't just about what you *produce*—it should also reflect how you *sustain*. Include movement, stillness, hydration, connection, and rest as intentional checkboxes. When you treat your body and soul like essential projects, they respond with energy, creativity, and resilience. You are the asset—protect it accordingly.

Don't confuse motion with progress. It's easy to chase dopamine hits from checking off tasks, even if they're irrelevant. True alignment means sometimes doing less, but better. Ask yourself: "If I only got *three things* done today, what would make the biggest impact?" That question cuts through the fog and makes excellence inevitable. When you lead with impact, the rest rearranges around your purpose.

Review and refine regularly. Alignment isn't a one-time event—it's a living process. Weekly reviews help you reflect on what worked, what drained you, and where you drifted from intention. This review is not judgment—it's *optimization*. Each cycle makes you sharper, more focused, more tuned to your soul's compass. Your to-do system becomes a mirror of your values, not just a list of obligations.

Celebrate completion with presence. Most people skip from task to task without acknowledgment. But your brain needs closure to encode success. When you finish something meaningful, pause. Breathe. Smile. Give thanks.

That moment of gratitude locks in confidence and reinforces the behavior loop. You're not just checking boxes—you're becoming someone new.

An aligned to-do system is a spiritual practice. It's not about control—it's about *creation*. It's how you declare, each day, who you are and what you stand for. When your calendar reflects your highest values, when your tasks echo your purpose, when your systems serve your soul—you stop managing time and start *shaping destiny*. That's when productivity becomes power. And that's when your life starts matching your mission.

Balancing Intuition and Structure

Success isn't born from chaos, and it doesn't thrive in rigidity. It lives in the sacred space where structure supports freedom and intuition guides movement. Too much structure, and you suffocate your soul. Too much spontaneity, and you scatter your power. The art of balancing intuition and structure is what allows the most aligned, fulfilled, and powerful lives to unfold—not by accident, but by design.

Structure is the soil. It's what grounds your vision and gives your gifts a place to grow. Without it, ideas stay ideas. Discipline creates the container for your genius to flourish. In fact, research from the American Psychological Association has shown that structured routines reduce decision fatigue, increase productivity, and improve emotional regulation. But the structure isn't meant to restrict you—it's meant to *serve* you.

Intuition, on the other hand, is the light. It's the inner compass that whispers when logic is too loud. It doesn't shout; it nudges. You *feel* it in your body long before your brain has the data to catch up. Neuroscience confirms that intuition often operates through the subconscious, which processes millions of bits of information the conscious mind can't access. Honoring it isn't mystical—it's strategic.

The key is knowing when to lean on each. Use structure to anchor your priorities and energy. Use intuition to choose the *how*, the *when*, and sometimes, the *if*. Let structure outline the map, and let intuition decide the route. The most visionary creators, CEOs, and leaders don't live by rigid checklists. They build systems—but stay flexible inside them.

Too much structure can become a cage. You become a machine—productive but disconnected. That's when burnout creeps in. That's when joy dries up. That's when life becomes a checklist instead of a creation. On the other hand, relying only on intuition without commitment can leave you aimless—floating through ideas, dabbling without depth, inspired but unrooted. The dance between both is what makes the difference.

Start your day with structured intention—but leave space for guidance. Define your top priorities, your non-negotiables, your strategic moves. But also ask, "Where am I being led today?" Listen. Adjust. Book-correct. Some of the greatest opportunities you'll ever receive won't show up on your to-do list—they'll come as a whisper. Make room for that whisper.

Intuition thrives in stillness. If your life is full of noise, notifications, and nonstop motion, you won't hear it. That's why silence isn't just spiritual—it's practical. Even five minutes of deep breathing or solitude can tune your frequency back to alignment. In that stillness, you'll know when to push and when to pause. When to say yes and when to walk away.

Structure is your masculine energy—directive, focused, organizing. Intuition is your feminine energy—receptive, fluid, responsive. Every powerful being knows how to embody both. You lead with discipline but stay open to downloads. You plan with precision but remain soft enough to pivot. This is not about balance in the traditional sense—it's about *integration*.

Let your intuition inform the creation of your structure. If a system drains you, redesign it. If a schedule feels constrictive, reimagine it. Ask yourself regularly, "Does this way of working still serve who I am becoming?" When structure evolves with your growth, it stops being a trap and starts being a launchpad. Your systems should never outgrow your soul.

Flow happens when structure supports the state of ease. You don't get into flow by accident—you set the stage. Block the time. Minimize distraction. But once you're in that space, let intuition *run the show*. The more often you enter this state, the more effortless high performance becomes. Flow is the result of disciplined preparation meeting surrendered execution.

Create rituals that marry both worlds. Morning routines that ground you in clarity but leave space for intention. Weekly planning that sets priorities but invites reflection. Movement, music, journaling—these aren't "woo-woo" add-ons. They're bridges between logic and spirit. They are how you remember that productivity without soul is just survival. But productivity with soul? That's *sovereignty*.

You were not designed to hustle like a robot or float like a leaf. You were designed to co-create with the Divine through systems that honor your essence. When you let intuition and structure dance together, life stops being a grind and becomes a masterpiece. You stop forcing. You start *flowing*. And the results aren't just better—they're *miraculous*. Because they come from a deeper power than hustle. They come from alignment. And alignment always wins.

Eliminating Procrastination at the Root

Procrastination isn't laziness—it's self-protection. It's your nervous system trying to keep you safe from perceived danger, not your character failing. At the root of every delay, avoidance, or excuse is a story your mind is telling you: "You're not ready." "You might fail." "It has to be perfect." These aren't flaws. They're defense mechanisms built on outdated beliefs that no longer serve you. But once you expose them, you reclaim your power to act.

At its core, procrastination is a *state*, not a personality trait. It's a symptom of disconnection between your vision and your self-worth. When you forget why something matters—or doubt your ability to rise to the challenge—your brain activates survival mode. It shuts down your prefrontal cortex (responsible for planning and decision-making) and lights up your limbic system (which seeks comfort and safety). That's why you scroll, snack, or binge content instead of taking action.

To eliminate procrastination at the root, you must first remove shame from the conversation. Shame perpetuates paralysis. It tells you, "You should be better than this," which only deepens resistance. Psychology research from the University of Carleton has shown that self-compassion—not guilt—is the most effective antidote to chronic procrastination. Kindness creates spaciousness. And spaciousness creates momentum.

The next step is to get curious. Ask yourself, "What am I protecting myself from?" Often, you'll find the fear isn't about the task itself—it's about what the task *represents*. Fear of being seen. Fear of not being enough. Fear of success and the pressure it brings. When you name the fear, you shrink its control. Awareness breaks the cycle. Because what the subconscious avoids in the shadows, the conscious mind can transform in the light.

You must also redefine your relationship to discomfort. Procrastinators often chase the feeling of "readiness" like a finish line that never comes. But the truth is, readiness is a *myth*. Action creates readiness, not the other way around. The body follows the cue of behavior. When you begin, even clumsily, your system starts to shift from fear to focus. Research from Columbia University shows that taking even tiny steps toward a goal activates the brain's reward circuitry and builds confidence.

Breaking a task into micro-movements is a powerful tool. Instead of writing the entire proposal, just open the document. Instead of building the whole business plan, write the first sentence. The brain registers completion, no matter how small, and releases dopamine. That momentum becomes addictive. Progress begets progress. You don't need massive willpower—you need a *starting ritual*.

Procrastination thrives in vagueness. When your to-do list says "work on presentation," your brain doesn't know where to start. But if it says "draft outline for slide 1," your brain receives clear direction. Specificity kills resistance. Decision fatigue disappears when every action is well-defined. This is how elite performers move fast: they remove ambiguity from their workflow and replace it with clarity.

Environment plays a massive role in eliminating procrastination. You become what you're around. If your space is cluttered, distracting, or uninspiring, your focus suffers. But when you create an environment that cues productivity—clear desk, intentional lighting, music that triggers flow—you shift your default behavior. According to behavioral design expert BJ Fogg, "Design beats discipline." Structure beats willpower.

Your identity also fuels or destroys procrastination. If you see yourself as "someone who always puts things off," your subconscious will find ways to stay congruent with that belief. But when you begin to affirm and act from a new identity—"I'm someone who follows through"—your behavior changes to match. Identity is destiny. And the fastest way to change your identity is to act like the person you want to become, *before* you feel like them.

Energy matters. If you're running on fumes, your mind will resist tasks that require creative or emotional bandwidth. Prioritize sleep, hydration, nutrition, and movement—not as luxury, but as leadership. Your brain can't operate in excellence when your body is in depletion. Fueling your body is fueling your follow-through.

Celebrate completion. Most procrastinators skip this. But your brain needs reward to reinforce behavior. When you finish a task, even a small one, anchor it with celebration. Smile. Acknowledge the win. Speak life over the action you just took. That tells your subconscious: "This is who we are now." It codes the action as successful and increases the likelihood you'll repeat it.

Eliminating procrastination isn't about fixing yourself—it's about *freeing* yourself. From shame. From fear. From old patterns that were meant to protect you but now only keep you small. You don't need more pressure. You need more alignment. More compassion. More clarity. Because when your actions match your highest self, procrastination has nowhere to live. And what's left is momentum, power, and purpose—finally unleashed.

Action from Soul vs. Ego

Ego-driven action often looks impressive from the outside—loud, strategic, calculated—but it lacks true fulfillment. It seeks applause, validation, and significance. It's reactive, fueled by comparison and the illusion of control. Soul-driven action, on the other hand, is rooted in purpose. It's quieter but more potent. It's not about proving your worth; it's about expressing your truth. When you act from your soul, your energy uplifts instead of drains. Your path expands instead of exhausts.

The ego is obsessed with the outcome. It needs results to justify the effort. But the soul moves for the sake of alignment. It asks, "Is this true for me?" not "Will this make me look good?" Ego uses force; soul uses flow. Ego chases performance; soul seeks embodiment. Studies on intrinsic motivation have shown that when actions are aligned with internal values instead of external rewards, long-term fulfillment and persistence skyrocket.

Acting from the soul feels like coming home. It doesn't mean you never feel fear or doubt—it means your decisions aren't dictated by them. The soul invites discomfort because it knows growth is on the other side. It's willing to risk rejection to stay in integrity. This is why soul-aligned choices often look illogical on paper but make perfect sense in your body. Your nervous system relaxes when your truth leads.

Ego-driven goals often come from societal programming. Be successful. Be admired. Be the best. But many who achieve those goals still feel empty. That's because they were chasing an identity that wasn't theirs. Soul goals, in contrast, are quieter—but they feel expansive. They honor your unique path, your deep desires, your authentic rhythm. And ironically, when you align with your soul, the success the ego craved often follows as a *byproduct*.

The ego fears stillness, because in stillness it loses control. But the soul *requires* stillness. It speaks in whispers. It won't compete with the noise of the world or the pressure of productivity. That's why meditation, solitude, and breathwork are essential—not just for calm, but for *clarity*. Studies show that even brief periods of mindfulness reduce reactivity and increase heart-brain coherence, giving the soul space to lead.

You'll know the difference by how your body responds. Ego-driven action feels tight, pressured, performative. Soul-led action feels grounded, open, alive. Your breath deepens. Your heart expands. The more you tune into these sensations, the more accurately you can discern your true compass. Your body was built to guide you—it just needs to be heard.

Soul-driven action honors timing. The ego is impatient. It wants it now, or never. The soul knows that some seasons are for planting, some for waiting, some for harvest. This is not laziness—it's wisdom. Studies in behavioral economics show that long-term thinkers outperform impulsive actors in almost every domain. Soul-aligned action trusts divine timing without surrendering responsibility.

Ego often acts from fear of lack. It says, "If I don't do this, I'll fall behind." The soul acts from trust in abundance. It says, "What's mine can't miss me." That mindset doesn't make you passive—it makes you powerful. When you trust the unfolding, you stop grasping. And when you stop grasping, your energy becomes magnetic. You attract rather than chase.

Soul-based action doesn't mean avoiding strategy or structure. It means letting your spirit inform the strategy. Letting your truth guide your plans. When your calendar reflects your purpose—not just your pressure—you stop burning out and start burning bright. The soul doesn't resist discipline—it refines it.

In relationships, ego acts to be liked. It people-pleases, performs, and postures. The soul speaks truth with love. It sets boundaries. It honors authenticity over approval. This shift transforms how you show up—not just in what you *do*, but in who you *become*. Soul alignment doesn't just change your results—it transforms your identity.

Ego compares; soul connects. When you act from ego, you see others as competition. When you act from soul, you see others as mirrors. Their success reminds you of what's possible—not what you're lacking. This shift dissolves jealousy and activates collaboration. You rise together, not apart. And that collective rise creates quantum growth, both individually and collectively.

The most powerful lives are built from the soul up. Not to impress—but to *impact*. Not to win—but to *wake up*. Action from the soul is sustainable, meaningful, and magnetic. It won't always make sense—but it will always make *truth*. And truth is the highest frequency you can move from. Because when your actions echo your soul, the universe has no choice but to respond. Fully. Boldly. Beautifully.

Soulful Productivity Tools

Productivity isn't just about getting more done—it's about getting the *right* things done in the right energy. Soulful productivity isn't driven by pressure, guilt, or hustle. It's anchored in presence, alignment, and purpose. When your to-do list reflects your highest values—not just your urgent demands—you move through your day with more peace, clarity, and impact. It's not just about efficiency. It's about *embodiment*.

The first tool of soulful productivity is intentional planning. Begin each week not with a massive list of obligations, but with a sacred pause. Ask: "What do I want to *feel* this week?" and "What outcomes will support my soul and mission?" When you prioritize from the heart, your calendar becomes a reflection of your truth—not a prison of external expectations. Studies show that people who plan with intention outperform those who react to tasks as they come, and they experience lower stress levels in the process.

Time-blocking is powerful when infused with soul. Instead of cramming tasks into every available minute, block spacious, focused segments for deep work, rest, and creativity. Protect your mornings for sacred routines and vision-aligned actions. Group similar tasks together to reduce cognitive switching and maintain emotional presence. Research has shown that multitasking significantly reduces IQ and performance; batching keeps you grounded and sharp.

Journaling is more than a mental health tool—it's a productivity compass. A few minutes each morning and evening to reflect, release, and recalibrate creates emotional clarity. It helps you identify what's draining your energy, what's aligning with your values, and what deserves your highest focus. The act of writing builds self-awareness, which is the foundation of conscious productivity. Your journal becomes your feedback loop.

Energy tracking is essential for sustainable output. Instead of forcing a rigid schedule, learn your natural rhythm. When are you most alert, creative, grounded? Build your work around your peak energy—not society's 9-to-5 model. Tools like chronotype assessments and mood journals can help you find your optimal flow windows. Working with your energy, not against it, reduces burnout and magnifies output.

Digital boundaries are non-negotiable. You cannot do soulful work in a distracted environment. Tools like website blockers, focus timers, and notification managers are sacred in this age of noise. Studies from Harvard and UC Irvine reveal it takes 23 minutes to refocus after a single interruption. That's why intentional disconnection is a revolutionary act of power. Protect your flow like it's a treasure—because it is.

The soul needs ritual. Build sacred rituals into your workday to activate presence. This can be lighting a candle before you create, a short breathwork session before calls, or a gratitude list after major tasks. These rituals aren't fluff—they're neural anchors. They train your body and brain to associate work with joy, meaning, and embodiment. Over time, these cues automate flow and make consistency feel *natural*.

Visualization is a multiplier. Before major tasks or meetings, close your eyes and see yourself moving with calm confidence and clarity. Feel the energy of the desired outcome already realized. Neuroscience shows that visualizing success activates the same brain areas as *experiencing* it. This primes your system for peak performance and helps reduce subconscious resistance.

Tracking progress soulfully means celebrating the *feeling* behind the milestone—not just the checkbox. Instead of only measuring how many emails were sent or tasks completed, ask: "Did I honor my truth?" "Did I express my voice?" "Did I protect my peace?" When you track alignment alongside output, you cultivate deeper trust with yourself. And trust is the bedrock of authentic productivity.

Tech tools can support your soul—if used wisely. Platforms like Notion, Asana, or Todoist can help organize your vision when used with intention. But the tool is never the source—it's the *servant*. Avoid falling into the trap of planning your purpose more than *living* it. Let the tech support your intuition, not override it. The most powerful app is still your inner guidance system.

Accountability with depth makes all the difference. Having an aligned accountability partner or coach who asks not just "Did you do it?" but "Did it feel true?" shifts the entire dynamic. It adds consciousness to your commitments and ensures your results are coming from love, not pressure. This is the difference between burnout and breakthrough. Surround yourself with people who hold your highest self—not your productivity addiction.

Soulful productivity is a way of life. It says your worth isn't in your output, your value isn't in your pace, and your power isn't in your performance. It's in your *presence*. It's in the love you infuse into what you do. It's in the courage to slow down enough to align with something bigger than your to-do list. When you lead with soul, every task becomes sacred. Every moment becomes a miracle. And productivity becomes a path to your purpose—not a detour from it.

Habits of High-Clarity Creators

High-clarity creators don't just produce—they *transmit*. Their work carries frequency. It cuts through the noise, not because it's louder, but because it's *truer*. Their clarity doesn't come from luck or talent. It comes from daily devotion. From rituals that sharpen vision and strip away distraction. Clarity isn't an accident. It's an identity. And behind every extraordinary creator is a set of invisible habits that anchor that identity in action.

The first habit is radical presence. High-clarity creators aren't scattered. They're here. Fully. They show up to the blank page, the canvas, the camera, or the call with *undivided* energy. They've trained themselves to resist multitasking and instead cultivate single-task immersion. Science backs them up: research from Stanford University shows that multitasking reduces both the efficiency and quality of output. Focus is not just a mental skill—it's a competitive advantage.

Clarity requires solitude. Not isolation—but intentional stillness. Time to think, feel, and hear your own inner voice above the world's noise. The best creators regularly step away to reflect, unplug, and reconnect with their core vision. It's in silence that you meet your deepest truths. It's in stillness that your next-level ideas download. You don't find clarity by doing more—you find it by *listening* more.

High-clarity creators guard their input. They don't binge endless content or drown in social comparison. They curate what they consume—books, mentors, media—like sacred fuel. They know that what enters their mind shapes their message. A 2022 study from the University of Pennsylvania found that digital content overload significantly reduces cognitive clarity and emotional resilience. Consumption without consciousness clouds creation.

They also simplify their systems. High-clarity creators don't need 17 apps and 50 strategies to stay productive. They design elegant, repeatable workflows that reduce decision fatigue and increase momentum. Whether it's a morning ritual, a weekly planning practice, or a creative batching system, they build structures that support *flow*. Not rigidity—rhythm. Not pressure—precision.

Another habit is emotional honesty. These creators don't hide from their feelings—they use them. Anger becomes insight. Grief becomes depth. Joy becomes spark. Their clarity comes from inner congruence. They tell the truth—even when it's messy. Because clarity is birthed in authenticity, not perfection. And when you speak from your realness, your audience *feels* it before they understand it.

They choose alignment over approval. That means saying no to opportunities that look good but feel off. It means holding their ground when others doubt their direction. Clarity demands courage. When you know what you stand for, not everyone will clap. But high-clarity creators aren't here to please—they're here to *provoke*. Not to offend, but to awaken. And awakening always disrupts the status quo.

Daily reflection is non-negotiable. Whether through journaling, meditation, or walk-and-talks with themselves, they track the inner terrain. They ask: "What's working?" "What's draining me?" "What truth am I avoiding?" This habit of self-inquiry keeps their work aligned and their message sharp. Reflection turns experience into wisdom. Without it, your actions become noise instead of signal.

They also move their bodies. High-clarity creators understand that stagnation in the body creates stagnation in the mind. Movement—whether it's yoga, walking, or strength training—flushes mental fog and reactivates purpose. According to Harvard Medical School, regular physical movement increases brain-derived neurotrophic factor (BDNF), which enhances focus, memory, and mental clarity. The body isn't a distraction from your genius—it's a gateway to it.

One of their most underappreciated habits? *Pausing*. Before reacting. Before answering. Before launching. They pause to feel. To check in. To ensure the next move is coming from soul, not ego. In a world addicted to speed, the pause is revolutionary. It prevents regret. It protects integrity. And it amplifies the power behind every decision they make.

High-clarity creators build from vision, not urgency. They aren't whipped around by the tyranny of the immediate. They know how to zoom out, see the big picture, and reverse engineer their daily actions. They lead with intention. They ask not "What should I do today?" but "What would my highest self *create* today?" From that place, everything changes. The work becomes art. The tasks become sacred. The output becomes legacy.

At the core of all these habits is one truth: clarity is a choice. It's a muscle. It's built through repetition, reflection, and devotion. When you choose clarity over chaos, truth over trends, soul over noise—you rise. Not just in productivity, but in *power*. Your message sharpens. Your mission ignites. And the world doesn't just watch—you *wake it up*. Because clarity doesn't compete. It commands. It leads. It liberates. And when you live from that frequency, you don't just create—you *transform*.

Consistency Without Burnout

Consistency is the engine of greatness, but too many people misunderstand it. They confuse consistency with grind, hustle, and exhaustion. They think being consistent means pushing through pain, ignoring the body, and sacrificing joy. But true consistency doesn't deplete—it *sustains*. It aligns with your energy, honors your rhythm, and builds momentum that compounds. The secret isn't doing more. It's doing what matters, steadily, without breaking yourself in the process.

Burnout isn't the result of working too hard. It's the result of working out of *alignment* for too long. It happens when you ignore your needs, suppress your truth, and run your life on adrenaline instead of purpose. Research from the World Health Organization defines burnout as a syndrome stemming from chronic workplace stress that has not been successfully managed. But this stress isn't always external—it often comes from internal pressure to be everything, to everyone, at all times.

High achievers often wear exhaustion like a badge. But fatigue isn't a trophy. It's a warning light. True consistency doesn't mean showing up at 100% every day—it means showing up at the level you *can*, every day, with integrity. It means understanding your capacity and honoring it. That's why self-awareness is a non-negotiable trait of sustainable high performers. Without it, consistency becomes self-destruction.

The nervous system plays a crucial role. When you're constantly operating in fight-or-flight, your body can't rest, repair, or restore. You may be taking action, but it's coming from tension, not alignment. And tension is not sustainable. Breathwork, nervous system regulation, and intentional rest aren't luxuries—they're tools for *longevity*. Studies confirm that regulated breathing patterns significantly reduce cortisol and increase resilience under stress. This isn't soft. This is strategy.

Rituals create consistency that flows. They remove decision fatigue and anchor you in presence. Morning routines, pre-task grounding practices, and weekly reflection rituals help you enter your work in a conscious state. When your day starts with intention, everything else flows more smoothly. You stop reacting to life and start *leading* it. Your rituals become your roots—steady, supportive, and sacred.

Another key to sustainable consistency is margin. Most people cram their schedules with tasks and wonder why they're always exhausted. But creativity and clarity need space to breathe. High performers build in white space—gaps between meetings, unstructured time for reflection, even entire days of recovery. That space isn't empty. It's *productive* in a different way. It allows integration, inspiration, and recovery to occur.

Boundaries are the guardrails of consistency. Without them, your energy leaks. You say yes to things that drain you and wonder why you can't stay focused. But when you protect your time, energy, and priorities, your efforts become concentrated and potent. You get more done with less effort. That's not luck—it's leadership. Protecting your power is not selfish. It's essential if you want to serve at your highest level.

Tracking progress builds emotional momentum. When you see your small wins stacking up, you stop needing external validation. Your motivation becomes *internal*. Neuroscience shows that the brain thrives on progress. Every micro-win triggers a dopamine release, reinforcing the behavior. That's why celebrating your follow-through—even if it wasn't perfect—is crucial. Progress over perfection is how consistency becomes a lifestyle.

Self-compassion is the fuel that keeps consistency alive. You will miss days. You will fall short. That's not failure—it's feedback. The question isn't "Did I mess up?" The question is "Will I return?" High performers aren't the ones who never slip. They're the ones who *bounce back* quickly because they don't shame themselves into paralysis. They realign. They recalibrate. They recommit.

Alignment is the compass that prevents burnout. When your actions are connected to your values, your energy replenishes itself. Purpose is the most sustainable fuel source on earth. When you're clear on why you're doing what you're doing, you tap into a deeper well of energy that hustle can never match. You're no longer chasing—you're *embodying*. And that's the kind of consistency that transforms lives.

Rest is a strategy, not a sign of weakness. It's during rest that integration happens. Muscles don't grow in the gym—they grow in recovery. Your mind is the same. When you pause, you allow wisdom to settle. You allow vision to deepen. You allow energy to renew. High performers who understand this use rest as a weapon. They're not working less—they're working *smarter*, from overflow rather than depletion.

Consistency without burnout isn't a myth. It's a mastery. It requires awareness, alignment, boundaries, and belief. It asks you to redefine success—not by how much you do, but by how *true* you stay to your path. The most powerful rhythm isn't relentless hustle—it's sacred devotion. Show up. Honor your truth. Protect your energy. And let your consistency become a reflection of your *wholeness*, not your exhaustion. That's how you build legacies that last.

Real-Time Action Calibration

Real-time action calibration is the secret weapon of the most aligned, fulfilled, and effective people in the world. It's not about charging forward blindly—it's about staying tuned to feedback as you move. Too many people think success is about setting a plan and never deviating. But true power comes from the ability to pivot, refine, and respond to life in the *moment*. When your internal GPS is turned on, you don't need to control everything—you just need to stay *connected*.

This level of responsiveness requires presence. You can't calibrate if you're distracted. You can't hear the whisper of intuition if your mind is consumed with fear, doubt, or noise. Presence is the foundation of accurate action. Neuroscience research shows that mindfulness increases cognitive flexibility, allowing you to respond rather than react. That means you become agile—not anxious. Strategic—not stubborn.

Action without awareness can look impressive but lead to burnout or misalignment. You can be productive and still be far from your purpose. But when you learn to take *conscious* action—action that checks in with your values, your body, and your results in real time—you become a master of momentum. You no longer need to push. You *adjust*. And that adjustment saves energy, increases results, and builds unshakable trust in yourself.

Your body is one of the best calibration tools available. When you're acting in alignment, your body feels expansive. Your breath is steady. Your nervous system relaxes. When you're out of alignment, your body contracts. Your chest tightens. Your energy drains. Most people override these signals. But elite performers use them as *data*. Listening to your body mid-action allows you to book-correct before breakdown.

The best way to practice real-time calibration is to pause frequently. In the middle of a task, ask: "Is this still the best use of my energy?" "Am I chasing the result or honoring the process?" These questions bring you back into alignment. You don't have to finish something just because you started it. Stopping, pivoting, or shifting direction is not quitting—it's *wisdom in motion*.

Emotional feedback is another powerful signal. Feelings of dread, frustration, or irritation mid-task are not always laziness or resistance. Sometimes they're alerts that your soul is out of sync. Rather than forcing yourself to push through, get curious. Ask, "What's really going on here?" You may need to shift your approach, your environment, or your expectations. Emotional honesty is a calibration compass.

External feedback matters too—but only when filtered through discernment. Feedback from clients, colleagues, or results can be valuable—

but don't let it override your inner knowing. Use it to refine, not define. The most powerful creators use feedback as a tool, not an identity. They stay open to growth while staying loyal to their truth. That's the sweet spot where evolution and integrity meet.

Technology can help, if used wisely. Real-time tracking apps, habit scorecards, and digital journals allow you to measure what matters. But don't get lost in metrics. Use data to *inform* your calibration, not to dominate it. A to-do list isn't the ultimate authority—your energy and alignment are. Let tools serve your soul—not replace it.

One of the most underrated tools of calibration is *breath*. A single intentional inhale and exhale can bring you back to clarity. Breath is the bridge between the mind and body. When you feel yourself spiraling, stalling, or spinning, pause and breathe. This physiological reset opens the door for intuitive recalibration. It's not about finding the perfect answer—it's about creating the space to hear it.

Environment is another calibrator. If you're struggling to focus, it might not be your willpower—it might be your surroundings. Cluttered space, draining people, or a noisy atmosphere can throw you off center. Pay attention to how your space is shaping your state. Shifting your environment, even slightly, can recalibrate your energy instantly.

Real-time action calibration isn't about perfection—it's about responsiveness. It's the ability to act and observe simultaneously. To execute and listen. To move with intention but stay open to change. It's not rigidity that creates results—it's adaptability. The tree that bends in the storm doesn't break. The mind that adjusts in the moment doesn't fail—it *rises*.

When you build this habit, your actions become more effective, your results more aligned, and your energy more sustainable. You don't just work hard— you work *wise*. You don't chase your goals—you *dance* with them. And in that dance, you learn that success isn't about the plan—it's about the *presence*. The ability to move, check in, and book-correct in real time. That's how leaders are made. That's how legacies are built. And that's how your destiny is shaped—one aligned moment at a time.

Journal: Your Aligned Action Plan

Your aligned action plan isn't just a list of goals—it's a declaration of identity. It's not about hustling through tasks for the sake of progress; it's about committing to the path your soul has already whispered is yours. True alignment doesn't come from strategy alone. It comes from intention, vision, and the courage to follow through with actions that reflect who you *really* are. This journal is your sacred mirror—the place where your desires meet your discipline.

Before writing anything down, pause. Tune in. Ask yourself, "What am I truly being called to create?" Let the noise fall away. Let the expectations fade. What remains is your truth. That's the foundation. Because aligned action cannot be built on false desires. If your goals are built from fear, comparison, or proving your worth, they'll drain you. But when they come from clarity and purpose, they'll energize you—even when they stretch you.

Use this journal to distill your soul's vision into tangible movement. Start with your why. Why does this matter to you? What legacy are you building? Neuroscience confirms that when goals are emotionally meaningful, the brain's motivation centers activate with greater intensity. This emotional charge becomes the fuel that carries you through resistance, distractions, and uncertainty.

Once your why is crystal clear, map the *what*. Define outcomes, not just activities. Don't just write "post on social media"—write "share a message that shifts someone's belief in their worth." Don't just write "make sales calls"—write "connect with five people I can serve deeply." Aligned action speaks the language of *impact*, not just activity. When you frame your goals around transformation, your energy rises to match.

Next, write down the how—but hold it loosely. Plan with structure, but leave room for soul-guided detours. Rigid strategies often become cages.

Flexibility invites miracles. Some of your greatest breakthroughs will come from spontaneous pivots, intuitive nudges, and divine timing. Your aligned action plan isn't a prison. It's a partnership—with life, with Source, with your higher self.

Track your energy, not just your results. Each day, reflect: "Which actions lit me up?" "Which drained me?" This is vital data. When your plan aligns with your natural rhythm, productivity becomes flow. When it fights your rhythm, even small tasks feel heavy. Optimize for alignment—not efficiency alone. Because what you love, you'll *repeat*. And what you repeat, you *master*.

Document your resistance too. Where did fear speak up? Where did you hesitate, procrastinate, or shrink? These aren't failures—they're gold. They reveal where your next breakthrough lives. When you write them down with compassion, you rob them of their power. You create space for healing. Awareness is the first step to liberation.

Use this journal as a space to rehearse your future. Visualize the version of you who already lives this plan. How do they think, speak, act, and decide? What do they no longer tolerate? What habits do they embody without negotiation? Neuroscience shows that mental rehearsal activates the same neural pathways as real experience. Writing as if it's already done trains your mind to close the gap between now and next.

Gratitude must also live on these pages. Not just for what's happened, but for what's coming. Gratitude in advance is a frequency that pulls your vision closer. It anchors you in faith, not fear. It reminds you that you are *creating*, not chasing. When you write, "I'm grateful for the impact I'm already making," you tell your subconscious it's safe to move forward. That you already belong to your vision.

Set milestones—but let them feel *magnetic*, not mandatory. Milestones help you measure alignment and momentum. Celebrate them fully. Let your wins land. This reinforces your identity as someone who follows through with power and purpose. Studies in behavior psychology confirm that reward accelerates habit formation. And what is alignment but a series of soul-aligned habits executed with devotion?

This journal isn't just paper and ink. It's a blueprint. A blueprint for becoming. A mirror of your higher self. A container for your brilliance. Return to it daily, not as a duty, but as a *devotion*. Let it remind you that you don't need to hustle harder—you need to align deeper. Your greatest breakthroughs will come not from doing more, but from acting in integrity with your truth.

Every word you write in this journal is a thread in the tapestry of your future. Don't just write what sounds good. Write what feels *real*. Don't just list goals. Declare intentions. Don't just track progress. Document your *becoming*. This is the work that changes lives. This is the work that changes *you*. And once you move from that place, there's nothing you can't create. Because aligned action isn't just powerful—it's *unstoppable*.

What you've just uncovered isn't theory—it's truth. But truth alone doesn't transform lives—**activation** does. And that's exactly what the *Clarity Confidence Code Course* delivers. It's not just a course. It's a mental reset, a total identity upgrade. Inside, you'll be guided step-by-step to reprogram your subconscious, eliminate limiting beliefs, and install the mindset of someone who creates results without effort or hesitation. If you're ready to stop reading about change and start **living it**, this is your invitation. Don't wait for confidence to show up—**create it**. Your next level begins right now at ☞ https://clarityconfidencecode.com

Let's move forward—because the next part of this journey requires the *real you* to step up and take the lead.

CHAPTER 11

YOUR MAGNETIC MESSAGE — OWNING YOUR VOICE AND VISIBILITY

Why Your Voice Matters

Your voice is not an accident. It is a distinct frequency, a unique vibration that no one else on this planet can replicate. There is a message inside you—shaped by your lived experiences, your triumphs, your pain, and your wisdom—that someone in the world is waiting to hear. When you withhold your voice, you're not just playing small. You're silencing the healing, the insight, the transformation that only *you* can offer. The world doesn't just need more noise—it needs your *truth*.

Every time you speak your truth, you send a ripple through the collective unconscious. Sound carries power. Neuroscientific research shows that speaking affirmatively out loud can actually rewire the brain by activating areas responsible for self-perception and emotional regulation. When you use your voice, especially with intention and authenticity, you reinforce new neural pathways that transform not only your mind—but your *identity*.

Many people stay silent because they fear judgment. But staying silent doesn't keep you safe—it keeps you *small*. The truth is, people will judge no matter what you do. Speak up, and you may be criticized. Stay quiet, and you'll be overlooked. Either way, there's a cost. But when you speak up in alignment with your values, your message attracts the right people, repels the wrong ones, and frees *you*. Silence isn't safety—it's self-erasure.

Your voice is a tool of liberation—not just for others, but for yourself. When you suppress your expression, you suppress your energy. Your throat chakra, tied to communication and authenticity, is the bridge between your heart and your mind. When it's blocked, you may feel stuck, anxious, or disconnected from your purpose. But when you express openly and clearly, your energy flows. Your confidence rises. Your power awakens.

History has proven that one voice—anchored in truth—can move mountains. It can birth revolutions, dismantle systems, heal communities, and awaken nations. From spiritual leaders to poets to everyday people who decided to *speak*, change was always preceded by someone who refused to stay silent. You may not realize it, but your voice could be the *permission slip* someone else needs to reclaim theirs.

The fear of "not being ready" is one of the most toxic lies ever sold. You don't find your voice by waiting. You find it by using it. Clarity comes through expression, not contemplation. As you speak, as you write, as you show up, your message refines. Your impact sharpens. Confidence grows through action—not perfection. Every time you show up, you calibrate to the next version of yourself.

Your story holds medicine. What you've overcome isn't just your testimony—it's a map for others. Research from the University of Massachusetts confirms that storytelling activates brain areas associated with empathy and connection, making it one of the most powerful ways to bridge differences. When you tell your truth, people *feel* it. They see themselves in your words. And that resonance heals.

Speaking your truth doesn't require a stage. Your voice matters in boardrooms, family dinners, friend circles, classrooms, and quiet journaling sessions that only you read. The world doesn't need you to be loud. It needs you to be *honest*. Voice is not volume—it's *vibration*. And when your vibration matches your values, it echoes through everything you do.

Expression is an energetic transaction. When you speak from ego, people resist. When you speak from truth, people *remember*. Words have weight, but *presence* gives them power. When you speak from alignment, your voice becomes a channel. You're not forcing impact—you're allowing it. And people don't just hear you—they *feel* you. That's the kind of voice that shifts lives.

It's also important to know that your voice evolves. What you believe today may not be what you believe tomorrow. That's not weakness—that's growth. Give yourself permission to outgrow your old opinions. To refine your message. To contradict your past in service of your future. A voice that never changes is a voice that stopped *listening*. Stay open. Stay humble. Stay in motion.

When you honor your voice, you reclaim your sovereignty. You stop outsourcing truth to others. You stop asking for permission. You stop waiting for signs that you're good enough. Your voice is the sign. Your life is the stage. Your truth is the script. Speak with intention. Speak with love. Speak with courage. Because your silence serves no one—not even you.

And when you do speak—whether it's to one person or one million—speak with the knowing that your words carry *impact*. Not because they're perfect. But because they're *yours*. The world doesn't need another copy. It needs your raw, real, powerful truth. And once you decide to use your voice from that place, you don't just participate in change—you *become* it.

Healing Fear of Visibility

The fear of visibility is one of the most silent dream killers in the world. It doesn't shout like failure or paralyze like rejection—it whispers, "What if they see the real you and it's not enough?" This fear hides in plain sight, disguising itself as perfectionism, procrastination, or the need for more credentials. But the truth is, your fear of being seen is not a sign you're weak—it's a sign you're powerful. Because deep down, you *know* your presence can move mountains. You're just afraid of the weight of that responsibility.

Being seen doesn't just mean being visible on social media or in front of crowds. It means being *witnessed*—in your rawness, your power, your vulnerability. And for many, that's terrifying. It triggers old wounds: childhood moments of shame, past betrayals, cultural conditioning that said "Don't shine too bright." But healing this fear begins by understanding it. Visibility isn't dangerous. What's dangerous is hiding your gifts behind fear, year after year, and calling it humility.

The nervous system plays a massive role in visibility blocks. When past experiences of judgment, embarrassment, or ridicule are stored in the body, any attempt to stand out triggers a fight-or-flight response. That's why your heart races before you speak. Why your voice shakes when you share truth. It's not just in your mind—it's in your *cells*. But the good news is, what was wired through repetition can be *rewired* through presence, breathwork, and safe exposure.

Healing the fear of visibility starts with reparenting the parts of you that believe being seen is dangerous. Affirm: "It's safe to be seen in my truth." Repeat it while breathing deeply. Speak it into the mirror. Write it in your journal until it becomes your new truth. Your subconscious mind responds to repetition, not logic. Neuroscientific studies confirm that the brain cannot distinguish between real and vividly imagined experience—so give your mind a new story to rehearse.

It's not about being fearless. It's about being *braver* than your fear. Courage isn't the absence of fear—it's the decision to act in alignment with your soul, even when fear is present. Every time you speak when you want to shrink, post when you want to hide, or show up when you want to disappear, you send a message to your system: "I am safe. I am capable. I am ready." That's how confidence is built—not in thought, but in *motion*.

Visibility is also deeply linked to worth. If you don't believe you *deserve* to be seen, you'll sabotage every opportunity to rise. That's why the real work isn't in perfecting your message—it's in *receiving your own value*. You are not visible because you're flawless. You're visible because your presence is a portal for transformation. What you've overcome, what you know, what you embody—it's worthy of being shared.

Comparison is a thief of both visibility and joy. The moment you measure your voice against someone else's highlight reel, you disconnect from your power. You forget that your journey, your tone, your energy, is not supposed to mimic *anyone*. It's supposed to resonate like a frequency only you carry. What people need isn't another polished performer—they need someone real enough to remind them of themselves.

Start small, but start *now*. Visibility isn't a leap—it's a series of micro-courage moments. A story shared. A truth spoken. A photo posted. A boundary set. Each one is a crack in the armor fear has built around your light. Over time, those cracks become windows. And eventually, you won't just be seen—you'll *shine*.

Supportive community is essential. You don't have to heal visibility wounds alone. Surround yourself with people who *see* you and still love you. Spaces where you can practice showing up without performance. Psychological safety is a catalyst for courage. When others mirror your worth back to you, your nervous system learns a new pattern: "It's safe to be visible *and* loved."

Celebrate your wins, no matter how small. Visibility is an edge that deserves acknowledgement. Journal your breakthroughs. Speak gratitude for every time you show up. Let your nervous system *feel* the reward of presence. That's how you make being seen feel safe—by pairing it with emotional and energetic payoff. Eventually, the fear becomes background noise, and the mission becomes the music that leads.

The world is not waiting for perfection—it's waiting for *you*. For your authentic, unfiltered, powerful presence. Your visibility isn't about ego—it's about *impact*. Someone is praying for the exact message you're hiding. And when you finally decide to stop dimming, they'll finally find the light they've been searching for. That's what your healing makes possible—not just for you, but for *them*.

Your visibility is your ministry. Your radiance is your revolution. And your decision to be seen is an act of sacred defiance against every system that told you to stay small. Speak. Stand. Shine. Not because you're unafraid—but because you're ready. The fear will rise. But so will *you*. Every time.

How to Clarify Your Soul Message

Your soul came here with a message—a divine assignment etched into your being long before you ever learned how to doubt it. This message isn't something you have to invent or fabricate. It's something you remember. Something you *reclaim*. It reveals itself not through force, but through quiet, consistent alignment. When you strip away the noise, the conditioning, and the "shoulds," what remains is your truth—and that truth is magnetic.

Clarifying your soul message begins by listening beneath the surface of your daily thoughts. It's not the message your ego wants to shout to impress—it's the one your spirit *aches* to share to impact. It's the message you'd whisper in someone's ear if you knew it could set them free. It's the medicine you most needed during your own darkest night. Often, the wound you've been most afraid to show is the doorway to your message.

Ask yourself what you've always been pulled toward—what themes, conversations, or causes light a fire in you that won't go out. Your obsessions are clues. The problems that break your heart are invitations. The injustices that trigger you are signposts. As Joseph Campbell taught through the hero's journey, we are all called into our own version of transformation so that we can return with a message that liberates others.

Your life story holds the blueprint. Reflect on your turning points, your rock bottoms, your silent victories. What patterns keep repeating? What pain have you turned into purpose? The soul speaks in symbols and synchronicities. When you begin to track your experiences with spiritual eyes, you see that nothing was random. Every setback refined your message. Every challenge shaped your voice.

Journaling is one of the most powerful tools for discovering your soul message. When you write without censorship, you bypass the logical brain and access your intuition. Try prompts like "If the world could hear only one thing from me, what would I say?" or "What truth do I avoid sharing because it feels too raw?" What flows from these questions isn't content—it's *clarity*.

Silence is sacred. Your soul message won't compete with the world's volume. It emerges in meditation, stillness, and solitude. Neuroscience supports this—studies show that the brain accesses deeper insight and problem-solving during quiet reflection. You don't need more noise to find your voice. You need space. Silence isn't empty. It's *full* of answers.

Discernment is key. Not every idea that excites you is your soul's truth. Some are distractions dressed as purpose. Others are echoes of someone else's mission. Don't just chase what's popular—lean into what feels *pure*. The message that moves your cells and softens your defenses—that's the one. The one that makes you feel more alive when you speak it. The one that doesn't need to be hyped because it already *resonates*.

Feedback matters—but only in doses. When you begin to share your soul message, some people will see you. Others won't. Some will celebrate you. Others will question you. Let it refine you, not define you. Truth isn't a popularity contest. If it's real, it will polarize. And that's good. The sharper your clarity, the more your people can find you—and the more the wrong ones will walk away.

Your message is bigger than your niche. It's not limited to a platform, a career, or a business model. It's an energy you carry into every room, every conversation, every piece of content. When it's real, it infuses *everything*. People don't just follow your brand—they feel your essence. And that essence becomes your legacy.

Don't wait until it's perfect. Start speaking it now. Share imperfectly. Post rawly. Teach what you're still learning. Your vulnerability is part of your message. Studies on authenticity show that people connect more deeply to those who share transparently than to those who perform expertise. Let your humanity *lead*. You don't have to be polished. You just have to be *true*.

Clarity expands through use. The more you speak your message, the more refined it becomes. The more you live it, the more embodied it gets. This is why clarity is never a one-time decision—it's a practice. A devotion. A daily return to what matters most. Speak it. Write it. Pray it. Declare it. Again and again until it shapes your path.

Your soul message is sacred. It's your contribution to collective healing. It's the ripple you were born to create. When you clarify it, you don't just align your voice—you align your *life*. And when you live in that alignment, everything changes. You stop chasing success. You become a vessel for *significance*. That's not marketing. That's *mission*. That's why you're here.

Sharing Without Performing

There is a profound difference between sharing and performing. One is rooted in truth; the other in approval. One is an offering; the other is a mask. When you share, you give from overflow. When you perform, you posture to be accepted. And in a world that has been trained to seek validation before vulnerability, many people forget how powerful it is to simply *be real*. Sharing from the soul doesn't need an audience—it needs *authenticity*.

Performing often begins as self-protection. Somewhere along the journey, you were taught that your rawness was too much, your truth too messy, your emotions too inconvenient. So you learned to package yourself—presenting only the polished, filtered, and socially acceptable version. But this performance, over time, suffocates your spirit. It builds success on the foundation of self-abandonment. And no external applause can fill the internal emptiness that comes from silencing your real voice.

Sharing, on the other hand, is freedom. It's the act of saying, "This is where I am. This is what I've learned. And I'm not here to impress—I'm here to *impact*." When you share without performance, your presence becomes magnetic. People feel your sincerity. Studies on social perception have shown that authenticity increases both trust and emotional engagement. You don't have to try to be relatable when you *are* relatable.

You are not a brand. You are a human being with a pulse, a past, and a purpose. Social media and stage culture have blurred the lines between storytelling and self-promotion. But your story doesn't exist to make you look good—it exists to set others free. And the moment you stop trying to manage perceptions, your energy becomes more powerful than any scripted pitch.

There is strength in softness. It takes courage to share your truth without a safety net, to speak from the wound instead of the scar, to show up in your fullness even when it feels risky. This is not weakness—it's leadership. Brene Brown's research confirms that vulnerability is the birthplace of innovation, connection, and transformation. When you speak without needing to be perfect, you create a bridge between hearts.

Performance is rooted in ego. Sharing is rooted in essence. The ego says, "Look at me." The essence says, "See *yourself* in me." One tries to prove; the other invites connection. One strives for likes; the other inspires *light*. And when you let go of the need to be impressive, you become *unforgettable*—because you touch something deeper than logic. You speak to the soul.

Real influence doesn't come from looking flawless. It comes from being fully alive. People don't remember the curated posts—they remember the moment you said what they were too afraid to say. They remember the time your eyes watered when you spoke your truth. They remember the pause in your voice when you shared what almost broke you. That's what pierces through the noise. That's what *transforms*.

To share without performing, you must trust that you are enough *as you are*. Not when you've healed everything. Not when your message is perfectly crafted. Not when your following hits a certain number. But now—in your wholeness *and* your messiness. The moment you give yourself that permission, your soul breathes. Your creativity flows. Your impact multiplies.

The nervous system doesn't lie. When you perform, your body contracts. When you share, your body expands. You feel calm, even if you're trembling. You feel clear, even if you're nervous. This is alignment. This is how your truth signals to others that they are safe to be honest too. Your presence gives them permission to lay their masks down. That's healing. That's leadership.

Consistency in truth-telling strengthens this muscle. The more you practice sharing from your heart—not your highlight reel—the more natural it becomes. You'll no longer need to rehearse authenticity; you'll *live* it. Your life will speak louder than your posts. Your message won't just inform—it will *transmit*. That's the real mark of a messenger.

Silence the inner critic that says you need to entertain to be valuable. Your value isn't in the reaction you get—it's in the truth you carry. Speak from that place. Share from that place. Let your life be the evidence. The world has seen enough polished performance. What it craves now is *presence*—honest, raw, embodied presence that doesn't demand approval but radiates *truth*.

You weren't born to perform for applause. You were born to *liberate*. And liberation begins with your own. When you stop performing and start sharing, you don't just change how people see you—you change how they see *themselves*. You remind them that real is rare. And rare is *revolutionary*.

Storytelling That Moves People

Storytelling is one of the most ancient and powerful tools of human influence. Long before we had charts, apps, or media empires, we had stories.

Stories passed through firelight, across generations, down bloodlines. They carried truths, warned of danger, inspired courage, and preserved legacy. And today, in a world oversaturated with information, it's not more facts we need—it's more *connection*. People don't change because of data alone. They change because of *emotion*. And storytelling is the bridge between heart and action.

The most moving stories aren't the ones with the most drama—they're the ones with the most *truth*. A well-told story makes someone feel seen. It bypasses logic and speaks directly to the nervous system. Neuroscience confirms that stories activate more areas of the brain than simple facts, triggering a phenomenon known as "neural coupling." When someone is immersed in a story, their brain lights up as if they are *experiencing* the events themselves. That's the power of a well-crafted narrative—it doesn't just inform; it *transports*.

But what makes a story *move* people isn't its perfection. It's its *resonance*. When you share from lived experience, when your voice carries the tremor of truth, people feel it. They remember it. Not because you hit every storytelling formula, but because you *felt* what you said. Authenticity isn't just a buzzword—it's a biological cue. We're wired to detect it. And when we do, trust is built instantly.

The best storytellers aren't trying to be heroes. They're willing to be *human*. They tell the whole truth—the tears and the triumphs, the detours and the doubts. They don't airbrush their story into a perfect arc. They show up with vulnerability and let their story *breathe*. Vulnerability is magnetic. According to research by Dr. Paul Zak, emotionally engaging stories cause the brain to release oxytocin—the hormone associated with empathy and connection. That's why we lean in when a speaker shares something raw. Our biology is designed to connect through emotion.

Clarity matters. Every powerful story has a clear takeaway—a soul-anchored message that sticks with the listener long after the story ends. It's not enough to tell what happened; we must reveal what it *meant*. What did you learn? What shifted in you? What truth does this story reveal about life, love, growth, or purpose? When your story has a spine of meaning, it transforms from entertainment to *enlightenment*.

Great stories follow energy, not just structure. While storytelling frameworks like the hero's journey or three-act structure can help organize ideas, they are tools—not rules. What matters more is emotional *rhythm*. The pacing, the pauses, the punchlines—they create a heartbeat. That rhythm keeps people present, leaning in, nodding along. In public speaking, rhythm is retention. In conversation, rhythm is rapport. Let your story *breathe*—then hit with power.

Your story doesn't have to be dramatic to be impactful. A moment of stillness, a quiet realization, or a subtle shift in perspective can change lives when shared with presence. Don't discount your own experiences because they aren't extreme. What matters is *honesty*. When you speak the truth of your experience with intention, you give others the gift of recognition. You help them name their own unspoken truths.

Use sensory language to bring your stories to life. Describe what you saw, heard, smelled, and felt. Sensory detail makes a story immersive. Instead of saying "I was scared," say "My throat tightened, and my chest buzzed like a live wire." That kind of language paints pictures in the mind. And our brains *remember* images more than abstract words. You're not just telling a story—you're building a *world*.

Repetition is a powerful tool. Repeating a core message throughout a story anchors the lesson. It makes it stick. Think of the best speeches you've heard—there's often a phrase or line that repeats like a drumbeat. That rhythm imprints the message into memory. Don't be afraid to return to your core theme again and again. When done with intention, it deepens impact without feeling redundant.

The purpose of storytelling is not self-glorification—it's *transformation*. Your story isn't just about you. It's about what it *unlocks* in others. When told well, your story becomes a permission slip, a map, a mirror. It shows others what's possible for them. It says, "If I made it through, maybe you can too." That kind of storytelling doesn't just inspire—it *empowers*.

Practice is essential. Even the best storytellers rehearse. Not to memorize, but to embody. To feel the emotional beats. To refine the delivery. Storytelling is a craft. The more you do it, the sharper your instinct becomes. You begin to sense where the energy dips or where the connection spikes. Feedback, reflection, and repetition will turn your truth into a transmission.

Finally, remember that your story is *enough*. You don't need to embellish it. You don't need to manufacture a punchline. What you've lived, what you've learned, what you *carry*—that is your power. Speak it boldly. Speak it clearly. Speak it as if one person in the room is waiting for it to save them—because they are. And when you tell your story from that place, you're not just speaking—you're *changing lives*.

From Private to Public Power

There comes a point in every person's journey when the inner work must translate into outer expression. You've done the journaling, the meditating, the healing. You've whispered affirmations into the mirror and found solace in your silence. But power that stays private can only go so far. At some point, the transformation within must *expand* into the world. This isn't about ego— it's about *expression*. Your growth was never meant to be kept hidden. It was meant to *serve*.

Private power is essential. It's where confidence is incubated, resilience is tested, and self-trust is forged. It's the foundation for everything. But public power—your ability to show up, speak up, and stand tall in front of others— is where your influence multiplies. It's not a betrayal of your inner work—it's the fulfillment of it. It's the moment your healing becomes *help*, your story becomes *service*, and your presence becomes *permission* for others to rise.

Many fear the spotlight because they associate visibility with vulnerability. And yes, to be seen is to be exposed. But it's also to be *available*. You can't touch lives from the shadows. You can't shift culture from the sidelines. To make an impact, you must be willing to step out—not perfectly, but powerfully. The fear of exposure only lingers when you forget that your presence is needed. Your voice, your truth, your energy—it all has a role to play in someone else's breakthrough.

Public power isn't about performance. It's not about being the loudest or most charismatic. It's about being *anchored*. Anchored in your values. Anchored in your message. Anchored in the quiet knowing that who you are is *enough*. That kind of presence transcends personality. It magnetizes. Because when you walk into a room with internal certainty, people feel it before you even speak.

Neuroscience shows that confidence is not something you're born with—it's something you *build* through repeated exposure to fear, followed by survival. Every time you speak up despite the flutter in your chest, every time you hold your truth in a tense room, you wire your brain for leadership. You're not just expanding your voice—you're expanding your *capacity*.

Public power also lives in your physiology. Your posture, breath, and movement affect how others perceive you—and how you perceive *yourself*. Harvard research confirms that adopting open, grounded body language increases feelings of confidence and reduces cortisol levels. So when you're stepping into visibility, remember: your body is your ally. Stand like your message matters. Speak like someone's life depends on it—because it just might.

The transition from private to public also requires boundaries. Not every part of your journey is meant for everyone. Public power doesn't mean sharing every scar—it means sharing what serves. It's about intentional vulnerability, not emotional dumping. Your audience isn't your therapist. They're your mission field. Share from the *healed*, not the wound. That distinction preserves your energy and protects your integrity.

Public platforms aren't just stages—they're sacred spaces. Whether it's a podcast, a workshop, a livestream, or a room full of five people, your presence is a catalyst. But only if you show up as your *real self*. People are starved for authenticity. They don't want perfection—they want *permission*. When they see you owning your power without apology, it gives them the courage to do the same.

Stepping into public power will challenge your inner critic. It will stir the old voices: "Who do you think you are?" "You're not ready." "They'll reject you." But here's the truth: your readiness doesn't come before the leap—it *awakens* through the leap. Courage isn't the absence of doubt. It's the decision to trust your *calling* more than your conditioning.

When you activate public power, you become a mirror. You reflect back to others what's possible. Your energy expands beyond you. You become a field of influence, not through force, but through *frequency*. And people remember how you made them *feel*. That's your legacy—not what you said, but the resonance of your presence.

Celebrate every moment you choose to be seen. Every word you speak, every stage you stand on, every time you hit "publish" when you're still trembling—that's victory. That's evidence that you're no longer hiding. And in a world addicted to appearance, your decision to show up as you *are* becomes a revolution. A reminder that real is rare—and real is what we're craving.

You've done the inner work. You've cultivated private power. Now it's time to share it. Boldly. Publicly. Purposefully. Not to prove, but to *pour*. Because the light you carry isn't meant to be contained—it's meant to illuminate. And when you rise, not just in private, but in *public*, you don't just find your power. You *become* it. And the world shifts because of it.

Creating Safe Visibility Practices

Visibility without safety is not empowerment—it's exposure. The journey to being seen, heard, and recognized must be built on a foundation of *internal security*, not external applause. You don't build power by throwing yourself into the spotlight unprepared. You build it by creating rituals, systems, and emotional safeguards that allow you to rise without fracturing. Visibility must feel *safe* to be sustainable.

Before you can fully step into visibility, you must first build nervous system resilience. When your body perceives being seen as a threat—because of past experiences like criticism, shame, or trauma—it will resist your rise. This is biology, not weakness. The amygdala, the brain's fear center, activates in response to perceived danger—even if that danger is just a comment or disapproval. Breathwork, grounding, and somatic regulation aren't luxury—they're *leadership tools*.

Creating safe visibility practices begins with setting clear *intention*. Why do you want to be seen? For validation, or for contribution? When your "why" is rooted in purpose, not performance, you're less shaken by judgment. Studies in positive psychology show that intrinsic motivation (doing something because it aligns with your values) increases emotional resilience. Invisibility rooted in self-protection slowly kills purpose. Visibility rooted in service *liberates* it.

Start with containers where you feel emotionally safe. This might mean sharing your truth in a small mastermind before posting it online. It might mean practicing your voice in front of a mentor before taking the stage. Micro-exposures to visibility build confidence. This is called "systematic desensitization" in cognitive behavioral therapy—exposing yourself to the fear in measured doses until your body learns it's safe. Courage is cumulative.

Protect your energy *before* you share. Energetic hygiene is real. Whether it's meditating, praying, visualizing light around you, or simply breathing with intention, create a ritual that clears your field and centers your spirit. You're not just showing up to be seen—you're showing up to *serve*. The clearer your channel, the stronger your impact. You don't want to perform—you want to *transmit*.

Boundaries are not just about saying no to others. They're about saying yes to *yourself*. Decide what aspects of your story are sacred, and what can be shared. You don't owe the world your trauma to be valid. You don't need to bleed to be believed. Speak from the scar, not the wound. This isn't hiding—it's honoring. Safe visibility honors timing, discernment, and sovereignty.

Prepare for visibility with *support*. You are not meant to rise alone. Whether it's a coach, a trusted friend, or a therapist, have someone who holds space for the emotions that surface. Visibility will bring up old patterns—fear of rejection, impostor syndrome, abandonment wounds. These aren't signs to stop. They're signs you're *stretching*. Support helps you expand without collapsing.

Rehearse your message in safe space. Speak your truth out loud before you broadcast it. Journal it. Record yourself. Sit with the discomfort and let it melt. When you say something enough times in a place where you are affirmed, it becomes easier to say it in places where you are not. Visibility becomes less about others' approval and more about *your own embodiment*.

Rest is part of safe visibility. After you share something big, protect your system. Take time off. Don't check notifications obsessively. Step back and breathe. This "vulnerability hangover" is real, and rest is the remedy. Recovery is not weakness—it's wisdom. Athletes don't grow during the game—they grow during *recovery*. So do thought leaders. So do visionaries.

Track how you feel after being visible. Journal what felt expansive, what felt draining, what felt aligned. This isn't about performance metrics—it's about *energetic intelligence*. What feels good? What doesn't? This is how you build a visibility rhythm that sustains your energy rather than depleting it. You don't need to go viral to be valuable. You just need to be *aligned*.

Visibility is a sacred act. It's not just showing up for others—it's showing up for your *calling*. And that deserves protection, reverence, and intention. Your voice is powerful. Your presence is potent. But it must be held with care. Safe visibility is how you build a legacy without burning out. It's how you rise in a way that doesn't cost your peace.

Let the world see you, but let it see the version of you that feels *ready*, supported, and rooted. You don't owe anyone your urgency. You only owe yourself your *honesty*. And when you create safe practices around visibility, your light doesn't flicker with feedback—it grows brighter with every breath. That's not performance. That's *power*. Real, rooted, unstoppable power.

Speaking to Be Understood, Not Liked

There's a profound shift that happens when you stop speaking to be liked and start speaking to be *understood*. One is rooted in fear, the other in clarity. One is about molding yourself to fit into someone else's box. The other is about *standing* in your truth and inviting others to meet you there. It's the difference between playing small for safety and rising in full power for impact. When your words come from a place of alignment rather than approval, they land with more precision, more conviction, and more *truth*.

The human desire to be liked is deeply biological. From an evolutionary standpoint, belonging to the tribe was a matter of survival. Rejection once meant isolation, and isolation meant death. That wiring still lives in our nervous system today. But the modern world doesn't reward people-pleasers with fulfillment—it rewards truth-tellers with *transformation*. According to psychological research, the need for social acceptance can override our decision-making unless we consciously choose integrity over image.

When you speak to be understood, you stop editing yourself to match the comfort level of others. You start telling the truth—even when it shakes. You say what you *mean*, not what you think will make you more palatable. And ironically, that's what creates real connection. People are drawn to those who are unapologetically clear, even if they don't always agree with them. Clarity builds trust. Authenticity creates magnetism. Performance only breeds pressure.

Speaking with clarity isn't about being aggressive. It's about being anchored. There's no need to over-explain, overcompensate, or overshare. It's simply owning your message, your perspective, your values—with love and strength. When you communicate from this place, your tone changes. Your energy shifts. You're not looking for permission—you're offering *perspective*. And that's leadership.

Language is energy. Words carry frequency. When you speak from a place of inner approval, rather than external validation, people feel it. Your words vibrate differently. They carry weight, depth, and sincerity. This is why emotionally honest speeches and stories move people more than polished scripts. They bypass the brain and go straight to the heart. Because they weren't trying to impress—they were trying to *connect*.

Clarity also protects your energy. When you focus on being understood instead of being liked, you waste less time managing perceptions. You speak your truth, let it land, and release control over the outcome. You trust that the right people will resonate and the wrong people will redirect. This saves hours of overthinking, people-pleasing, and emotional leakage. You conserve energy for your *purpose*.

Fear of not being liked is often a symptom of not fully liking yourself. When you build self-respect, you no longer need every listener to nod in agreement. Your worth isn't up for debate. You're not holding your breath, hoping they approve. You're exhaling truth, knowing it's valid—even if it's misunderstood. When you love yourself, you speak *for* yourself, not just *to* others.

You don't need a perfect script. You need *presence*. Being liked may win attention, but being understood wins hearts—and hearts drive change. The most influential voices in history weren't always popular. But they were clear. They were consistent. They didn't water down truth to fit into trends. They spoke because they *had to*, not because they wanted to be applauded.

To master this way of communication, practice asking yourself before you speak: "Am I speaking to express or to impress?" "Am I diluting this truth so they'll like me, or am I delivering it with the respect it deserves?" That kind of awareness creates alignment. And alignment is what makes your message *land*.

Be prepared: clarity will challenge people. It will trigger those still living for applause. But your job is not to coddle egos—it's to deliver *impact*. Not to avoid discomfort—but to walk in *truth*. And truth doesn't need to yell. It just needs to be *clear*. The more direct you are, the more trustworthy you become.

Real power isn't in how many people like you—it's in how many lives you *touch*. And you don't touch lives by performing. You do it by speaking the truth, in love, with strength. Every time you choose understanding over approval, you free a part of yourself. You reclaim a piece of your voice. And your voice, when clear and connected, is a tool for liberation.

Speak your truth not to be liked, but to be *heard*. Speak not to impress, but to *impact*. Speak from your core, not your conditioning. And watch as the world shifts—not because everyone agrees with you, but because they *felt* you. They saw you. They understood you. And in that understanding, something opened. That's the real work. That's the real power.

Attracting the Right Audience

Attracting the right audience doesn't start with algorithms—it starts with alignment. You don't magnetize the people meant for you by chasing trends or copying formulas. You attract them by being so authentically yourself that the resonance is unmistakable. When your message comes from soul—not strategy—it doesn't just reach minds, it *moves hearts*. That's how the right audience finds you. Not because you're loud, but because you're *clear*.

The first step is knowing who you are, not just who you're trying to reach. Your brand is an extension of your essence. If it's built on roles, masks, or marketing hype, it will attract confusion and misalignment. But when it's built on purpose, clarity, and truth, it creates a signal that only the right people can hear. It's like tuning into a radio station—those on your frequency will find you effortlessly.

Psychology teaches us that people are drawn to what feels familiar, safe, and emotionally congruent. If your message carries integrity and emotional resonance, it creates immediate trust. According to Harvard research on trust and influence, authenticity is one of the strongest triggers for engagement. When your words match your walk, people can feel that—and that's when they lean in.

Trying to appeal to everyone is the fastest way to dilute your power. The truth is, not everyone will resonate with your mission—and that's a good thing. Repelling the wrong people is as important as attracting the right ones. Clarity is magnetic, but it's also polarizing. The sharper your message, the more it acts like a filter. And that filter protects your energy and your mission.

Speak to one person, not to a crowd. When your message feels personal, it cuts through the noise. Picture your ideal client, student, or listener. What are they afraid of? What do they secretly hope for? What's keeping them up at night? Speak to that. When you make one person feel deeply seen, you'll reach a thousand others who recognize themselves in that same truth.

Consistency builds credibility. If your message keeps changing with the wind, your audience won't know what to trust. But when you consistently anchor in your values, your story, and your purpose, your message becomes a lighthouse. People return to your content not for novelty—but for *stability*. In a world of noise, clarity is a *sanctuary*.

Visibility with intention is key. Don't just post to be seen. Post to *serve*. Every caption, video, or podcast is an opportunity to deliver transformation, not just information. Ask yourself, "Will this help someone shift?" The right audience isn't just looking for entertainment—they're looking for elevation. And when you commit to serving over selling, your audience becomes not just followers, but *family*.

Use your own story as the foundation. Your lived experience is your most valuable asset. When you share from what you've overcome, you offer a bridge to those still in it. According to research from the University of Massachusetts, storytelling increases empathy and retention, making your message more memorable and meaningful. People don't just want expertise—they want *evidence* that you've walked the path.

Create content that calls people *into* something. Don't just describe the pain—paint the vision. The right audience doesn't want to dwell in the problem. They want to see the possibility. Give them hope. Give them strategy. Give them proof that what they want is *reachable*. Empowerment is more magnetic than complaint. Speak to potential, not just problems.

Make it easy for your audience to recognize themselves. Use language they use. Address the emotions they're afraid to say out loud. When they read your message and think, "That's me," you've made the connection. This is empathy marketing at its highest level—not manipulation, but mirroring. When they feel understood, they'll *trust* you.

Invite engagement. Ask questions. Encourage conversation. The right audience doesn't just want to consume—they want to connect. Create community, not just content. When your space becomes a mirror for their growth, they won't just follow—they'll *stay*. Loyalty is built on belonging, not performance. Make your message a place they feel *home*.

The right audience is never found through chasing—it's revealed through *alignment*. When you stop trying to please everyone and start showing up as your most powerful, unfiltered, mission-led self, the people you're meant to serve will not only hear you—they'll *feel* you. That's not branding. That's frequency. And that frequency is what makes you unforgettable.

Expressing the Whole You

Expressing the whole you is not an act of indulgence—it's an act of liberation. The world has conditioned many to segment themselves into digestible pieces, to present only what's palatable and hide what's raw. But true power, the kind that commands without control and inspires without effort, comes from *wholeness*. Not from playing roles. Not from being "on brand." But from being *real*. When you bring your full self to the table—flaws, brilliance, quirks, soul—you become undeniable.

You weren't born to fit into anyone's box. You were born to *expand*. To embody a frequency that hasn't existed before in this exact way. And that means bringing forth every part of you that society told you to dim. Your rage has wisdom. Your softness has strength. Your dreams have direction. Your wounds have wisdom. You are not too much—you are exactly right when you stop *shrinking* to be accepted.

Psychology confirms that emotional congruence—the alignment between internal experience and external expression—leads to higher well-being and stronger relationships. When you suppress parts of yourself, it creates cognitive dissonance and drains energy. But when you express all of who you are, your energy flows freely. People feel your *aliveness*. And aliveness is magnetic.

Wholeness doesn't mean constant confidence. It means radical honesty. It's the courage to say, "I'm still figuring this out," while also saying, "And here's what I know for sure." You don't need to be fully healed to show up fully human. In fact, your transparency becomes someone else's roadmap. They don't connect to your perfection—they connect to your *process*.

In a culture obsessed with curation, authenticity is revolutionary. When others are editing their truth, your decision to share all of you becomes a beacon. You no longer perform for acceptance—you *embody* truth. You no longer chase applause—you *radiate* presence. And that shift? That's what opens doors you didn't even know existed. Because people follow clarity. They trust realness. They crave *permission* to be whole.

Bringing your whole self doesn't mean dumping your story on everyone. It means showing up with coherence. It means letting your inner life match your outer message. You don't preach peace while living in chaos. You don't post joy while drowning in resentment. You integrate. You align. And from that alignment, your words don't just inform—they *transform*.

The nervous system is your partner in this process. When you've lived in environments where expression was punished, your body learns to shut down. But that's not a life sentence—it's a signal. A signal that healing is possible. Through breath, movement, and safe relationships, you can retrain your system to feel safe in being seen. This isn't just spiritual—it's *somatic*. Your body holds the key to expressing the full truth of who you are.

Spiritual teachings and scientific findings agree—suppressed energy becomes stagnant energy. Whether it's unexpressed grief, unspoken dreams, or unshared opinions, what you bottle up weighs you down. But when you express it, you become lighter. Freer. More magnetic. Expression is not just about communication—it's about *circulation*. What flows through you, frees you.

You were not created to be one-dimensional. You are an entire galaxy of wisdom, intuition, emotion, fire, and grace. The more you allow each part to be seen, the more potent your impact becomes. You don't need to choose between being strategic and spiritual, logical and emotional, bold and gentle. You are the *bridge*. You are the integration. And the world needs *wholeness*, not fragmentation.

To express the whole you is to live unapologetically aligned. You don't water yourself down in rooms that can't hold your truth. You don't shrink your light to comfort those afraid of their own. You walk in with integrity, speak with clarity, and lead with compassion. You let every part of you have a seat at the table. And in doing so, you give others the courage to do the same.

You don't attract your people by pretending. You attract them by *revealing*. When you stop editing your essence, you find the tribe that was waiting to recognize you. The ones who love you not in spite of your wholeness, but *because* of it. That's not coincidence—it's *alignment*. That's not strategy—it's *truth*.

The world doesn't need another filtered copy. It needs *you*. All of you. The soulful, the struggling, the rising, the radiant. And when you finally decide to bring your full self to every space you enter, you don't just find success—you find *sovereignty*. And from that place, everything changes. Not because you performed—but because you *arrived*. Whole. Honest. Unapologetically *you*.

Magnetic Messaging in Business or Life

Magnetic messaging is not about clever slogans or fancy copy—it's about *resonance*. The words that move people are the ones that feel like truth echoing in their chest. In both business and life, the most powerful message isn't the loudest or most polished—it's the one that's *aligned*. Aligned with your values, your story, your soul. When your message comes from that deep place, it becomes more than communication—it becomes a *transmission*.

In today's oversaturated world, attention is currency. And the only thing more valuable than attention is *trust*. Magnetic messaging doesn't just grab eyes—it builds hearts. According to Edelman's global trust report, 88% of consumers say trust is a deciding factor in who they buy from, follow, or support. That trust is built when your words match your walk. When your message is consistent—not just across platforms, but across moments.

You can't create magnetic messaging by copying others. You must distill your own essence. What have you overcome? What do you stand for? What are you unwilling to compromise on? These questions are the foundation. When you speak from conviction, not convenience, people feel it. You don't need to shout your message—you need to *embody* it. That's what makes it stick.

Great messaging doesn't try to convince. It *connects*. It doesn't chase attention—it creates alignment. The most successful brands and leaders don't speak to the masses. They speak to the *one*. The one who's stuck, who's searching, who's ready. And because they speak with such clarity, their message finds not just one—it finds *millions*. It scales not through hype, but through *honesty*.

Emotional relevance is the secret. People buy with emotion and justify with logic. They choose leaders, brands, and movements that make them *feel* something. Neurological studies confirm that emotional storytelling increases both memory and motivation. If your message doesn't stir the heart, it won't stick in the mind. It's not about being sentimental—it's about being *real*.

Simplicity is power. The most magnetic messages are clear and direct. They don't rely on jargon or fluff. They speak the language of *humanity*, not hype. "I see you." "You're not alone." "There's another way." These kinds of messages cut through noise because they speak to universal truths. Strip away the fluff. Speak like a human. Say what matters, and say it *well*.

Magnetic messaging is also about rhythm. The cadence of your words can carry just as much impact as the meaning. That's why speeches and messages with repetition, emphasis, and flow linger in the soul. Think about some of the greatest orators in history—their words landed not just because of content, but *delivery*. Rhythm makes your message memorable. Repetition makes it *unforgettable*.

Authenticity cannot be faked. You can't market your way into being magnetic. You have to *live* it. Your energy, your presence, your posture all reinforce your message. If your words say one thing but your tone says another, people will feel the dissonance. Integrity is magnetic. Incongruence is repelling. The more you align what you say with how you show up, the stronger your pull becomes.

Messaging isn't just about promotion—it's about *positioning*. It tells the world what you stand for, who you serve, and why it matters. Whether you're launching a product, pitching a client, or standing up for a belief, your message positions you as either noise—or *necessity*. Position yourself with purpose. Speak like your message is a *mission*, not a marketing tactic.

Feedback refines your message, but it shouldn't *reshape* your truth. Listen to how people respond. Let their questions clarify your language. But don't twist your voice to fit every ear. The more you dilute your message to please everyone, the more you lose its potency. Feedback is a mirror, not a master. Use it to grow—but not to *shrink*.

You don't need a massive platform to start. You need a *message that matters*. Speak it where you are, with what you have. One post. One video. One conversation. When it's magnetic, it spreads. People *share* what hits their soul. And the right message in the right moment can ripple through millions—not because of budget, but because of *boldness*.

At the end of the day, magnetic messaging is about owning your truth so completely that the world can't ignore it. Whether it's in a boardroom, a bio, or a bedtime story to your child, your words shape *worlds*. Speak with clarity. Speak with courage. And most of all, speak with *intention*. Because when your message is magnetic, it doesn't just get heard—it *heals*. It doesn't just influence—it *activates*. That's the real power of your voice. Use it wisely. Use it fully. Use it now.

Exercise: Craft Your Signature Voice

Your signature voice isn't just how you speak—it's how you *resonate*. It's not limited to tone or vocabulary; it's the energy behind your words, the truth you stand on, and the conviction that pulses through everything you say. Crafting your signature voice isn't about inventing something new—it's about remembering who you are beneath the noise. It's peeling back the layers of expectation, performance, and fear until what's left is *you*, unfiltered, undeniable, and unforgettable.

Your voice is your soul in motion. It carries your life story, your triumphs, your heartbreaks, your beliefs. It is the fingerprint of your experience translated into language. When aligned with purpose, it has the power to influence, to uplift, and to awaken. But when disconnected from truth, it can sound polished yet hollow. True resonance doesn't come from perfection. It comes from *presence*.

Start with your story. Your voice is shaped by where you've been. What have you overcome? What lessons have you earned—not just learned? What values have emerged from the fire? The more honest you are about your journey, the more depth your voice gains. Research shows that storytelling increases oxytocin in the brain, making your audience feel more connected and empathetic. When people feel you, they trust you.

Then, define your message. What is the core truth you want the world to hear through you? Not the curated version, not the trendy slogan—but the soul-anchored statement that burns in your gut. Maybe it's freedom. Maybe it's truth. Maybe it's awakening. Your voice becomes magnetic when it orbits a central purpose. That message is your compass, and it must be revisited often to keep your communication powerful and pure.

Next, notice your patterns. When do you speak with the most ease and power? Is it when you're teaching? Sharing stories? Giving encouragement? Your signature voice thrives where you feel most at home. Some voices are fire—bold, direct, catalytic. Others are water—calm, fluid, nourishing. There's no right tone—there's only the *truthful* one. The one that flows when you stop trying to sound like someone else.

Emotion fuels your voice. Speak with feeling, not just facts. Tone, pacing, and inflection are tools of influence backed by science. Studies from UCLA and other institutions have shown that nonverbal cues account for the majority of communication impact. When your tone matches your message, it creates coherence. Coherence creates trust. Trust creates transformation.

Your signature voice also requires boundaries. Not every space deserves your deepest truth. Not every audience earns access to your most sacred message. Discernment is wisdom. Protect your energy, refine your words, and reserve your highest truth for those ready to receive. Authenticity doesn't mean oversharing—it means speaking with *integrity*.

Practice is the polish. You don't craft your signature voice once and walk away. You test it. You refine it. You record, review, revise. You speak it in small rooms until you can own it on global stages. Mastery is not a moment—it's a rhythm. Speak often. Listen deeply. And let your voice evolve as you do. It's not fixed—it's *alive*.

Environment matters. Surround yourself with people who see your voice as sacred. Feedback is valuable, but only when it's given by those who understand your mission. If someone's critique is rooted in conformity, discard it. Your voice is not meant to be trimmed to fit in—it's meant to *expand* to lead.

Write as much as you speak. Your written voice strengthens your spoken one. Free-write without filters. Let your truth pour out. Over time, your written rhythm will begin to mirror your spoken cadence. This alignment is powerful—it brings consistency to your message across platforms. And consistency builds credibility.

Your signature voice will challenge you. It will ask you to shed every borrowed sound and every fear-based silence. It will demand your truth. It will test your courage. But in return, it will give you *legacy*. Because the world doesn't remember noise—it remembers *frequency*. And your voice, once clear, becomes a vibration that moves mountains and *hearts*.

The most powerful thing you can do is own your voice without apology. Not because it's perfect, but because it's *yours*. Craft it. Honor it. Let it stretch. And when it's ready, let it *soar*. Because the moment you fully claim your voice, you don't just speak—you *ignite*. And the world, aching for something real, turns its head and listens.

By now, you've felt it—that inner shift. A spark of awareness, a deeper truth stirring. But here's the reality: reading about change isn't the same as living it. If you're serious about upgrading your identity, dissolving doubt, and operating from absolute certainty, then the **Clarity Confidence Code Course** is your next move. This is where theory becomes transformation. It's a step-by-step system that installs the beliefs, emotions, and subconscious wiring of someone who *just knows* they're meant for more—and finally lives like it. If you're done playing small and ready to *lock in* unshakable clarity and confidence for good, your moment is now. Join the full experience at https://clarityconfidencecode.com

Now, let's take what's been awakened—and unleash it in the next chapter of your evolution.

CHAPTER 12

LIVING THE CODE — INTEGRATION, EXPANSION & NEXT-LEVEL IDENTITY

Review of the Code and Core Shifts

The journey through the Clarity Confidence Code isn't about adding more to who you are—it's about *remembering* who you've always been. This code isn't external doctrine; it's an inward awakening. It doesn't hand you answers—it reactivates your power to ask better questions. The core shifts you've experienced weren't designed to temporarily motivate you; they were designed to *rewire* your default settings, to challenge your limiting beliefs at the root and help you build a life from the inside out.

The first shift is the most radical: clarity over confusion. Confusion is not a permanent state—it's often a symptom of disconnection from your truth. When you begin reclaiming your desires, your direction sharpens. You're no longer bouncing between opinions or hiding behind indecision. You stop waiting for permission and start acting from alignment. According to neuroscience research from Yale and Stanford, clarity in goals improves motivation and action by activating the brain's goal-oriented pathways.

Confidence is no longer a mask. It's now embodied—rooted not in how loud you are, but how aligned you are. You've learned that true confidence comes from keeping promises to yourself, not from impressing others. This is backed by behavioral psychology: self-integrity is one of the strongest predictors of self-trust. The more consistent your actions are with your inner values, the more confident you become—not as a role, but as a *reality*.

You've also released the addiction to "maybe" energy—the chronic indecision that leaks power. You've stepped into decisiveness as a muscle. No more wavering between paths, fearing the "wrong" choice. You now understand that aligned decisions aren't about guarantees—they're about *growth*. As you practiced embodied decision-making, you rewired your nervous system to tolerate risk and uncertainty without collapse.

The shift from fear-based action to soul-led action changes everything. No longer are you driven by urgency, scarcity, or proving energy. You are now motivated by vision, contribution, and resonance. This realignment has a physiological impact—decreasing cortisol and increasing dopamine, the brain chemical responsible for motivation and satisfaction. When your actions reflect who you *really* are, your body supports your mission, not resists it.

You've traded performance for presence. Instead of projecting an image, you now radiate from essence. This transition is subtle but powerful. Your authenticity isn't a branding tactic—it's your *birthright*. Harvard research confirms that people trust and engage more with those who display vulnerability and coherence between message and behavior. Your willingness to be real makes your presence magnetic.

Another key shift is your relationship with fear. Rather than avoiding it, you've learned to listen to it, map it, and move with it. Fear became a feedback system, not a stop sign. You're no longer hijacked by fight, flight, freeze, or fawn. You now ask, "What is this fear protecting?" and "What would courage look like here?" That change alone reclaims more energy than any productivity hack ever could.

Boundaries became sacred, not selfish. You realized that saying no doesn't make you mean—it makes you *clear*. You learned that honoring your energy is an act of service to your purpose. Energetic clarity attracts the right relationships, opportunities, and momentum. As you strengthened your boundaries, you deepened your *worthiness*. Because when you believe you're worthy, you stop tolerating what drains you.

One of the most transformative shifts has been how you speak. You stopped using language to shrink or apologize. You began using it to shape reality. Your words became declarations, not disclaimers. And as you practiced owning your truth, your voice shifted from performance to *presence*. This is not just personal—it's neurological. Language shapes identity, and identity dictates behavior. You rewrote your story by *speaking* it differently.

You also broke the cycle of overthinking. Action replaced paralysis. You no longer needed all the answers before you moved—you just needed *alignment*. Through micro-courage and embodied consistency, you reclaimed momentum. This is the neuroscience of action in motion: small wins generate dopamine, which fuels bigger risks. Confidence is no longer something you chase. It's something you *build*.

Most importantly, you reconnected with your soul's signal. You stopped outsourcing authority. You remembered that intuition isn't vague—it's a guidance system. You've learned to clear the static, tune in, and move from knowing. That is the ultimate shift—from conditioned noise to *internal clarity*. And in a world that's always trying to pull you outward, this inward anchoring is your most powerful revolution.

The Clarity Confidence Code wasn't a lesson—it was a *return*. A return to truth. A return to power. A return to self. These shifts aren't fleeting. They are the foundation of a new way of being. One where you don't just survive—you *soar*. One where clarity replaces chaos, confidence replaces comparison, and you speak, act, and create from the most magnetic source of all: your *authentic truth*. Now, you don't just know the code—you *embody* it.

How to Lock in the New Identity

Locking in a new identity isn't about repeating affirmations until they stick—it's about living from the *frequency* of the person you've decided to become. Identity is not simply who you *say* you are. It's who you *act* like, think like, move like—consistently. Lasting transformation happens when alignment becomes your standard, not your exception. You don't become your next level self through willpower alone—you *embody* it until it's automatic.

Neuroscience shows that the brain doesn't distinguish between imagined and real experiences when they're emotionally charged and repeated. This is how Olympic athletes mentally rehearse gold-medal performances with the same brain activity as physically executing them. When you visualize your new identity with detail and feeling, you begin reprogramming your neural pathways. Your brain begins to adopt that identity as truth—not someday, but *now*.

This isn't just theory—it's proven. Dr. Joe Dispenza's work, grounded in measurable EEG brain scans, shows that focused intention paired with elevated emotion changes both the brain and body. Identity change is a *biological* event, not just a mindset game. When you feel the feelings of your future self in the now, you activate the biochemical signature of that version. You literally begin *broadcasting* a new signal to the world.

But identity isn't locked in without *behavioral evidence*. You must act in integrity with the version of you that already lives that life. You stop asking, "What do I feel like doing?" and start asking, "What would the *next-level me* do?" Would they avoid the call, or take it boldly? Would they scroll, or show up?

Would they doubt themselves or move decisively? Behavior becomes the proof that the identity is not a wish—it's *reality*.

Identity requires *environmental reinforcement*. Who and what surrounds you will either support your evolution or sabotage it. Curate your inputs—your media, your conversations, your spaces. Neuroscientists confirm that mirror neurons in the brain pick up on the behavior and energy of those around us. When you regularly engage with environments aligned with your new self, you fast-track integration. Elevation requires intentional *exposure*.

Habits become the scaffolding for your identity. When you ritualize success, discipline becomes effortless. Atomic habits, as James Clear puts it, are "votes for the person you want to become." Every time you honor a morning routine, speak powerfully, or complete a task you once avoided, you cast a vote for your new identity. Enough votes and it becomes *inevitable*. It's no longer "I'm trying." It's "This is who I am."

But locking in identity also means *releasing* the old one. You must let go of narratives, roles, and wounds that kept you small. The identity of the past isn't bad—it was just built to survive. Now, you're building to *thrive*. This might mean grieving comfort zones or friendships that reflect your former frequency. But freedom demands space. You cannot ascend while clutching what no longer fits.

Language is a key. Speak as the new self. Not "I hope I can," but "I *am*." Not "I'm working on it," but "This is what I do." Words are instructions to your subconscious. The more you speak with certainty, the faster your mind obeys. Psycholinguistics proves that identity-based language ("I am a writer" vs. "I try to write") strengthens behavior consistency. Speak it until it's normal. Live it until it's undeniable.

Emotion is your fuel. Don't just mechanically go through the motions. Feel the pride of honoring your word. Feel the expansion when you act boldly. Emotions create chemical memory in the body. When you celebrate each small win with joy, gratitude, or pride, your body begins associating growth with *pleasure*, not pain. That's how identity becomes *sticky*—when it feels good to be you.

Accountability accelerates embodiment. Whether it's a coach, a friend, or a public declaration, let others *witness* your new standard. The psychology of commitment says we are more likely to follow through when someone is watching. It's not about pressure—it's about *ownership*. When you declare, "This is who I am now," and others see you live it, your identity crystallizes in community.

Resilience is part of locking it in. You will wobble. The old self will whisper. But slippage doesn't mean failure—it means *integration*. Your task is not to be perfect. It's to *return* faster. To remind yourself that this is who you are now. Each bounce back is a signal to the subconscious that this identity is here to stay. Over time, the wobble disappears, and the new self becomes *automatic*.

To lock in your new identity is to stop trying to become—and to *be*. You make a decision. You live it. You reinforce it with action, feeling, and intention. And then one day, without forcing, you realize: the old you is just a memory. The new you? It's your *home*. It's not temporary. It's not fragile. It's not performative. It's real. It's rooted. And it's *locked in*.

Integration Rituals and Daily Anchors

Integration is where transformation becomes reality. You don't change your life in a breakthrough moment—you change it in the *anchoring*. The flash of insight, the emotional high, the big declaration—they're all powerful. But without rituals to root the change, they evaporate. Integration rituals and daily anchors turn your growth into identity. They shift your transformation from *event* to *embodiment*. This is how new beliefs become your baseline, and new behaviors become your norm.

Your nervous system craves rhythm. In a world addicted to unpredictability and overstimulation, rituals offer stability. Studies in neuroscience confirm that predictable routines reduce cortisol, regulate emotional states, and increase motivation. When you create intentional rituals—morning grounding, evening reflection, midday resets—you're not just managing time, you're managing *state*. And your state determines your results more than your strategy ever will.

Start your day with *alignment*, not reaction. Don't check your phone before checking in with your mission. A magnetic morning ritual doesn't have to be long—it just has to be *intentional*. Breathwork, visualization, gratitude, stretching, or even silence—it's the signal to your subconscious that you are leading your day, not following it. When you command your energy first, you step into your power before the world makes demands on it.

Language is a powerful anchor. Declare who you are becoming aloud. Speak your vision as if it's already done. Neuroscience shows that identity-based affirmations rewire the brain faster than goal-based ones. So instead of saying, "I want to be confident," say, "I *am* confident." Instead of "I hope to lead," say, "I *lead with clarity and power.*" These declarations aren't empty—they're *instructions* to your mind and body to act accordingly.

Movement locks it in. The body remembers what the mind tries to forget. Integrate your intentions with physical anchoring. Stand tall while declaring. Walk in power after visualizing your next level. Train your posture to match your purpose. Research from Harvard shows that physical power poses increase testosterone (confidence) and decrease cortisol (stress), literally shifting how you feel in your body. Embodiment isn't a metaphor—it's a mechanism.

Create mini rituals for moments of resistance. A deep breath before responding. A mantra before speaking. A pause before a decision. These micro-habits create *space* between your programming and your potential. That space is sacred—it's where old patterns dissolve and new choices are born. This is how you stop reacting and start *responding* as the person you've chosen to become.

Evening rituals are just as vital. Before you sleep, review the day through the lens of *identity*. What did you do today that aligned with your new self? What lesson did you extract? What deserves to be celebrated, not just corrected? Sleep is when the subconscious mind reorganizes data. When you reflect with intention, you feed it the narrative you want to reinforce. This is where momentum is multiplied overnight.

Anchors can also be physical. A specific candle, song, or piece of jewelry can become an identity trigger. Neuroscience calls this an "anchor stimulus." The brain links emotional states with sensory cues. So when you wear the bracelet, light the candle, or hear the song, your body recalls the energy you associate with it. This is not superstition—it's *conditioning*. And it works.

Don't underestimate the power of *tracking*. Journaling, habit apps, or even a simple daily checklist can become powerful reinforcement tools. Why? Because what gets measured gets magnified. Dopamine, the brain's reward chemical, spikes not just when you reach goals—but when you *see* progress. Tracking becomes proof that your change is real, and proof feeds belief.

Community matters. Shared rituals—like group meditations, weekly check-ins, or live declarations—amplify accountability and integration. We become who we're witnessed to be. Mirror neurons in the brain mimic what we observe, making group environments powerful containers for identity stabilization. When others see you rise, it reminds your subconscious that this new version of you is *seen* and supported.

Anchors are not burdens—they're *freedom codes*. They reduce decision fatigue, eliminate distraction, and automate alignment. You don't need more willpower—you need *structure*. Because structure liberates energy. And when your life runs on rituals that reflect who you've chosen to become, your transformation becomes not just sustainable—but *inevitable*.

Integration is not the final step—it is the *foundation*. Without it, growth is fleeting. With it, growth becomes your baseline. These rituals, these anchors, these daily decisions—they are not small. They are everything. They are the bridge between insight and embodiment, between the person you were and the person you now live as. And when practiced consistently, they don't just remind you of your power—they *reveal* it. Daily. Relentlessly. Unapologetically.

From Healing to Leadership

Healing is not the end of the journey—it's the beginning of *true* leadership. The world tells us to lead from credentials, from performance, from polished perfection. But the deepest leadership emerges from *integration*—when your past no longer defines you, but refines you. When your wounds are no longer hidden or raw, but *alchemized* into wisdom. You lead not in spite of your pain, but because you've *transformed* through it.

Real leadership isn't about standing above—it's about *rising from within*. The journey of healing gives you authority not granted by titles, but by experience. When you've walked through fire and stayed standing, your presence carries weight. People don't follow charisma alone—they follow congruence. They feel when your words come from lived truth instead of intellectual theory. That's why healed people *heal people*—not by force, but by *frequency*.

According to trauma researchers like Dr. Bessel van der Kolk, healing the nervous system not only restores internal peace but also enhances empathy and relational intelligence—two non-negotiables in powerful leadership. When you've regulated your own emotional chaos, you can hold space for others without projection. Your presence becomes a safe haven, not a battlefield. And in that safety, people *grow*.

Healing also births *vision clarity*. Pain distorts perception. Unhealed stories filter how you see the world, often narrowing your focus to survival. But healing expands your aperture. Suddenly, possibilities appear. You dream bigger. You speak bolder. Because you're no longer trying to protect a wound—you're building from *wholeness*. You're not just reacting—you're *creating*.

The shift from healing to leadership is marked by responsibility. Healing asks, "What happened to me?" Leadership asks, "What can I do with what happened to me to serve others?" That's the difference between self-focus and soul-purpose. When you turn your pain into a platform—not to exploit it, but to elevate others—you step into the sacred territory of *impact*.

This isn't about being fully healed—because healing is never linear. It's about leading from *integration*, not identity. You are not your trauma. You are the alchemist who transmuted it. You are not your past. You are the steward of a future that others can step into. This evolution from victimhood to vision is what makes your voice trustworthy. Not because it's perfect, but because it's *anchored*.

The best leaders model *resilience*, not invincibility. When you show that you can fall and still rise, doubt and still act, break and still rebuild—you give permission for others to do the same. Vulnerability isn't weakness. It's leadership currency. In fact, studies from Brené Brown and others have shown that vulnerability increases trust, collaboration, and creativity in teams and communities.

Healing gives you the ability to *listen* differently. You no longer listen to reply—you listen to understand. You don't impose your truth—you illuminate others' own. This makes you not just a speaker or a strategist, but a *guide*. People don't need more gurus. They need grounded leaders who see their wholeness even when they can't. And that level of sight only comes through *inner* clarity.

From healing to leadership also means moving from *protection* to *expression*. When you're no longer hiding your truth, your energy expands. Your voice gets stronger. Your message becomes a force, not a request. This kind of presence isn't taught in classrooms—it's forged in the furnace of transformation. It's the kind of voice that doesn't just communicate—it *moves*.

True leaders born of healing lead with both fire and compassion. Fire to call people into greatness. Compassion to honor their pace. Fire to challenge mediocrity. Compassion to recognize trauma. This duality is rare. But it's magnetic. And it's exactly what the world needs more of—not influencers, but *initiators* of healing through their embodiment.

As you lead, you continue to heal. Leadership becomes your next level of growth. It exposes your edges, expands your capacity, and requires deeper embodiment. Every stage calls you to revisit your roots not with pain, but with power. Not to repeat—but to *reintegrate*. You lead not because you've arrived, but because you've committed to walking with *awareness* and *integrity*.

So, from this moment on, understand this: your healing was not just for you. It was the initiation into your next identity. Not just the survivor, but the visionary. Not just the student, but the *steward*. Your leadership is needed—not when you're perfect, but when you're present. And your presence, when forged in healing and anchored in truth, becomes not just influential—but *transformational*.

Creating Long-Term Expansion Plans

Expansion isn't a moment—it's a movement. Creating long-term expansion plans isn't about setting goals that sound good in a journal. It's about *constructing a future* so aligned with your soul that it pulls you forward with clarity, certainty, and momentum. Expansion, by its very nature, requires vision beyond the current environment. It demands a level of thinking that stretches past your comfort zone and a commitment to consistency even when emotions fluctuate.

The first key to real expansion is foundation. Before building upward, you must build *inward*. This means anchoring your values, clarifying your mission, and understanding your "why" at a cellular level. Research by Simon Sinek and other leadership theorists proves that people and organizations with a clearly defined "why" outperform those focused only on what and how. When your plan stems from purpose, it becomes unshakable—no matter what storms come.

Sustainable expansion also demands time-based *mapping*. Dreams without dates remain fantasies. When you place timelines, checkpoints, and tangible actions on your vision, you create a bridge between the spiritual and the strategic. Neuroscience confirms that when we visualize specific time-bound goals, our brain treats them as achievable tasks, increasing our likelihood of success by engaging the prefrontal cortex—our planning and execution center.

But a long-term plan must be flexible. It must allow for evolution. You are not a fixed being—you're a dynamic creation. As your clarity deepens, so will your desires. Expansion isn't linear—it's spiral. You return to certain lessons with greater awareness and build on them. Rigidity breaks momentum. But flexible structure—sacred discipline with space for growth—creates *resilience*.

Another anchor of long-term expansion is *identity alignment*. Who must you become to fulfill this vision? What beliefs, habits, and standards must you adopt? Every long-term plan is secretly an identity upgrade plan. As you act in congruence with your future self, you strengthen the neural pathways that make that identity automatic. Psychologists call this "habit stacking"—linking identity to behavior creates long-lasting transformation.

Energy management is a non-negotiable. You cannot expand sustainably from depletion. Every long-term plan must include rituals for rest, recalibration, and renewal. Leaders who thrive over time are those who honor their energetic capacity as much as their ambition. Burnout is not a badge—it's a barrier. According to the World Health Organization, chronic burnout impairs decision-making, creativity, and emotional regulation—three pillars of effective leadership and long-term success.

You must also develop systems that multiply your impact. Systems create scalability. Systems reduce decision fatigue. Whether it's automating repetitive tasks, building strong teams, or documenting processes, long-term expansion requires that you no longer operate as the bottleneck. Delegation is not weakness—it's wisdom. It allows you to stay in your zone of genius, where your impact is exponential, not incremental.

Relationships become a catalyst. Your five-year plan must include *people*. Who do you need to connect with, serve, or partner with to elevate your mission? Studies show that proximity to high-level thinkers increases your own level of execution through mirror neuron activation. If your vision doesn't stretch your network, it's too small. Surround yourself with those who reflect your future, not your past.

Data is your ally. Measure what matters. Track your progress. Reflect on trends. The most expansive leaders aren't just intuitive—they're *informed*. They don't wait until December to evaluate—they make weekly and monthly book corrections. Metrics don't limit you; they *liberate* you from assumptions. They reveal what's working, what needs adjusting, and where momentum is building.

Your long-term expansion plan must include *legacy thinking*. Ask, "What impact will this create beyond me?" Real visionaries don't just build income—they build *inheritance*. Whether that's intellectual, emotional, spiritual, or financial, legacy isn't reserved for the end of life. It's built in the *now*. Every aligned action plants seeds you may never see—but others will *harvest*.

Mindset reinforcement is the fuel. Without renewing your mind daily, your plans remain vulnerable to sabotage. Doubt, fear, and distraction will knock, but your mental practices—meditation, visualization, declarations, journaling—fortify your resolve. Cognitive behavioral science confirms that thought patterns directly influence behavior outcomes. Train your thoughts like you train your body: with intensity, repetition, and purpose.

Long-term expansion isn't about someday—it's about *starting now*. Your clarity, your planning, your rituals, your action steps—they all begin today. One step leads to a rhythm. That rhythm becomes a routine. That routine becomes a lifestyle. And that lifestyle becomes your *legacy*. You are not waiting for the perfect moment. You *are* the perfect moment. Your expansion has already begun—the plan is simply the proof. So dream boldly. Structure wisely. Move daily. And build the future that your soul has always whispered was possible.

Spiritual Confidence and Faith

Spiritual confidence is not loud—it's unwavering. It's the quiet, rooted knowing that no matter what the outer world shows, something greater is working *through* you, *for* you, and *with* you. Faith is not passive hope—it is *activated belief*. When you merge confidence with faith, you become unstoppable. You no longer question your worth or your path because you trust the divine orchestration that is always unfolding behind the scenes.

This kind of confidence doesn't come from ego—it comes from *alignment*. When you are in sync with the higher intelligence that governs the universe, you no longer need constant validation from others. You become guided by *conviction*, not consensus. Quantum physics has shown that particles respond to observation. In the same way, your reality responds to the *energy of your expectation*. Faith activates the field.

Faith is the substance of things hoped for, the evidence of things not seen. It is the frequency that calls what is invisible into form. When you cultivate spiritual confidence, your energy becomes magnetic—not because you chase, but because you *trust*. You radiate calm in chaos, vision in the fog, and power in moments that would unravel most people. That's not delusion—it's divine connection.

Confidence rooted in spirit means you don't just believe in yourself—you believe in the *source* that created you. You understand that you were not randomly assigned a purpose; you were *designed* for it. Your desires are not arbitrary. They are spiritual GPS signals pointing to your soul's curriculum. And when you stop treating your calling like a suggestion, your confidence becomes divine *obedience*.

There is power in surrender. Spiritual confidence doesn't require that you control everything. It teaches you to *co-create*. You do your part, and then you *release*. Neuroscience has shown that stress decreases when people adopt a surrender mindset. When you trust that you're guided, your nervous system shifts out of fight-or-flight and into flow. You're no longer hustling—you're *aligning*.

Every spiritual tradition speaks of trust—not just in the divine, but in the process. Confidence deepens when you realize delays aren't denials—they're recalibrations. What feels like stagnation is often *gestation*. Seeds germinate underground long before we see the sprout. Your vision is doing the same. Faith gives you the strength to water your goals with belief even when nothing seems to be growing.

You build spiritual confidence by *remembering*. Remembering who you are beyond the limitations, beyond the labels, beyond the lies. You are not your past. You are not your fear. You are not your bank account, your followers, or your titles. You are spirit having a human experience. And when you root into that truth, you become immovable. Not because you've mastered life, but because you've *trusted life*.

Spiritual confidence speaks a different language. It says, "Even when I don't see it, I *know*." It walks into the unknown with peace. It doesn't rush to prove—it stands in *presence*. It doesn't shout to be heard—it *vibrates* truth so powerfully that the right people are drawn without force. This isn't just mysticism—it's energetic reality. What you believe deeply shapes what you experience tangibly.

Faith isn't fragile—it's fierce. It's what allows you to act boldly without guarantees. You start the business, speak the truth, write the book, walk away from what doesn't serve—not because you know exactly what's next, but because you *know who's leading you*. That kind of faith is unshakable. That kind of confidence changes *everything*.

Your spiritual power multiplies when you embody gratitude. Not just for what has happened, but for what *is* happening—even the unseen. Gratitude tells the universe, "I trust your timing." It raises your vibration, opens your heart, and aligns your frequency with abundance. Studies from UC Davis show that gratitude boosts well-being, increases optimism, and activates the brain's reward pathways. Gratitude is not a nicety—it's a *strategy*.

Confidence becomes unbreakable when your foundation is the divine. You're not just standing on personal development—you're standing on *principle*. On the truth that the same power that spins planets lives in *you*. That's not a metaphor—it's a *mandate*. You were not made to shrink. You were made to shine. When you remember that, no circumstance can intimidate you again.

Let your confidence be a declaration of your faith. Let your walk be evidence of your trust. Let your life be a *sermon without words*—not because you never doubt, but because you *choose belief anyway*. That choice will separate you. It will elevate you. And it will align you with a life far greater than what you could've ever strategized. Because spiritual confidence doesn't just open doors—it parts seas.

Navigating the Next Level

The next level isn't a destination—it's a *dimension*. It's a new frequency of responsibility, clarity, and expression. And stepping into it isn't just about having more; it's about *becoming more*. More present. More honest. More disciplined. More *you*. Most people want elevation, but they aren't prepared for the shedding that comes with it. The truth is, the doorway to your next level is guarded by your current limitations—and only you can walk through.

At every new level, a new version of you is required. Not because the old you was bad, but because they were built for survival at a lower altitude. The identity that got you here—through the pain, through the hustle, through the learning curve—isn't the identity that will get you *there*. Growth demands that you release familiar patterns to step into your future with intention, not inertia.

The higher you rise, the subtler the sabotage. It's not the loud fears anymore—it's the whispers of "Maybe I'm not ready," or "Let me just stabilize before I expand again." That's comfort speaking the language of logic. But logic is a lousy leader when you're called to evolve. Neuroscience tells us that the brain is wired to seek safety, not success. Your job is to override that default with *deliberate action*.

Elevation will test your integrity. The higher you climb, the more power you hold. And with power comes visibility, responsibility, and temptation. At the next level, shortcuts become seductive. But true expansion doesn't come from speed—it comes from *alignment*. Real leaders double down on their values when things get good, not just when things are hard. They don't compromise for applause—they *anchor* for legacy.

Your next level isn't just about doing more—it's about *being more intentional* with less. Complexity is not always progress. Simplification is power. High performers often fall into the trap of over-engineering their lives, when in fact, mastery comes from *clarity*. What's essential? What moves the needle? What brings peace *and* performance? Strip away what's excessive so what's extraordinary can shine.

The people around you may shift. Your next level will require deeper boundaries, tighter circles, and clearer communication. Everyone can't go with you. Some will misunderstand the new you because they were attached to the old one. That's not betrayal—that's *graduation*. Honor those who supported you, bless those who fall away, and keep your vision sacred. Elevation requires energetic hygiene.

The next level also comes with new *emotional muscles*. You will have to navigate higher stakes without higher stress. Emotional regulation becomes your superpower. Studies show that leaders with high emotional intelligence make better decisions, manage teams more effectively, and experience less burnout. Calm is not weakness. It is the *quiet confidence* of someone who trusts their mission.

Expect resistance—not as punishment, but as proof. Every breakthrough comes with friction. Not because you're off book, but because you're *breaking old programming*. Your subconscious will fight to pull you back into the familiar. You must choose to hold the line. Declare who you are becoming louder than the fear of who you've been. That is the essence of momentum—*alignment over anxiety*.

Your next level will ask you to trust invisible data. You won't always have external validation, yet you'll be called to act boldly. That's when you rely on intuition sharpened through integrity. The more you honor your internal guidance, the more accurate it becomes. In fact, studies in the field of heart-brain coherence show that intuition often arrives faster than conscious reasoning and leads to better decisions.

You will also be called to serve on a bigger stage. Your voice, your story, your presence—it will impact more lives. That's not an ego trip. That's a *responsibility*. You've earned your voice by healing, learning, and showing up. Now, use it with wisdom. Not to impress, but to uplift. Not to dominate, but to *liberate*. The next level isn't just about receiving more—it's about *giving more* with strategy and soul.

Investing in yourself becomes non-negotiable. Whether it's mentorship, coaching, education, or environments that elevate your thinking—you must stay in rooms that reflect where you're going, not where you've been. Your environment is either reinforcing your greatness or reinforcing your doubt. Choose wisely. Long-term success is rarely about talent. It's about *alignment and exposure*.

The next level doesn't require perfection. It requires *permission*. Your permission. To grow. To shine. To lead. To fail forward. To let go. To start again. To evolve publicly and privately. You don't wait until you're flawless to rise. You rise because your calling *won't wait*. So breathe deep, stand tall, and walk boldly. The next level isn't waiting for the perfect version of you. It's waiting for the *present* version—the one who's ready *now*.

Creating a Life of Alignment

A life of alignment isn't something you stumble into—it's something you *design* with intention, truth, and courage. Alignment means living in harmony with who you are, what you believe, and what you're here to do. It's the intersection where purpose meets presence, and decisions are no longer driven by pressure but by *principle*. When your thoughts, words, and actions reflect your deepest values, you unlock a state of flow where fulfillment and success are no longer opposites—they become partners.

Alignment starts with radical self-honesty. You can't live in truth if you're afraid to look at it. Most people are exhausted not because they're doing too much, but because they're doing things that *aren't aligned*. When you abandon your inner voice to please others or follow someone else's version of success, your energy leaks. The body feels the cost of misalignment before the mind does—fatigue, anxiety, burnout. These aren't random—they are *feedback*.

The greatest lie we're sold is that we have to hustle harder to be worthy. But alignment teaches the opposite: when you honor who you truly are, you no longer have to *chase*—you begin to *attract*. Research on values-based living has shown that individuals who align their actions with their internal values experience higher well-being, lower stress levels, and greater resilience. This isn't fluff—it's neuroscience and soul combined.

To live in alignment, you must first define your *true north*. What do you believe in so deeply that you'd live it, speak it, and protect it—even when it's inconvenient? These aren't your surface preferences—they are your soul's non-negotiables. When you don't know your values, every opportunity looks tempting and every obstacle feels disorienting. But when you know what you stand for, you move with *conviction*.

Your environment plays a critical role in your ability to stay aligned. You cannot consistently thrive in spaces that require you to shrink, lie, or pretend. Alignment doesn't mean perfection—it means *congruence*. Your surroundings should reflect your values, support your vision, and elevate your energy. Studies in behavioral psychology confirm that environment strongly influences identity. If you want to live aligned, create surroundings that speak to your highest self.

Boundaries are a non-negotiable in a life of alignment. When you say yes to things that don't reflect your truth, you betray yourself in small ways that eventually add up to *disconnection*. Boundaries aren't walls—they're doors. They protect what matters. They create the space where your aligned life can breathe, expand, and flourish. Saying no is not rejection—it's *direction*.

Decision-making becomes clearer in alignment. You no longer overanalyze or look for endless signs. You ask, "Does this resonate with my truth?" and "Does this move me closer to the life I've declared?" That's not impulsivity—it's *integrity*. You stop outsourcing authority and start honoring your inner compass. And the more you do, the more precise it becomes. Alignment sharpens discernment like nothing else.

Living in alignment doesn't mean life becomes easy—it means it becomes *authentic*. You'll still face challenges. But they won't shake you the same way because your roots are deep. You're no longer acting—you're *embodying*. And embodiment is magnetic. People can feel when someone is grounded in truth. It inspires trust, admiration, and influence—without manipulation.

Your habits become sacred. They're no longer chores or checkboxes. They're expressions of identity. You journal because clarity matters. You move your body because vitality matters. You speak affirmations because your words shape your world. Habits in alignment are not about control—they are about *conscious creation*. They're how you prove to yourself every day that your life is a reflection of who you *really are*.

Aligned living calls you to let go of false timelines. Society may say you're behind or ahead—but alignment isn't on a clock. It's on *truth time*. You begin to understand that the most powerful results come from alignment, not urgency. You release comparison. You respect your pace. And in doing so, you often accelerate faster than the ones trying to rush their way to peace.

Service becomes a natural byproduct of alignment. When you are aligned, your overflow blesses others. You don't have to force influence—it flows from who you are. You become a mirror, a reminder, a lighthouse for others still navigating confusion. And you don't lead from above—you lead from *within*. That's how movements are born—not from performance, but from *presence*.

In the end, a life of alignment is the most rebellious and liberating thing you can create. It is a declaration that your life is yours. That your truth matters. That peace is more valuable than performance. That purpose is more important than approval. And when you live that way—every day, in every decision—you don't just feel successful. You *become whole*. And wholeness? That's the real wealth. That's the real win. That's the life that changes everything.

Building Your Personal Manifesto

A personal manifesto is more than a motivational list—it's your sacred declaration. It's a soul-stamped commitment to who you are, what you believe, and how you will show up in the world. It becomes your compass in chaos, your anchor in doubt, your fuel in fatigue. When life throws distractions, delays, or detours, your manifesto reminds you: *This is who I am. This is what I stand for. This is the future I'm creating*. It's not written for others—it's carved for your spirit.

Most people drift because they've never decided what they actually *believe*. They mimic, they follow, they adapt—but they never *declare*. Without declaration, you have no filter for decision-making. You say yes to things that drain you. You entertain people who dishonor you. You pursue goals that aren't even yours. But when you've written your manifesto, clarity is no longer negotiable—it's your *standard*.

Your manifesto doesn't begin with who the world told you to be. It begins with *truth*. What lights you up? What infuriates you? What breaks your heart and makes you want to change the world? These emotional activators are not random—they are divine breadcrumbs. According to leading psychologists, core emotional values are often predictors of lifelong purpose. Your manifesto gives them voice and structure.

Language is everything. Words don't just describe your reality—they *create* it. Studies in cognitive linguistics show that affirming language rewires the brain through neuroplasticity. So when you write "I am a leader of change," your brain begins reorganizing itself to match that truth. Your manifesto becomes a reprogramming tool. It's not just what you say—it's what you *speak into existence*.

A powerful manifesto includes your highest truths. These are the unshakable beliefs you choose to live by, even when tested. Maybe it's: "My worth is not earned—it is inherent." Or "My vision is more powerful than my fear." These truths are not clichés—they're spiritual contracts. When life tries to shrink you, these statements pull you back into your greatness. They are vows, not suggestions.

Clarity leads to conviction. And conviction leads to consistency. When you've taken time to articulate your core values—truth, freedom, love, growth, impact—they stop being abstract. They become filters. You begin asking: "Does this decision honor my manifesto?" If not, it's a no. Not from fear, but from alignment. This is how you stop people-pleasing and start *purpose-living*.

Every great leader, movement, or revolution started with a manifesto. Not because they had power—but because they had a *promise*. Martin Luther King Jr.'s "I Have a Dream" speech? A spoken manifesto. Steve Jobs' vision for

Apple? A corporate manifesto that reshaped industries. When you declare who you are and what you stand for, you become a force of nature—not just personally, but *publicly*.

Your manifesto is not fixed. As you evolve, so should it. Review it monthly. Refine it as you grow. What once felt true may deepen. What once felt bold may now feel basic. That's not inconsistency—that's *elevation*. A living manifesto grows with you. It becomes both mirror and map—reflecting who you are and guiding who you're becoming.

Write it in your voice. Raw, real, and rhythmically yours. It doesn't need poetic flair. It needs *power*. Say what must be said. Speak what you've been scared to say. Declare what your soul has always known but your mouth never gave permission to articulate. This is not the time for politeness. This is the time for *proclamation*.

Read your manifesto daily. Out loud. With conviction. Don't mumble your truth. Don't whisper your future. Speak it like your life depends on it—because it *does*. Your cells are listening. Your subconscious is watching. Your energetic field is responding. Daily declaration is not ritual—it's *recalibration*.

When challenges arise, your manifesto becomes your armor. When opportunities appear, it becomes your filter. When fear speaks, it becomes your rebuttal. This is not fluff—it is frequency management. Neuroscientific studies confirm that when we regularly remind ourselves of our values and identity, we are more resilient, focused, and decisive under pressure.

Building your personal manifesto is not just an exercise—it's a revolution. It's the moment you take your power back from conditioning, from confusion, from compromise. It's your written permission slip to live unleashed, unfiltered, and unshakeable. You are no longer drifting. You are declaring. And with that declaration, your life begins to respond. Not because you hoped— but because you *decided*.

Accountability & Next-Step Vision

Accountability is the bridge between intention and implementation. You can have the clearest vision, the strongest desire, and the most powerful affirmations—but without accountability, momentum collapses under the weight of distraction and delay. Accountability transforms "someday" into *now*. It converts vague goals into measurable progress. It makes your word matter—not just to others, but to *yourself*. Because integrity isn't just about being honest with others. It's about *keeping promises to your future self*.

Vision without structure is like a river without banks—powerful but scattered. Accountability creates the banks. It channels your energy into direction. Studies in behavioral psychology show that people who publicly commit to their goals are up to 65% more likely to achieve them. That's not just motivation—it's science. When your actions are witnessed, your follow-through increases. You become a person of *completion*, not just a dreamer of beginnings.

But accountability is not punishment—it's partnership. The right kind of accountability doesn't shame or police. It supports, stretches, and *mirrors* your greatness. It's a sacred container that says, "I see who you're becoming, and I won't let you forget it." True accountability doesn't rescue—it *reminds*. It doesn't control—it *calls forth*. And when it's rooted in respect and vision, it becomes one of your greatest tools for transformation.

Your next-step vision should not be a mountain of vague ambitions. It should be *clear*, *measurable*, and *emotional*. What are the next three things that move your life, business, health, or purpose forward? Don't get stuck in ten-year fantasies while neglecting ten-day execution. Long-term vision must be *anchored* in short-term alignment. What you do in the next seven days says more about your destiny than what you post on your vision board.

Write it down. The simple act of writing down your goals increases the likelihood of achievement by over 40%, according to research from Dominican University. Your vision must leave the realm of thought and enter the physical world. On paper. In ink. With *intention*. This isn't just productivity—it's spiritual responsibility. Writing signals to the brain, "This matters." And what matters gets *momentum*.

Create feedback loops. If you don't track it, you can't improve it. Build rituals that reflect your commitment—daily check-ins, weekly progress reviews, monthly recalibrations. These aren't corporate buzzwords—they're life rituals. Consistency isn't sexy, but it's *sovereign*. Your results don't come from occasional greatness. They come from *daily truth*.

Accountability partners matter—but choose wisely. Don't partner with people who enable your excuses. Partner with those who elevate your execution. You want allies who remind you of your *identity*, not just your goals. Your future is too sacred to share with people who only see your current version. Surround yourself with believers, builders, and bold thinkers. Energy is contagious—choose wisely what you catch.

Technology can be your ally if used intentionally. Set reminders, track habits, log progress, automate routines. Use tools like Notion, Habitica, or Google Calendar to create digital accountability structures. But remember—tools don't build discipline. *Decisions* do. Apps can help, but your *standard* must lead. You're not just building routines. You're building *identity alignment*.

Your next-step vision must also include *emotional clarity*. Why does this matter to you? What will shift in your life when it's done? How will it feel to live on the other side of completion? Neuroscience proves that emotion intensifies memory and motivation. When you link action steps to emotional rewards, you create a neurochemical cocktail that amplifies commitment. This is how goals become *magnetic*.

Celebrate progress, not just perfection. High performers often skip their wins in pursuit of the next milestone. But celebration isn't indulgence—it's reinforcement. Every time you acknowledge your growth, your brain releases dopamine, reinforcing the behavior. Over time, this creates a habit loop of *self-generated motivation*. Progress becomes its own reward.

Don't just hold yourself accountable to the goal. Hold yourself accountable to the *standard*. Goals change. Circumstances shift. But your standard—your energy, your integrity, your discipline—that's what creates long-term transformation. Standards make results inevitable. When your standard is excellence, the outcome takes care of itself. You stop chasing results and start *embodying inevitability*.

Your next-step vision is not separate from your identity—it *is* your identity. When you hold yourself accountable, when you act with precision, when you commit with heart—you're not just achieving things. You're *becoming someone*. And that someone doesn't wait for permission. That someone doesn't negotiate with doubt. That someone lives in truth, leads with clarity, and creates impact *on purpose*. The next step is not complicated. It's just waiting for you to decide: *Will I lead myself or leave myself waiting?*

Celebrating Your Breakthroughs

Celebrating your breakthroughs is not just a feel-good practice—it's a *spiritual imperative*. When you recognize and honor the progress you've made, you anchor that growth into your identity. Without celebration, transformation feels incomplete. Breakthroughs that go unacknowledged quickly fade into the background of your consciousness, leaving you chasing the next goal without integrating the last victory. Recognition is retention. And retention becomes reinforcement.

Too often, society glorifies the grind and downplays the growth. We're taught to keep moving, keep striving, never pause. But the truth is, celebration is a form of energetic integration. According to neuroscience, the brain releases dopamine—the "reward" chemical—when we recognize achievement. This dopamine reinforces neural pathways, making the behavior that led to the breakthrough more likely to be repeated. Celebration is not indulgence—it's *neuroplasticity in motion*.

You are not the same person you were last year, last month, or even last week. But you'll never feel the magnitude of that growth if you don't *mark the moment*. One of the most powerful things you can do for your confidence and momentum is to pause and say, "I did that." Not out of ego, but out of *embodiment*. Because if you don't believe in your own progress, why should anyone else?

Breakthroughs come in many forms—some loud and dramatic, others quiet and subtle. Don't wait for the massive external shift to celebrate. That moment you spoke your truth? Breakthrough. That time you chose peace over people-pleasing? Breakthrough. The day you finally honored a boundary you used to violate? That's *evolution*. Don't miss the miracle because you were waiting for the fireworks.

Celebration also reminds your subconscious that this path is *safe*. When we pair achievement with tension, burnout, or self-criticism, the brain begins to associate growth with danger. But when we link it with joy, gratitude, and pride, the body relaxes—and says, "Let's do this again." This is critical for sustainable success. According to the Harvard Business Review, progress—even small wins—triggers powerful positive emotions that drive performance and creativity.

How you celebrate matters. It doesn't have to be extravagant, but it should be *intentional*. Write it down. Speak it aloud. Share it with someone who can mirror your excitement. Take a victory walk, light a candle, dance to your favorite song. The ritual itself isn't the point—the energy is. Celebration puts punctuation on your progress. It tells your system, "This moment is worthy of recognition."

Your journey hasn't been easy. You've navigated doubt, discomfort, and disruption. You've released old identities, dismantled limiting beliefs, and shown up when it would've been easier to quit. That deserves more than a passing thought. It deserves *presence*. Every time you acknowledge a breakthrough, you are telling your nervous system, "This is who I am now." You're reinforcing the frequency of greatness.

You also give others permission to celebrate themselves. When you normalize acknowledgment, you elevate the collective vibration. People don't just learn from your lessons—they expand through your *liberation*. Your celebration becomes a testimony. It says, "You're allowed to own your growth. You're allowed to shine." And in a world addicted to self-judgment, that's revolutionary.

Your breakthroughs are evidence. They are proof that the work is working. They are signals that your clarity, commitment, and courage are *moving mountains*. Whether internal or external, subtle or seismic, every breakthrough shifts your trajectory. Don't let them go undocumented. You are writing a legacy. And legacies aren't just built on results—they're built on *remembrance*.

Let your celebrations become part of your rituals. Schedule them. Plan for them. Track them. When you build celebration into your rhythm, you train yourself to be fueled by appreciation, not only anticipation. And when you're fueled by appreciation, your power becomes sustainable. You stop burning out and start *burning bright*.

Celebration breaks the cycle of always needing to be "better." It invites you to rest in the moment, to feel the joy of progress, and to realize that you are already *becoming* what you once prayed for. You're no longer chasing transformation—you're *embodying* it. That shift changes everything. Because you stop proving and start *proclaiming*.

So today, pause. Look back. Feel the shift. Honor the leap. Let gratitude flood your system. You didn't get here by accident—you got here by decision, by devotion, by design. Your journey is sacred. Your progress is valid. And your breakthroughs are worth celebrating—not later, but *now*. Because celebration isn't just how you end a chapter—it's how you prepare for the *next one*.

Exercise: Your Future Identity Embodiment

Your future identity isn't just a concept—it's a *frequency*. It's a version of you that already exists on the timeline of possibility, waiting for you to step into it with full conviction. Embodiment is the bridge. When you begin to act, speak, think, and move like the person you say you're becoming, you collapse time. You bring that future self into the now. Not by wishing—but by *becoming*.

You don't become your future self by thinking harder—you become them by behaving differently. Studies in behavioral psychology confirm that identity is shaped not only by internal belief but by consistent external action. When your daily habits reflect your future reality, your nervous system begins to recognize it as *normal*. This is the foundation of neuroplasticity—your brain changes as your behavior does.

Start with vision. Who is this future version of you? What do they believe about themselves? What boundaries do they hold? How do they dress, speak, eat, lead, and respond to fear? Get specific. Vague identity produces vague results. Clarity turns the abstract into actionable. And once you define it clearly, you can begin practicing it *intentionally*. Embodiment is not theory—it's rehearsal.

Write a declaration as if your future self were speaking to you now. "I am…" statements carry immense power. According to neuroscience, affirming identity-based statements activates the brain's reward centers and embeds new beliefs deeper than mere goals. Don't just say, "I will be confident." Say, "I *am* someone who speaks with clarity, leads with integrity, and trusts their inner knowing." Speak it until your cells believe it.

Now align your environment. You can't embody a new identity in the same energetic space that supported the old one. Remove what contradicts your future self. Upgrade your digital, physical, and social environments to reflect the version of you who already lives this reality. When your surroundings match your soul, embodiment becomes *natural*, not forced.

Movement anchors embodiment. Your posture, gestures, and breath communicate to the subconscious mind who you are. Embodied confidence stands taller. Embodied clarity moves with intention. Embodied leadership breathes deeper. The body doesn't lie. Train it to express your new identity even before your mind fully catches up. This is why somatic coaching and power posing are proven tools for self-regulation and performance.

Your relationships will shift as you embody your future. Not everyone is meant to evolve with you—and that's okay. Some will cling to your past because it's comfortable for them. But the version of you you're stepping into is not here to be *palatable*. It's here to be *powerful*. Let your embodiment become the permission slip others didn't know they needed.

Don't wait for external validation. Your embodiment isn't a performance—it's a *practice*. Some days will feel awkward. Some choices will challenge your comfort. But every time you act in alignment with the future you, you're casting a vote for that reality. Over time, those votes become *evidence*. And evidence becomes identity.

Use visualization to rehearse your embodiment. Mental imagery activates the same neural pathways as real experience. Olympic athletes have used this technique for decades to enhance performance. You can use it to embody character. Visualize your future self navigating challenges, leading conversations, receiving abundance. Make it vivid. The brain doesn't know the difference between real and rehearsed when emotion is involved.

Track your shifts. Journaling your embodiment moments helps you reflect and reinforce. What did I do today that reflected my future self? Where did I revert? What would the embodied version of me do next? Reflection turns motion into mastery. It helps you book-correct without judgment and grow with grace.

Let celebration amplify the shift. When you embody your future self and *feel it*, mark it. Celebrate with words, rituals, or rewards. This trains your nervous system to link expansion with pleasure, not pressure. It creates positive feedback loops that make your new identity sticky, sustainable, and *satisfying*.

You are not waiting to arrive—you're choosing to *embody* now. Your future is not out of reach. It's already coded into you. The only thing required is the decision to live it daily. Not when you're ready. Not when the world approves. But now. Because the future isn't something you step into—it's someone you step *as*. And that someone is already within you. Waiting. Ready. Real.

Now that you've seen the truth about how clarity and confidence are created from within—not through willpower, but through subconscious reprogramming—you're standing at a crossroads. You can close this chapter and let the momentum fade… or you can take the next step and *lock in* the transformation. That's exactly what the **Clarity Confidence Code Course** was built for. It's a complete step-by-step system to rewire your mind, dissolve self-doubt, and activate the version of you that moves with power, certainty, and magnetic energy—naturally. This isn't about hype. It's about results. If you're ready to go beyond inspiration and fully embody the shift, the full course is waiting. Step into it now at https://clarityconfidencecode.com

Because the next chapter is where your new identity takes the lead. Let's go.

BIBLIOGRAPHY

Abraham-Hicks. Ask and It Is Given: Learning to Manifest Your Desires. Carlsbad, CA: Hay House, 2004.

American Psychological Association. "Gratitude and Well-Being." Accessed May 31, 2025. https://www.apa.org/news/press/releases/2011/03/gratitude.

Carnegie, Dale. How to Win Friends and Influence People. New York: Simon & Schuster, 1936.

Chopra, Deepak. The Seven Spiritual Laws of Success: A Practical Guide to the Fulfillment of Your Dreams. San Rafael, CA: New World Library, 1994.

Dweck, Carol S. Mindset: The New Psychology of Success. New York: Random House, 2006.

Emmons, Robert A., and Michael E. McCullough. "Counting Blessings Versus Burdens: An Experimental Investigation of Gratitude and Subjective Well-Being in Daily Life." Journal of Personality and Social Psychology 84, no. 2 (2003): 377–89.

Fredrickson, Barbara L. "The Role of Positive Emotions in Positive Psychology: The Broaden-and-Build Theory of Positive Emotions." American Psychologist 56, no. 3 (2001): 218–26.

Harvard Business Review. "Research: Confidence Matters More Than You Think." Accessed May 31, 2025. https://hbr.org/2014/11/research-confidence-matters-more-than-you-think.

Harvard Business School. "Clarity of Purpose in Leadership." Accessed May 31, 2025. https://www.hbs.edu.

Hill, Napoleon. Think and Grow Rich. Cleveland: The Ralston Society, 1937.

Journal of Behavioral Decision Making. "Inaction Regret vs. Failure Regret." Journal of Behavioral Decision Making 36, no. 2 (2023): 201–212.

Journal of Cognitive Neuroscience. "Identity-Based Change and Belief." Journal of Cognitive Neuroscience 28, no. 4 (2016): 512–519.

Lyubomirsky, Sonja, Kennon M. Sheldon, and David Schkade. "Pursuing Happiness: The Architecture of Sustainable Change." Review of General Psychology 9, no. 2 (2005): 111–131.

Ma, X., Yue, Z.-Q., Gong, Z.-Q., Zhang, H., Duan, N.-Y., Shi, Y.-T., Wei, G.-X., and Li, Y.-F. "The Effect of Diaphragmatic Breathing on Attention, Negative Affect and Stress in Healthy Adults." Frontiers in Psychology 8 (2017): 874. https://doi.org/10.3389/fpsyg.2017.00874.

McKinsey & Company. "The Case for Clarity: How Leaders Outperform in Complexity." 2022. https://www.mckinsey.com.

MIT McGovern Institute. "The Brain's Plasticity: Rewiring Through Repetition." Accessed May 31, 2025. https://mcgovern.mit.edu.

Nature Neuroscience. "Identity Rewiring and Emotional Focus." Nature Neuroscience 23, no. 6 (2020): 745–752.

Psychological Science. "Gut Decisions: Intuition Outperforms Logic." Psychological Science 25, no. 4 (2020): 789–798.

Psychology Today. "Seeing Is Believing: The Power of Visualization." Accessed May 31, 2025. https://www.psychologytoday.com/us/blog/the-power-prime/201303/seeing-is-believing-the-power-visualization.

Robbins, Tony. Awaken the Giant Within. New York: Free Press, 1991.

Sincero, Jen. You Are a Badass: How to Stop Doubting Your Greatness and Start Living an Awesome Life. Philadelphia: Running Press, 2013.

Stanford University. "Neuroplasticity and Emotional Engagement." Accessed May 31, 2025. https://neuroscience.stanford.edu.

Tang, Yi-Yuan, Yihong Ma, Yong Fan, Hongbo Feng, Jianhui Wang, Shigang Feng, Qingbao Lu, Bin Hu, Yijun Lin, Jing Li, Yanchun Zhang, Yan Wang, Lei Zhou, and Michael I. Posner. "Central and Autonomic Nervous System Interaction Is Altered by Short-Term Meditation." Proceedings of the National Academy of Sciences 106, no. 22 (2009): 8865–70. https://doi.org/10.1073/pnas.0904031106.

The Lancet Psychiatry. "Cognitive Reappraisal and Emotional Safety." The Lancet Psychiatry 7, no. 8 (2020): 655–662.

Tolle, Eckhart. The Power of Now: A Guide to Spiritual Enlightenment. Novato, CA: New World Library, 2004.

Tracy, Brian. Goals! How to Get Everything You Want—Faster Than You Ever Thought Possible. San Francisco: Berrett-Koehler, 2004.

UCLA Mindful Awareness Research Center. "Affect Labeling and Emotional Regulation." Accessed May 31, 2025. https://www.uclahealth.org/marc.

Yale Center for Emotional Intelligence. "Emotional Suppression and Burnout." Accessed May 31, 2025. https://ei.yale.ed

www.ingramcontent.com/pod-product-compliance
Lightning Source LLC
Chambersburg PA
CBHW050851160426
43194CB00011B/2112